British Culture of the Postwar

The second half of the twentieth century was a period which saw huge political, social, technological and economic changes. These upheavals are mediated in often controversial innovations in literature, art and cinema.

From Angus Wilson to Pat Barker and Salman Rushdie, *British Culture of the Postwar* is an ideal starting point for those studying these cultural developments in Britain of recent years. Chapters on individual people and art forms give a clear and concise overview of the progression of different genres. They also discuss the wider issues of Britain's relationships with America and Europe, and the idea of Britishness.

Each section is introduced with a short discussion of the major historical events of the period. Read as a whole, *British Culture of the Postwar* will give students a comprehensive introduction to this turbulent and exciting period, and a greater understanding of the cultural production arising from it.

Alistair Davies teaches literature and film at the University of Sussex. He has published widely on British modernism, modernist poetics, and contemporary literature.
Alan Sinfield is Professor of English at the University of Sussex. His recent publications include *Literature, Politics and Culture in Postwar Britain* (1997) and *Out on Stage* (1999).

Contributors: Nannette Aldred, Andrew Crozier, Alistair Davies, Margaretta Jolly, Siobhán Kilfeather, Drew Milne, Minoli Salgado, Alan Sinfield.

British Culture of the Postwar

An introduction to literature and society 1945–1999

Edited by Alistair Davies
and Alan Sinfield

London and New York

First published 2000 by Routledge
11 New Fetter Lane, London EC4P 4EE

Simultaneously published in the USA and Canada
by Routledge
29 West 35th Street, New York, NY 10001

Routledge is an imprint of the Taylor & Francis Group

Typeset in Goudy and Gill Sans by
Curran Publishing Services Ltd, Norwich
Printed and bound in Great Britain by
TJ International Ltd, Padstow, Cornwall

British Library Cataloguing in Publication Data
A catalogue record for this book is available from the British
Library.

Library of Congress Cataloging in Publication Data
British culture of the postwar: an introduction to literature
and society, 1945–1999/[edited by] Alistair Davies and Alan
Sinfield.
    p.   cm.
Includes bibliographical references (p.) and index.
1. English literature–20th century–History and criticism. 2.
Literature and society–Great Britain–History–20th century. 3.
World War, 1939–1945–Literature and the war. 4. Great
Britain–Social conditions–1945– 5. Great Britain–Civilization–
1945– 6. World War, 1939–1945–Influence. 7. Social problems
in literature. I Davies, Alistair. II Sinfield, Alan.

ISBN 0–415–12810–2 (hbk)
ISBN 0–415–12811–0 (pbk)

Contents

Plates

Plates

Contributors

Nannette Aldred is based in the Centre for Continuing Education at the University of Sussex where she teaches courses on visual culture. She has written about national identity in the films of Powell and Pressburger and about double portraits and significant others in the work of David Hockney. She recently published *Teaching Cultures: The Long Revolution in Cultural Studies* (NIACE 1999) which she co-edited with Martin Ryle.

Andrew Crozier teaches English and American Literature in the School of English and American Studies at the University of Sussex. His edition of John Rodker's *Poems and Adolphe 1920* was published by Carcanet Press in 1996.

Alistair Davies teaches literature and film in the School of English and American Studies at the University of Sussex. He has published widely on British modernism, modernist poetics and contemporary literature.

Margaretta Jolly lectures in literature, life history and lesbian studies in the School of Cultural and Community Studies at the University of Sussex. She is author of *Dear Laughing Motorbike: Letters from Women Welders of the Second World War*, and is the editor of the *Encyclopaedia of Life Writing*.

Siobhán Kilfeather teaches British and Irish literature in the School of English and American Studies at the University of Sussex. She is an editor of *The Field Day Anthology of Irish Writing* and has published several articles on Irish women's writing since the eighteenth century.

Drew Milne is the Judith E. Wilson Lecturer in Drama and Poetry at the University of Cambridge. He co-edited *Marxist Literary Theory:*

A *Reader* with Terry Eagleton and is currently completing a book entitled *The Philosophy of Modern Theatre: A Critique*.

Minoli Salgado is a Lecturer in English in the School of African and Asian Studies at the University of Sussex where she specialises in the teaching and study of post-colonial literature. She has published widely on literature from the South Asian diaspora and is currently co-editing a book on critical approaches to short fiction.

Alan Sinfield teaches English and lesbian and gay studies in the School of English and American Studies at the University of Sussex. His recent publications include *Cultural Politics: Queer Reading* (1994), a new edition of *Literature, Politics and Culture in Postwar Britain* (1997), and *Out on Stage: Lesbian and Gay Theatre in the Twentieth Century* (1999).

Acknowledgements

When was 'the postwar'? For some, the displacement of 1950s stuffiness by the social experimentation of the 1960s brings the period to an end; for others, it is concluded by the abrupt assault by Margaret Thatcher's Conservative government on the prospect of sharing that had been envisaged as the pay-off for the war; or perhaps the embracing of market forces by Tony Blair's New Labour government of 1997 is decisive. Or maybe such views are (typically) parochial, and international developments are more important: the ending of the Cold War, or the pressures towards globalisation.

The contributors to this volume offer no single perspective on the postwar period in Britain and its culture. In discussing the literature, film and visual arts of the past fifty-five years, they discover radical discontinuities and underlying continuities. We would like to thank them for the enthusiasm and care they have brought to the project.

Lines from poems by W. H. Auden and Paul Muldoon in chapter six are quoted with permission of Faber and Faber.

Nannette Aldred and the editors would like to thank all those at the Tate Gallery Archives who helped to locate material from the ICA Archives. Plates 7.1 to 7.4 are from the early exhibitions organised by the ICA, and are reproduced courtesy of the *Architectural Review*. Plate 7.5, a Reg Butler photomontage showing the working model for a monument to 'The Unknown Prisoner' on the proposed site, the Humboldt Hohe, West Berlin, is reproduced courtesy of Rosemary Butler. Plate 7.6, an installation shot of Victor Burgin's 'Photopath' in the exhibition *When Attitudes Become Form: Live in Your Head*, ICA 1969, is reproduced courtesy of Simon Wilson, Tate Gallery (ICA Archives).

The editors are also grateful for the support of Joanna Cheetham, Gowan Hewlett, Vincent Quinn, Talia Rodgers and Kate Wilcox.

Part I

From imperial to post-imperial Britain

The postwar world order

When the Second World War ended, millions of Britons took to the streets to celebrate. After six years of suffering, their joy was understandable, but the cost of victory was huge. 264,000 servicemen and 90,000 civilians had been killed in the war. The industrial and commercial centres of cities and towns, in Northern Ireland, Scotland and Wales as well as in England, had been destroyed in the blitz. Much of Britain's housing stock and physical infrastructure – railways, roads, schools and hospitals – had suffered severe bomb damage. Basic foodstuffs were in short supply, while industry faced disabling shortages of raw materials, machinery and markets. The British economy, which had been one of the strongest before the war, was now technically bankrupt, sustained only by America's ability and willingness to extend credit. Those dancing in the streets were largely oblivious to the ways in which the war had transformed the global political and economic order and Britain's position within it.

In 1939, Britain was the world's greatest imperial power; by 1945, even though the empire remained intact, Britain was an enfeebled state in a world divided between two new superpowers, the USA and the Soviet Union. Britain's wartime defeats had convinced many under British rule that the British Empire was no longer invulnerable. The ease, for instance, with which the Japanese overwhelmed Singapore in 1942 had an immediate impact on the region, with the result that British troops had to be stationed in India to keep nationalist agitation in check. Winston Churchill, the wartime Prime Minister, could not conceive of an independent India, declaring that he had not become the King's chief minister to oversee the dissolution of the British Empire. However, the new Labour Prime Minister Clement Attlee, following his landslide election victory of 1945, made Indian independence a priority, in part because it had been a long-standing Labour Party commitment, in part because he realised that Britain lacked the resources to hold India. Nevertheless, after India became independent in 1947, the Labour government was as keen as the Conservatives to hold on to what remained of the empire, for without it, Britain had no hope of preserving its status as a world power (Robbins 1998; Morgan 1999).

Suez and Europe

The Conservatives returned to power in 1951. Their most dramatic attempt to slow down the pace of de-colonisation, however, had the effect of speeding it up. In 1956, the British, French and Israeli governments conspired to invade Egypt, in retaliation for its nationalisation of the strategic Suez Canal, the British empire's direct link by sea with Arab oil and its colonies in South-East Asia. The action not only divided public opinion in Britain with an unprecedented intensity, it was also condemned by the rest of the world, most significantly by the USA which threatened to speculate against the pound. British troops were withdrawn and the Prime Minister, Sir Anthony Eden, was forced to resign. Five years later in 1961, Eden's successor, Harold Macmillan made the first (unsuccessful) attempt to join the recently formed European Economic Community. The decision, like Suez, again divided public opinion, but for the political elite (on the left as on the right), the lesson of Suez was that Britain was no longer a world power. While its traditional ties with the empire and the Commonwealth and its close postwar alliance with the USA were important, its future lay in a still to be defined relationship with Europe. British politics have ever since been preoccupied with the attempt to define the exact nature of that relationship.

Post-imperial melancholy

'Great Britain has lost an empire and not yet found a role,' one American politician famously remarked in 1962. Many of the leading British and American commentators on postwar British culture have echoed his sentiments. For them, the politics and culture of postwar Britain have been defined by evasive inwardness and nostalgia (Hewison 1977, 1981, 1986), cultural retardation (Wiener 1981), middle-class conformism (Nehring 1993), anti-technological romanticism (Veldman 1994) and insularity (Piette 1995). The cultivation of empiricism in philosophy, of the figurative in painting, of realism in fiction, of the personal voice in poetry, and of the comic and the domestic in film and television has involved a very conscious refusal of the dominant forms of artistic modernity in postwar America and Europe (Appleyard 1989).

Most strikingly, the postwar period reveals a loss of confidence and ambition amongst British writers (Kenner 1987). Critics of the postwar novel in Britain have suggested that the turn to fabulation, allegory and self-reflectiveness – from William Golding to John Le Carré, Iris Murdoch to J. G. Farrell, Elizabeth Bowen to Paul Scott – mirrors the end of imperialism's confidence in historical narrative (Scanlan 1990; Connor 1996). Similarly, critics of postwar poetry and drama in Britain have found writers (John Osborne, Kingsley Amis, Philip Larkin and Donald Davie) either expressing a profound resentment and anxiety at Britain's loss of imperial status or (Trevor Griffiths, David Edgar, David Hare and Geoffrey Hill) analysing that resentment and anxiety (Morrison 1980; Sinfield 1983; Moore-Gilbert 1994).

The popular success in the 1980s of the 'Raj revival' in films and TV dramas and of 'heritage' films set in the Edwardian period (no less than support for the Falklands/Malvinas War in 1982) convinced many that post-imperial British culture remained, four decades after the end of the Second World War, in a state of unresolved mourning for a glorious past, when the empire gave Britons (or rather the English) an unshakeable sense not only of their intrinsic superiority but also of their central position in world affairs (Wright 1985; Hewison 1987; Corner and Harvey 1991; Samuel 1994; for discussion of 'heritage culture' in Scotland, McCrone *et al.* 1995; and Northern Ireland, Brett 1996).

Counter-cultural Britain

For other leading interpreters, however, this is not the whole story. The rise of the counter-cultural movements of the 1960s, they suggest, has had decisive effects in creating a positive, post-imperial culture in Britain, a culture coinciding with or provoking profound social and political re-alignments and transformations: 'the harvest of the sixties' in Patricia Waugh's memorable phrase (Sinfield 1989 and 1997; Marwick 1991 and 1998; Waugh 1995). Women writers appeared – notably Doris Lessing and Margaret Drabble – who devoted themselves to the disadvantaged position and distinctive insights of women. In Northern Ireland, Scotland and Wales, as the demand for devolution or separation became more powerful (Bogdanor 1999), a new generation of dissident intellectuals began to make fundamental challenges to the subordinate position of the regions within what they considered to be Britain's English dominated unitary state. (Tom Nairn's seminal *The Break-Up of Britain* was published in 1977, a Marxist *critique* of nationalism which has been central to subsequent debates about the topic (Nairn 1988; Beveridge and Turnbull 1989; McCrone 1992; Craig 1996; Nairn 1997).)

From the 1960s onwards, writers and intellectuals began to reflect on the ways in which the influx of immigrants, largely from the Caribbean, India, Pakistan and East Africa, was changing British culture. Even while detailing the politics of racism in the postwar period and the riots of the early 1980s, recent commentators have argued that since the 1970s, youth and popular cultures have shaped new trans-ethnic identities in Britain (Gilroy 1987; Hebdige 1987), while post-colonial critics, examining the globalisation both of the economy and of culture, have taken the migrant experience – the loss of home, the crossing of borders, the inhabiting of different selves – to define the experience of the majority under globalisation (Bhabha 1994; Chambers 1994).

Post-colonial metaphors and post-colonial actualities

Nations, however, are not just imaginary states but actual formations of power. For a new generation of British historians and cultural critics, Britain is less a unitary state than a unionist one with long-standing affiliations to a Protestant monarchy, an established Church, and a national parliament (Kearney 1989; Colley 1992; Samuel 1998). While unionism has made possible the relative cultural autonomy of Northern Ireland, Scotland and Wales, it has also set inevitable limits to change (Paterson 1994; Mitchell 1996; Bogdanor 1999). Recent proposals to end the civil war in Northern Ireland by sharing sovereignty between Britain and Ireland (a solution made easier by the pooling of sovereignty within the European Union) have confirmed for some Irish post-colonial thinkers not only a positive detachment in both states of the idea of nationality from the idea of the nation-state, but also in Britain a willingness to question unionist institutions (Kearney 1997). As Siobhán Kilfeather reminds us in her essay in this book, writing in Ireland, Scotland and Wales has taken place within and against the structures of the unionist state. Indeed, many Scottish and Welsh writers, she argues, have taken inspiration from Ireland's successful political and cultural independence from Britain (even if the newly independent Irish state was to prove a culturally repressive one). Migration also, as Minoli Salgado argues in her essay on Salman Rushdie, is not merely a metaphorical condition but is experienced by many in Britain as a condition of profound social and economic inequality. There is an essential difference between those like Rushdie who migrate between two elites and those who migrate for reasons of economic necessity. These are both timely interventions in key post-colonial debates: debates which more than any other continue to raise questions about the nature and possibility of Britain's post-imperial identity.

Bibliography

General studies on postwar British politics and history

Childs, D. (1997) *Britain since 1945: A Political History*, 4th edn, London: Routledge.

Marwick, A. (1996) *British Society since 1945*, 3rd edn, Harmondsworth: Penguin.

Morgan, K. O. (1984) *Labour in Power, 1945–51*, Oxford: Clarendon Press.

—— (1999) *The People's Peace: British History since 1945*, 2nd edn, Oxford: Oxford University Press.

Robbins, K. (1998) 'Fragile bearings 1945–' and 'Losing (domestic) bearings? 1945–', in *Great Britain: Identities, Institutions and the Idea of Britishness*, London: Longman: 297–343.

Sked, A. and Cook, C. (1993) *Post-War Britain: A Political History, 1945–1992*, 4th edn, Harmondsworth: Penguin.

General studies on postwar British culture and identity

Appleyard, B. (1989) *The Pleasures of Peace: Art and Imagination in Postwar Britain*, London: Faber.

Hewison, R. (1977) *Under Siege: Literary Life in London 1939–45*, London: Weidenfeld and Nicolson.

—— (1981) *In Anger: Culture in the Cold War, 1945–60*, London: Weidenfeld and Nicolson.

—— (1986) *Too Much: Art and Society in the Sixties, 1960–1975*, London: Methuen.

—— (1987) *The Heritage Industry: Britain in a Climate of Decline*, London: Methuen.

—— (1995) *Culture and Consensus: England, Art and Politics since 1940*, London: Methuen.

Kenner, H. (1987) *A Sinking Island: The Modern English Writers*, New York: Knopf.

Marwick, A. (1991) *Culture in Britain since 1945*, Oxford: Blackwell.

—— (1998) *The Sixties: Cultural Revolution in Britain, France, Italy, and the United States, c.1958–c.1974*, Oxford: Oxford University Press.

Nehring, N. (1993) *Flowers in the Dustbin: Culture, Anarchy and Postwar England*, Ann Arbor: University of Michigan Press.

Piette, A. (1995) *Imagination at War: British Fiction and Poetry, 1939–1945*, London: Papermac.

Sinfield, A. (1989) *Literature, Politics and Culture in Postwar Britain*, Oxford: Blackwell.

—— (1997) *Literature, Politics and Culture in Postwar Britain*, 2nd edn, London: Athlone.

Veldman, M. (1994) *Fantasy, the Bomb and the Greening of Britain: Romantic Protest, 1945–1980*, Cambridge: Cambridge University Press.

Waugh, P. (1995) *The Harvest of the Sixties: English Literature and Its Background, 1960–1990*, Oxford: Oxford University Press.

Wiener, M. J. (1981) *English Culture and the Decline of the Industrial Spirit 1850–1980*, Cambridge: Cambridge University Press.

General studies on post-imperial Britain

Beveridge, C. and Turnbull, R. (1989) *The Eclipse of Scottish Culture: Inferiorism and the Intellectuals*, Edinburgh: Polygon.

Bhabha, H. K. (1994) *The Location of Culture*, London: Routledge.

Bogdanor, V. (1999) *Devolution in the United Kingdom*, 2nd rev. edn, Oxford: Oxford University Press.

Brah, A. (1996) 'Constructions of the "Asian" in post-war Britain: culture, politics and identity in the pre-Thatcher years', in *Cartographies of Diaspora: Contesting Identities*, London: Routledge.

Brett, D. (1996) *The Construction of Heritage*, Cork: Cork University Press.

Chambers, I. (1994) *Migrancy, Culture, Identity*, London: Routledge.

Colley, L. (1992) *Britons: Forging the Nation 1707–1837*, New Haven: Yale University Press.

Corner, J. and Harvey, S. (1991) *Enterprise and Heritage: Crosscurrents of National Culture*, London: Routledge.

Curtis, T. (1986) *Wales: The Imagined Nation. Essays in Cultural and National Identity*, Bridgend: Poetry Wales Press.

Gilroy, P. (1987) *'There Ain't No Black in the Union Jack': The Cultural Politics of Race and Nation*, London: Hutchinson.

Harvie, C. (1998) *Scotland and Nationalism: Scottish Society and Politics, 1707 to the Present*, 3rd edn, London: Routledge.

Hebdige, D. (1987) *Cut'n'mix: Culture, Identity and Caribbean Music*, London: Routledge.

Kearney, H. F. (1989) *The British Isles: A History of Four Nations*, Cambridge: Cambridge University Press.

Kearney, R. (1997) *Postnationalist Ireland: Politics, Culture, Philosophy*, London: Routledge.

McCrone, D. (1992) *Understanding Scotland: the Sociology of a Stateless Nation*, London: Routledge.

McCrone, D., Morris, A. and Kiely, R. (eds) (1995) *Scotland the Brand: The Making of Scottish Heritage*, Edinburgh: Edinburgh University Press.

Miller, D. (ed.) (1998) *Rethinking Northern Ireland: Culture, Ideology and Colonialism*, London: Longman.

Mitchell, J. (1996) 'Scotland in the union, 1945–95: the changing nature of the union state,' in T. M. Devine and R. J. Finlay (eds), *Scotland in the 20th Century*, Edinburgh: Edinburgh University Press: 85–101.

Morgan, K. O. (1981) *Rebirth of A Nation: Wales 1880–1980*, Oxford: Clarendon Press.

—— (1995) *Modern Wales: Politics, Places and People*, Cardiff: University of Wales Press.

Nairn, T. (1977) *The Break-Up of Britain: Crisis and Neo-Nationalism*, London: New Left Books.

—— (1988) *The Enchanted Glass: Britain and its Monarchy*, London: Radius.

—— (1997) *Faces of Nationalism: Janus Revisited*, London: Verso.

Paterson, L. (1994) *The Autonomy of Modern Scotland*, Edinburgh: Edinburgh University Press.

Pocock, J. G. A. (1995) 'Contingency, identity, sovereignty', in A. Grant and K. J. Stringer (eds), *Uniting the Kingdom? The Making of British History*, London: Routledge:292–302.

Samuel, R. (1994) *Theatres of Memory, vol. 1: Past and Present in Contemporary Culture*, London: Verso.

—— (1998) *Theatres of Memory, vol. 2: Island Stories: Unravelling Britain*, London: Verso.

Wright, P. (1985) *On Living in an Old Country: the National Past in Contemporary Britain*, London: Verso.

General studies on postwar British poetry, fiction and drama

Connor, S. (1996) *The English Novel in History 1950–1995*, London: Routledge.

Corcoran, N. (1993) *English Poetry since 1940*, London: Longman.

—— (1997) *After Yeats and Joyce: Reading Modern Irish Literature*, Oxford: Oxford University Press.

Craig, C. (1996) *Out of History: Narrative Paradigms in Scottish and English Culture*, Edinburgh: Polygon.

Crawford, R. (1992) *Devolving English Literature*, Oxford: Clarendon Press.

Day, G. and Docherty, B. (eds) (1995) *British Poetry 1900–1950: Aspects of Tradition*, Basingstoke: Macmillan.

—— (1997) *British Poetry from the 1950s to the 1990s: Politics and Art*, Basingstoke: Macmillan.

Elsom, J. (1979) *Post-War British Theatre*, 2nd edn, London: Routledge.

English, J. F. (1994) *Comic Transactions: Literature, Humor and the Politics of Community in Twentieth-Century Britain*, Ithaca, N.Y.: Cornell University Press.

Gasiorek, A. (1995) *Post-War British Fiction: Realism and After*, London: Arnold.

Goodman, L. (1993) *Contemporary Feminist Theatres: To Each Her Own*, London: Routledge.

Moore-Gilbert, B. J. (ed.) (1994) *The Arts in the 1970s: Cultural Closure?*, London: Routledge.

Morrison, B. (1980) *The Movement: English Poetry and Fiction of the Nineteen-Fifties*, Oxford: Oxford University Press.

Rebellato, D. (1999) *1956 And All That: The Making of Modern British Drama*, London: Routledge.

Scanlan, M. (1990) *Traces of Another Time: History and Politics in Postwar British Fiction*, Princeton: Princeton University Press.

Sinfield, A. (ed.) (1983) *Society and Literature 1945–1970*, London: Methuen.

Wandor, M. (1986) *Carry on Understudies: Theatre and Sexual Politics*, new edn, London: Routledge.

Chapter 1

Disunited kingdom

Irish, Scottish and Welsh writing in the postwar period

Siobhán Kilfeather

Naming names

In my reading of the Irish, Scottish and Welsh writing of the postwar period, I place emphasis on the tension, awkwardness and embarrassment that Irish, Scottish and Welsh people experience with the English language: as they use it, as they are described by it and as they transform it. Amongst other features of this tension there is a history of controversy over naming peoples, territories, languages and literatures that may not be obvious to readers from elsewhere.

The United Kingdom is a name that attempts to encompass two kingdoms, Scotland and England; a principality, Wales; and a province, Northern Ireland, (which incorporates most of the old Irish province of Ulster), partitioned since 1920 from the rest of Ireland. Many people in Ireland, Scotland and Wales regard the terms 'kingdom', 'principality' and 'province' with unease and there is a continuing dispute over whom to include in the adjectives 'Irish', 'Scottish' and 'Welsh'. It is difficult to find neutral descriptions even of territory. Many of the Irish dislike the 'British' in 'British Isles', while the Welsh and Scottish are not keen on 'Great Britain'. As the Scottish poet Douglas Dunn (b. 1942) puts it:

> At certain points the cultures of Wales, Ireland, Scotland and England overlap. But there's too much resistance from each of them – and, quite rightly so, from England too, for these tentatively shared concerns to make a 'Britain'.
>
> (Crawford 1992: 290)

In response to these difficulties, 'Britain and Ireland' is becoming a preferred usage although there is also a growing trend amongst some critics to refer to Britain and Ireland as 'the archipelago'.

Part of the difficulty in using 'Irish', 'Scottish' and 'Welsh' in a discussion of culture is that each country has literature in at least two languages. For Ireland I use 'Irish language' or 'Gaelic' and 'anglophone'. The three languages of Scotland I describe as 'Scottish Gaelic', 'Scots' and 'anglophone Scottish'. I follow recent practice in using Welsh as an inclusive category and distinguishing 'Welsh language' from 'anglophone Welsh' (in preference to Anglo-Welsh). There are some writers who still identify themselves as Anglo-Irish, Anglo-Scottish and Anglo-Welsh, but the majority reject the implication that they are half-English even if they accept other hyphenated identities. In Ireland Unionists prefer the terms 'Northern Ireland' and 'Ulster', while other people prefer 'the north of Ireland' and 'the six counties'. Again, there is no neutral position and I use these descriptions as I think people would describe themselves, unless there is some striking advantage apparent in placing a writer in a new category.

Should writers be identified as 'unionist' or 'anti-unionist', 'nationalist' or 'anti-nationalist', 'catholic' or 'protestant'? I do not believe that any of the writings I discuss are simply unionist or nationalist and I do not think there is any value in ascribing these opinions to writers unless they are actively espousing a cause. In Ireland, as in Wales and Scotland, knowledge of a person's religious background (even when it is not a major theme in the work) may contribute to an understanding of her/his outlook and material circumstances. It would, of course, be handy if there were a collective term for the Irish, Scots and Welsh. In this essay, I use the term 'Celtic', while acknowledging my own Celtic embarrassment at doing so.

Disunited kingdom

One way of reading the presence of Irish, Scottish and Welsh writing in contemporary British culture is to see that presence as a contribution to the richness, density and particularity of the whole, to see it as one of the terms by which Britishness has had to re-define itself in the last fifty years. Another way of looking at the same history might suggest that Celtic writers, whatever their politics, have drawn attention to the breakup of Britain, perhaps even contributed to that breakup, to such an extent that it is almost impossible to name and describe something called British culture. Like other disaffected groups within the United Kingdom, the Celts have at times squirmed uneasily at their presumed incorporation into Britishness.

It is a common perception among the Scottish, Welsh and Irish populations that they face personal discrimination in England, and that for much of the last fifty years they have been discriminated against *en masse* by the Westminster government. Northern Irish Catholics, Ulster Unionists, Scottish and Welsh peoples may have very different and quite specific grievances against English dominance within the British Isles, but they have shared, for much of the postwar period, the experience of being ruled by Westminster governments which have received little mandate from the non-English provinces of the United Kingdom. The Irish, and more particularly the Scottish and Welsh, differ in one significant way from other minorities in that the imagined communities described by the terms 'the United Kingdom' and even 'Great Britain' depend on the fiction of their consent to inclusion within Britishness, and for the last fifty years that fiction has been under increasing pressure. This is not to say of the Northern Irish, Scottish and Welsh populations that each manifests a complete nationalist disaffection from the United Kingdom. The tension between unionist and anti-unionist opinion in Northern Ireland is well known and the Scottish and Welsh devolution referendums of 1979 and 1997 indicated substantial unionist feeling. Many Scottish and Welsh people have been divided in themselves over the question of national identification, and one useful consequence of thinking about postwar culture is to remind oneself that the war represents a high point in loyalty to the union.

National and nationalist consciousness

What relevance does the development of national or nationalist consciousness have to a discussion of literature in the postwar period? (For some people, a national consciousness allows them to make a cultural identification while a nationalist consciousness implies a desire to see political self-determination.) Peter Kravitz remarks, with regard to the failure to achieve Scottish devolution in 1979, that there is 'a school of thought that says that when the politics of a country run aground, the people look for self-expression in culture' (Kravitz 1997: xiii).

One might argue with some plausibility that most significant postwar Celtic writing has demonstrated a nationalist consciousness of disaffection, even if it has not espoused nationalist politics; yet before assenting to the proposition that culture is an alternative to, or an alternative form of political action, one might want to examine the possibility that the literature of the Irish Republic represents a counter-example; of a more achieved and self-sufficient culture, speaking to an international as well as a home audience, its self-sufficiency made possible by the political independence that has allowed Ireland to differentiate itself from Britain. Certainly, since Independence, Irish writers have generally been more productive and have had a higher profile, in Britain as well as internationally, than their Welsh and Scottish counterparts. Because of exile and diaspora, Irish writing also confounds those descriptive projects that map national culture onto a national territory.

Since the 1970s, Northern Irish writers have increasingly identified themselves as Irish, while some of the leading Irish writers of the postwar period, including the novelists and short story writers William Trevor (b. 1928) and Edna O'Brien (b. 1930), have lived in Britain and set much of their fiction there. It would be perverse, even if it is not uncommon, to exclude figures such as the novelists John McGahern (b. 1934) and John Banville (b. 1945) and the dramatist Brian Friel (b. 1929) from a discussion of British literature since much of their work was originally published or performed in Britain and had an immediate influence on British writers and audiences.

Provincial and parochial

No one surveying British culture in the postwar period could fail to notice the numbers of Celts prominent in publishing, performance, broadcasting, journalism and the cinema. In the immediate postwar period, however, the perceived asymmetry in cultural relations between the English and the Celts was manifest in a widespread Celtic anxiety about provincialism. In the 1940s and 1950s, the poet, novelist, journalist, editor and cultural commentator Patrick Kavanagh (1904–67) repeatedly denounced what he saw as an abject provincialism in Irish culture, involving, on the one hand, a cliquish self-involvement amongst Dublin intellectuals and, on the other hand, an unnecessary deference to London, where most Irish writers were published. Kavanagh argued instead for the value of what he termed the parochial: the writer's ability to pay close attention to the detail of his or her specific location, and by the quality of that attention to create a universal interest:

> Parochialism and provincialism are opposites. The provincial has
> no mind of his own; he does not trust what his eyes see until he has

> heard what the metropolis – towards which his eyes are turned – has to say on any subject. . . . The parochial mentality . . . is never in any doubt about the social and artistic validity of his parish.
>
> (Kavanagh 1967: 282)

This was to prove a particular inspiration for later writers of rural origin, not least Seamus Heaney (b. 1939). From the opening poem 'Digging', in his first full collection, *Death of a Naturalist* (1966), Heaney asserts the validity of country observations and pursuits in and of themselves and as an appropriate analogue for poetic endeavours. He opens an essay on Kavanagh by quoting Kavanagh's 'I have never been much considered by the English critics' (Heaney 1980: 115; Kavanagh 1964: xiii). It is not, of course, something that Heaney could now say about himself, but it was until recently a common note struck by other Celtic writers. One meets it, for instance, in Scotland's greatest twentieth-century poet Hugh MacDiarmid (1892–1978) writing about his Welsh contemporaries:

> It is a sufficient exposé of contemporary criticism in the English-speaking world that a host of names would be mentioned as contemporary poets of consequence before coming to, if at all, the names of David Jones and Saunders Lewis, who alone of poets in the United Kingdom today are worth mentioning at all.
>
> (MacDiarmid 1973: 158; Jones 1996: 22)

This frustration with English metropolitan culture has pushed Celtic writers into modes of address that by-pass English audiences. For some, from MacDiarmid and other major Scottish poets such as Edwin Muir (1887–1959) and Edwin Morgan (b. 1928) to more recent Northern Irish poets such as Derek Mahon (b. 1941) and Tom Paulin (b. 1949), the turn has been towards Europe, particularly the literatures of Russia and Eastern Europe (Muir, Morgan and Mahon have all been notable translators); but more recently, as we shall see, the USA has become a stronger influence.

The contrast between a European interest and an American interest may *loosely* equate with a contrast between two different attitudes to tradition, one modernist and the other post-modernist, and that shift in attitudes may be partly attributed to a change over the postwar period in the way intellectuals live their public lives. Heaney's career is a good example of that change. He was born and reared in Co. Derry, in Northern Ireland, of Catholic background, and attended Queen's University, Belfast, where he later worked as a lecturer. He had published three book-length collections of poetry by 1971–2, when he spent a year as guest lecturer at the University of California, Berkeley. When he returned to Ireland it was to live in the Republic, at first writing full time, then from 1975 as head of English at a teacher training college. From 1981 he divided his time between home in Dublin and a professorship at Harvard. He has won every major literary prize and distinction including election as Oxford Professor of Poetry in 1989 and the Nobel Prize for Literature in 1995.

Few contemporary writers have been as successful as Heaney, but most are affected by the globalisation of literary culture and the collapse of a simple opposition between home and exile or emigration, themes which figure prominently in Heaney's recent volumes of poetry, *The Haw Lantern* (1987), *Seeing Things* (1991) and *The Spirit Level* (1996). In an essay entitled 'Englands of the Mind' (1980) he described three English poets – Philip Larkin, Ted Hughes and Geoffrey Hill – as 'afflicted with a sense of history that was once the peculiar affliction of the poets of other nations who were not themselves natives of England, but who spoke the English language' (Heaney 1980: 150). One way of differentiating Celtic modernists from post-modernists would be to suggest that the latter feel liberated from the responsibilities of literary and political representation into an embracing of the notion that there is no real Ireland or Scotland or Wales other than that of the mind. It is a view which has been strongly contested, but the fact that it has been expressed at all reveals some of the profound transformations of the postwar period.

War and the postwar: re-figuring Celtic identities

For many Celtic writers, the deaths of W. B. Yeats (1865–1939) and James Joyce (1882–1941) seemed to mark a generational shift to coincide with the war. The most recognisably cosmopolitan Irish writer of the postwar period and the one who seemed most intimately con-nected to Joyce and his pre-war inheritance was Samuel Beckett (1906–1989), but Beckett's chosen exile in Paris contributed to the sense that he was exceptional to debates about the nature and signifi-cance of Irish literature, even though he remained an aid and inspiration to writers in Ireland.

There were still major writers who linked both pre-war and postwar

England and Ireland. Born into the Anglo-Irish gentry, Elizabeth Bowen (1899–1973) spent only part of her time and creative energies in Ireland, yet she set some of her pre-war and her postwar fiction (including her finest novel, *The Heat of the Day* (1949) and *A World of Love* (1955)) wholly or in part in Ireland. One might argue that her meditations on loyalty and betrayal, her concern with houses and with place, and her many ghost stories were intrinsically 'Irish' in their interests. Francis Stuart (b. 1902), who had been educated at a major British public school, focused in his pre-war and his postwar fiction on the figure of the artist: violence, shame, alienation and the suffering of the innocent scapegoat informing his vision. Yet their different relationships to Britain during the war revealed powerful doubts and self-divisions within Irish culture. During what was termed 'the emergency' (1939–45), the Irish Free State maintained its neutrality. Bowen gathered intelligence in Ireland for the British government. Stuart (who explored his decision to do so in his extraordinary autobiographical novel, *Black List, Section H*, (1971)) broadcast anti-British propaganda for the Nazis on German radio. Imprisoned briefly by the French after the war, he did not return to Ireland until 1958.

To a lesser extent, support for the British cause during the Second World War caused division within Scotland and Wales, where some nationalists sought to oppose the war effort on the grounds that it was England's imperialist war. The dominant figure in twentieth-century Welsh language writing, Saunders Lewis (1893–1985), was at the forefront of this. Indeed, Celtic writers who fought in the war were not unaware of the contradictions of fighting in the British Imperial Army. The brilliantly gifted Welsh poet Alun Lewis (1915–44), who died while on military service in Burma, possibly by his own hand, movingly captured in the first volume of his masterly short stories, *The Last Inspection* (1943), the dislocation experienced by Welsh soldiers in the British army and, in *In the Green Tree* (1948), the difficulties of a Welsh-born officer faced in India with the suppression of nationalist agitation.) By contrast, MacDiarmid, Scotland's leading literary figure, supported the war-effort by working in a factory in Glasgow.

It has been suggested that Hugh MacDiarmid and the Welsh poet and painter David Jones (1895–1974) arrived late at the table of high Modernism, but in both cases one might prefer to attribute their continuing preoccupations with modernist aesthetics in the postwar period (they had both produced outstanding work in the 1930s) to their desire to maintain reference and allusion to Celtic traditions. Throughout his career, MacDiarmid hoped for a literary and political

Scottish Renaissance, equivalent to the Irish literary Renaissance at the beginning of the century. (An explicitly political writer, he had founded the National Party of Scotland in 1928, from which he was expelled in 1933 for being a communist. He was in turn expelled from the communist party in 1938 for being a nationalist.) Jones took a more conciliatory view of the idea of Britain. For, in a poetic style which owed much to Joyce's *Finnegans Wake* (1939), Jones celebrated in *The Anathemata* (1952) and his other densely written postwar prose and poetry, the Celtic substratum of the Romano-British culture from which, in his view, 'the matter of Britain' was formed. Jones actually lived in Wales for only a very short part of his life, but the interest in his Welshness which he inherited from his father was reinforced by his time in a Welsh regiment of the British army during the First World War. Jones is thus an uncharacteristic Welsh writer in some respects, but he shares with many other Welsh writers an interest in pre-conquest Wales, in the figures of storyteller and bard, and in translation from medieval Welsh tales, particularly *The Mabinogion*. In all the Celtic countries translation has been a central cultural activity (as we have seen most recently in Heaney's Sweeney poems), a debt to the past and also a source of relatively little known and 'exotic' narrative.

MacDiarmid, however, drew attention to one important difference between Scotland and the other Celtic nations: Scotland has literatures in three languages. The exotic vocabularies and eclectic allusions of modernist poetry authorised MacDiarmid's revival of Scots language poetry as capable vehicle for a dialogue with a Western European tradition, but he was even more particularly inspired by Joyce's 'taking on the English language itself and wrestling its genius with his bare hands' (Heaney 1980: 196) and by the Irishman's demonstration as to how 'the panorama of human existence could be presented in a modern "provincial" town which was, like Edinburgh, a lapsed European capital' (Crawford 1992: 252). *In Memoriam James Joyce* (1955) is the most obvious acknowledgement of this debt but it is also present in an aspect of MacDiarmid's poetry that often exasperates critics, the apparently awkward juxtapositions of vernacular Scots as still spoken with an archaic Scots mined from etymological dictionaries.

In 1961, Caradog Prichard (1904–80) published the one undoubted masterpiece of postwar Welsh-language fiction, *Un Nos Ola Leuad*. (Translated into English in 1973, this was re-issued by Penguin in 1999 under the title *One Moonlit Night*.) Set in a Welsh slate-quarrying village during the First World War, it not only undermined idealistic representations of Welsh rural life by presenting a world of isolation, madness, violence and sexual perversion; it also used the techniques of the English and European modernist novel to explore consciousness, sexuality and the nature of time. With this exception in mind, one might still be tempted to polarise postwar Welsh writing into two camps: one rural, nationalist and Welsh-language, the other industrial, socialist and anglophone. The first tradition has been memorably captured in Paul Turner's 1992 Oscar nominated Welsh-language film *Hedd Wyn*: a biography of Ellis H. Evans (1887–1917), a young Welsh-language poet who won the National Eisteddfod Chair a month after he was killed in action. In a not unsubtle way Evans is represented as inhabiting a pre-modern, family-centred, idyllic rural life doubly assaulted by the arrival of the English language, which in the film signifies both sexual corruption and modern technologies, specifically the technology of the Englishman's war.

Although much Welsh literature is preoccupied with self-divisions and hostilities that might seem to pit the Welsh-language and anglophone communities against one another, there have been significant alliances and exchanges between writers in the two languages. Born in Cardiff but brought up in England during the first six years of his life, R. S. Thomas (1913–2000) (whom many regard, along with Larkin, as the outstanding English-language poet of the postwar period) only became sufficiently at home in the Welsh language to write prose, and his (anglophone) poetry often reflects on language as a site of struggle in Wales. In one obvious way his poetry dwells on the question *What is a Welshman?*, the title of his 1974 collection, and in the early poetry, particularly *Song at the Year's Turning* (1955) which established his reputation, this seems to be addressed through modes of observation. Thomas was a Church of Wales priest, whose early work records aspects of the lives of his rural parishioners in Manafon. Yet, in his later work, he is a writer who seems particularly aware of the contradictions in his own work, using the English language, as in 'Reservoirs', to criticise the English degradation of Wales, while also alert to the dangers of certain Welsh complicities with that degradation. The English, he complains, scavenge 'among the remains / Of our culture. . . .' They elbow 'our language / Into the grave that we have dug for it.' Thomas' alienation from England and from English has become so intense that this pre-eminent anglophone poet declares in his recent *Autobiographies* (1997) that he pretends not to speak English when asked for directions by English tourists in Wales (Thomas 1997: 147).

Stage Celts, screen Celts

As the author of some of the most celebrated English lyrics of the century (*Deaths and Entrances*, 1946), Dylan Thomas (1914–1953) remains Wales's most famous literary figure outside Wales. Born in Swansea to Welsh-speaking parents, he felt the loss of the Welsh language which his own parents had not passed on to him, and in his best known work, the verse-play *Under Milk Wood* (1954) and the auto-biographical *Portrait of the Artist as a Young Dog* (1940), he gave English poetry, fiction and drama a distinctively Welsh setting and inflection.

Brendan Behan (1923–1964) is a figure like Dylan Thomas, almost as famous for his definition of an artistic life of excess as for his writing, and like Thomas he was taken up as something of an idiot *savant* by English and American critics. In the 1950s and 1960s, he entertained and scandalised the British with his drunken appearances on the BBC. He had been released from prison in 1946 and carried *a frisson* of danger about him. To some Irish critics he was a bogus figure, merely catering to English fantasies of the stereotypical drunken Irishman. Recently his reputation has risen again, with greater appreciation of the ways in which his bi-lingual and bi-sexual writings challenged taboos in their exploration of gender and nation. An exciting writer in both languages and across a number of genres, Behan made a particular impact on the otherwise relatively unmemorable field (Beckett excepted) of Irish drama in the 1950s, with *The Quare Fellow*, produced at The Pike Theatre Dublin in 1956 and *An Giall* produced by Joan Littlewood in London, in translation as *The Hostage* (1958).

The Quare Fellow was made into a film (dir. Arthur Dreifus, GB, 1962), which toned down its anarchic elements. It was one of a number of films in the 1940s and 1950s representing Celts on the screen. *Odd Man Out* (dir. Carol Reed, GB, 1946) was filmed in Belfast, and is a moody and evocative example of what was to become an increasingly popular genre of films about Ireland; the story of the IRA gunman torn by guilt and conflicting loyalties. It is a world apart from *The Quiet Man* (dir. John Ford, USA, 1952), in which Sean Thornton (John Wayne) is an Irish-American who returns to the West of Ireland to buy the cottage in which he was born, and to bury his own violent past as a boxer. His courtship of Mary-Kate Danagher (Maureen O'Hara) is played out against a background of folk-custom and romantic rural landscape that seems to deny Ireland a place in the modern world, or any world but that of the imagination. The film may well have contributed to an American image of Ireland as fundamentally pastoral and innocent, but Ford's sentimentalism is by no means unintelligent or simply socially conservative. *The Quiet Man* represents an important moment in the preoccupation of film makers with finding ways of using and ways of interpreting the Irish landscape. (In later films as divergent as *Ryan's Daughter* (dir. David Lean, GB, 1970) and *Maeve* (dir. Pat Murphy and John Davies, IR, 1980) the representation of landscape is a major theme.)

One film, *This Other Eden* (dir. Muriel Box, IR, 1959), deserves to be better known. It tells the story of a small town's plan to commemorate a hero of the War of Independence (clearly modelled on Michael Collins) and the revelation of long-kept secrets; there is a richly comic treatment of the contradictions inherent in modern Ireland's attitude to remembering history.

Probably the two best known films set in Scotland in the period 1945–59 are *I Know Where I'm Going* (dir. Michael Powell and Emeric Pressburger, GB, 1945) and *Whisky Galore!* (dir. Alexander Mackendrick, GB, 1948). It is not to denigrate their fine achievements to suggest that these two films work within conventions of caricature of the Celt that, on the one hand, involve feudalism, loss, mourning, mythic and mystical attributes, and, on the other hand, comic deviousness and insubordination. Ford had used Maureen O'Hara and other Irish actors in a sentimental film about childhood in a Welsh mining village, *How Green Was My Valley* (USA, 1941), adapted from Richard Llewellyn's novel of the same name. One might infer from this that the Welsh stereotype was less clearly identifiable in Britain and America than the Scottish or Irish equivalents.

Censorship and conservatism: postwar Irish writing

With Independence, Irish writers and intellectuals developed some sense of material and moral separation from Britain but they also encountered a growing alienation from the institutions of Irish society which they found repressive: the churches, the government, and the structures of family life. In 1949 the Free State became a Republic, marking a further degree of separation from the United Kingdom and British Commonwealth. A parallel *malaise* was felt in Northern Ireland: the forms of optimism associated with the new Labour government in Britain after the war were in marked contrast to the re-establishment of an Ulster Unionist government socially conservative and rigorously sectarian. From 1945 to 1959 Ulster writers, led by poets such as John Hewitt (1907–1987) (the most interesting of the Northern Irish poets to write about landscape and dialect) and W. R. Rodgers (1909–1969) attempted to carve out a space loosely termed 'regional'. By contrast, Dublin-based intellectuals attempted to situate their work within and against the larger body of anglophone writing. *The Bell*, a periodical founded and edited in Dublin by Sean O'Faoláin (1900–1991) in 1940, and from 1946 until its closure in 1954 edited by the novelist Peadar O'Donnell (1893–1986), was a major site of debate on cultural, social and economic issues.

In its early years *The Bell* was particularly noted for its critique of the Irish Censorship Board. The Censorship of Publications Act (1929) had established the Board to advise the Minister of Justice on the proscription of corrupt literature. It is possible to read the early enthusiasm for censorship in Ireland as part of a wider trend in favour of cultural and social differentiation from Britain. It was, however, not very long before censorship began to blight the careers of Irish writers. In 1936 O'Faoláin's own novel, *Bird Alone*, was banned, as was Kate O'Brien's (1897–1974) *Mary Lavelle* (1936); and there was particular scandal in 1941 when O'Brien's novel, *The Land of Spices*, was banned for the sake of a single sentence referring to homosexuality. It is not clear, however, that the general public beyond liberals and intellectuals greatly noticed the censorship of publications, even while their public libraries and education system were impoverished by it. It might rather be argued that the most significant impact of censorship was in its provocative effect on literary production. It became almost an act of responsibility for Irish writers to defy the law, and this may have influenced novelists in particular in favour of the apparent formal realism that characterises the early fiction of banned writers such as O'Brien and McGahern. Censorship may have been intended to promote a distinction between Britain and Ireland favourable to the latter's self-esteem, but for writers it had the opposite effect, with many banned writers, or those who feared censorship, migrating to Britain.

Northern Ireland may have been free from the censorship of the Republic but life there was characterised by social conservatism and repression. Louis MacNeice (1907–1963), who had been born in Northern Ireland, was the pre-eminent northern poet of the immediate postwar period, but it took a long time for his juniors to digest and respond to his work, particularly to the Irish section of his *Autumn Journal* (1939). To his immediate contemporaries MacNeice, who worked for the BBC in London, seemed to belong much more to the world of Auden and Spender. It was only in the 1970s that one begins to see homage to MacNeice in the work of poets such as Michael Longley (b. 1939) and Derek Mahon, equivalent to that offered by younger Irish poets to Kavanagh's writings. For Ulster novelists, 'lonely passion', often played out across a sectarian divide, is the central trope. Brian Moore (1921–99) wrote about the bleak Belfast of his adolescence from the perspective of exile in Canada and later the USA. Anne Crone (1915–1972) and Janet McNeill (1907–1992) may well have suffered in terms of reputation, as have many other women writers in similar circumstances, because their novels on the same subject appeared to be arriving at *genres* and conventions just as their male contemporaries were departing from them.

The Field Day Company: theatre and nation

The economic modernisation of Ireland in the 1960s led to increasing challenges to the status quo. Indeed since the 1960s, modernisation has been accompanied by what has come to be known as a 'revisionist' turn in academic and perhaps in more popular Irish attitudes to the past, a critique of nationalist mythology around certain key events in history such as the famine and the War of Independence. Revisionism, which was originally a feature of academic debates between historians, became a feature of more widespread cultural criticism and provoked counter-arguments. Journals such as *Atlantis* (1970–74) and *The Crane Bag* (1977–85) attempted to fill the role once played by *The Bell* in addressing the state of the nation, and situating Irish cultural debate within a European context. From the outset, *The Crane Bag* sought to identify itself with a mythical 'fifth province', 'a no-man's land, a neutral ground where things can detach themselves from all partisan and prejudiced connection and show themselves for what they really are' (M. P. Hederman and R. Kearney 1982: 10).

The Field Day Theatre Company, founded in 1980 by dramatist Brian Friel and the actor Stephen Rea, and emulating the work of the 7: 84 Company in Scotland, became another important platform for critique. The company was initially pledged to touring theatre in Ireland, for theatre had played an important role in the Irish Revival at the beginning of the century and could be seen as a significant place for consciousness-raising. (From the 1970s amateur theatre groups were part of a mushrooming in community action in Northern Ireland.) By opening their plays in Derry and moving to all-Ireland tours, Field Day contributed to the presumption of a culturally united Ireland. Field Day's first production was of Friel's *Translations* (1980), an instant critical and popular success. Describing the confrontation between British soldiers and a small Irish-speaking village during the Ordnance Survey of Ireland in the 1830s, the play explored the ways in which identity was tied to language and to place names. Seamus Deane (b. 1941), Heaney and Paulin joined the Board of Directors, and their early productions included both new plays by Friel and others and translations of classical plays given an Irish resonance by Heaney and Paulin. Field Day not only rapidly became the most controversial cultural project in Ireland but also ensured that the theatre (energised by the work of Friel) was the place in which the competing traditions in Ireland were explored. In *Observe the Sons of Ulster Marching Towards the Somme* (1986), for instance, Frank McGuinness (b. 1953) represented Unionist identity critically but with imaginative understanding, while in *The Steward of Christendom* (1995), Sebastian Barry (b. 1955) dramatised the plight of those Catholic Irishmen after Independence who had been loyal to the Crown.

Anthologising the nation

To the theatrical productions were added a pamphlet series, which included contributions from distinguished international leftist critics, and a large multi-volume historical anthology of Irish writing. For critics of Field Day the importation of post-colonial perspectives, such as that of Edward Said, far from enlarging debates on Irish culture, rather revealed Field Day's covert nationalist bias. Field Day was attacked by Edna Longley (b. 1940) for mixing up poetry and politics, helping to reinforce the literary streak that makes Irish Nationalism 'more a theology than an ideology' (Longley 1986: 185). The publication in 1991 of *The Field Day Anthology of Irish Writing* drew a different and more widespread critique. In spite of all of the ways in which the editors, in particular Deane, the general editor, had argued for a diverse and inclusive vision of Irish writing, informed by new and post-modern definitions of 'writing', the anthology was actually received as authoritarian and exclusive, particularly in its apparent evaluation of women's contributions to Irish culture.

The controversy stirred by *The Field Day Anthology* can partly be accounted for by observing that anthologies, literary histories, dictionaries and atlases were all sites of debate about nationhood in the Celtic countries from the 1970s onwards. As the easiest texts to produce, anthologies were the most frequent occasions of debate. The arguments about names, for example, which I describe in my foreword, is largely conducted in the introductions to anthologies. In 1983 Heaney responded to his inclusion in *The Penguin Book of Contemporary British Poetry* (1982) with 'An Open Letter' addressed to the anthology's editors, Blake Morrison and Andrew Motion, refusing the adjective 'British':

> For weeks and months I've messed about,
> Unclear, embarrassed and in doubt,
> Footered, havered, spraughled, wrought
> Like Sauneen Keogh,
> Wondering should I write it out
> Or let it go.
>
> (Heaney 1983: 8)

Heaney's verse-letter was a declaration of independence from the semi-colonial status that characterised much of Irish, Scottish and Welsh literature, thought and culture for most of this century. Embarrassment, he suggests, is a key term in appreciating the relationship that anglophone Celtic writers have negotiated with metropolitan English culture. They have felt their difference paraded in order to establish their minor status, but ignored whenever their work is co-opted into claims for the strength, in international terms, of contemporary British poetry or the English novel. (After the death of his friend, the British poet laureate Ted Hughes in 1998, Heaney's name repeatedly appeared in press speculation on candidates for the post since it seemed that his 1995 Nobel Literature Prize made him the pre-eminent living English-language poet. Such speculation drew attention to British confusion as to whether 'English' refers to language, culture or nation.) Nor was he the only poet to take exception to the anthology. Douglas Dunn, who complained that Morrison and Motion referred to him as 'provincial' rather than 'Scots' in their anthology, has a collection of poems, *Barbarians* (1979), which explicitly represents the various ways in which 'barbarians' – the Celts, the provincials, the working class – are made to feel 'embarrassed' in Britain.

Language and dialect

The theatrical work of the Scottish poet and dramatist Liz Lochhead (b. 1947) is regarded by many as amongst the most significant achievements of the postwar Scottish theatre. Her Scots adaptations of Molière (*Tartuffe* in 1986 and *Patter Merchants*, a Glaswegian version of *Les Précieuses Ridicules* in 1989) are, for instance, both 'democratic' – they open up classical theatre to wider audiences – and also attempt to connect the local to the universal, in ways that parallel the adaptations of Sophocles and Chekhov by Heaney, Friel and Paulin for Field Day. In her most popular play, *Mary Queen of Scots Got Her Head Chopped Off* (1987), written in a dialogue between Scots and standard English, Lochhead offers a revision of Scottish and British history that encompasses the historical roots of contemporary sectarianism, the suppression of women's knowledge and experience and the state's investments in the control of female sexuality and reproduction. Finally, in texts such as *Them through the Wall* (1989), co-written with Agnes Owens (b. 1926), Lochhead maintains a commitment, most evident in Scottish fiction through the twentieth century, to represent Scottish working-class life. Heaney's use of 'footered', 'havered', 'spraughled' in the poem above similarly draws attention to the ways in which class and ethnic conflicts in late twentieth-century Britain have often been figured in struggles over voice. Accent, dialect and pronunciation, like multilingualism, have been controversial in debates over proper British identities, with conservative educationalists advocating minority assimilation through the school system, and a repression of ethnic dialects, languages and cultures.

For much of Heaney and Lochhead's childhood the broadcast media and school curriculum were dominated by 'standard English' and 'received pronunciation'; yet for Irish and Scottish writers the use of non-standard grammatical forms and dialect vocabulary connects them respectively to the Irish language and the evolution of Hiberno-English as Gaelic dwindled in common usage and to Lallans Scots and Gaelic. Simon Armitage and Robert Crawford have suggested that the 1944 Butler Education Act 'heralded and later schooled' an emergent 'democratic' voice in postwar British and Irish poetry (Armitage and Crawford 1998: xx), with the result that provincial and working-class poets such as Tony Harrison and Peter Reading, immigrants and, of course, women, like Fleur Adcock (who came to Britain from New Zealand), Grace Nichols (originally from Guyana) and, one might add, Northern Ireland's most accomplished female poet, Medbh McGukian

(b. 1950), shared in the liberation from the Oxbridge tones of pre-war poets and critics.

One might suppose that writers working in the Welsh language, the Irish language and in Scots Gaelic would have had little impact on any common sense of British culture. It is certainly true that most students of twentieth-century British literature have never heard of *Traed mewn Cyffion* (1936) (trans. *Feet in Chains*) by Kate Roberts (1891–1985) or *Cré na Cille* (1949) by Máirtín Ó Cadhain (1906–1970). Somhairle MacGill-Eain/ Sorley MacLean (1911–1966), the Scottish-Gaelic poet is better known, not least through his own translations of his work. Yet, for writers committed to the survival of minority languages, the question of whether or not to engage in or even to permit translations from their work has been a vexed one. The Irish poet, Biddy Jenkinson (b. 1949), for example, will not allow her poetry to be translated into English, the language of the conqueror, although she permits translations into other languages. Another Irish poet, Michael Hartnett (b. 1941), titled his 1975 volume *A Farewell to English* and subsequently wrote in Gaelic for a decade. All Scottish, Irish and Welsh writers, however, even if they are mono-lingual, are aware that another language thrives and another literature exists in their own places.

It is a recognition particularly felt in the writing of the Northern Irish poets Ciaran Carson (b. 1948) and Paul Muldoon (b. 1951), which explores one of the familiar themes of Celtic literatures: the threat of cultural contagion that issues from close linguistic proximity. For Carson and Muldoon (as for many other Celtic writers), the clash of the two languages has been productive, a source of macaronic wit and resource. They refresh the vocabulary and syntax of English poetry by interrogating it through 'quotation' from Irish and other languages. Carson's book, *The Irish for No* (1987), involves a punning as much of grammar and syntax as of vocabulary, particularly in the title poem, which invokes one of the most celebrated differences between English and Irish, the fact that Irish has no words for 'yes' and 'no':

> *I cannot see what flowers are at my feet*, when *yes* is the verb repeated,
> Not exactly yes, but phatic nods and whispers.
>
> (Carson 1987: 49)

The quotation from Keats's 'Ode to a Nightingale' invokes in a specific way the partial poetic inheritance from the English tradition. While the recollection of English poetry necessarily informs Carson's use of language, in this case it refers to an alien experience of nature: there are no nightingales in Ireland. Muldoon has an omnipresent romance with real and imagined lexicography. In 'The Right Arm' (*Quoof* 1983), 'English' hovers unspoken behind his speculations on the Irish place-name, Eglish:

> I would give my right arm to have known then
> how Eglish was itself wedged between
> *ecclesia* and *église*.
>
> (Muldoon 1983: 11)

Muldoon's careful meanderings delicately displace meaning, so that in *Meeting the British* (1987), in the volume of the same name, (where the native Americans are given 'two blankets embroidered with smallpox') a little passage of French seems to save the poem from the kind of direct political allegorization that many saw in Heaney's controversial volume, *North* (1972).

Celtic chic and the nineties iconoclasts

> So it was I gave up the Oona for the Susquehanna,
> the Shannon for the Shenandoah.
>
> (Muldoon 1998: 41)

The international success of Irish cinema and popular music (with artists such as Van Morrison, U2, Clannad and Sinéad O'Connor achieving huge international audiences), the acclaim for the 'magical realist' fiction of the Scottish novelist Alasdair Gray (b. 1934), and the admiration (particularly amongst the young) for 'hard-boiled' Scottish writers such as Iain Banks (b. 1958), James Kelman (b. 1946) and Irvine Welsh (b. 1958) have undoubtedly contributed to the widespread sense that it is now fashionable to be Celtic, in ways that writers such as Kavanagh could never have imagined. (Since the late 1980s the annual Booker Prize shortlist has almost always featured an Irish or a Scottish novel: McGahern's *Amongst Women* (1990), Kelman's *How Late it Was, How Late* (1994), Deane's *Reading in the Dark* (1996), Bernard MacLaverty's *Grace Notes* (1997), Patrick McCabe's *Breakfast on Pluto* (1998) and Colm Tóibín's *Blackwater Lightship* (1999).)

Neil Jordan (b. 1951) brought international recognition to Irish cinema with films such as *The Crying Game* (GB, 1992), *Michael Collins* (USA, 1996) and *Butcher Boy* (IR/USA, 1997), adapted from Patrick McCabe's novel of the same name, while the film of Welsh's novel *Trainspotting* (1993) (dir. Danny Boyle, GB, 1996) brought sensational glamour to drug-users and the poor.

Recent Irish writing, including *Ripley Bogle* (1996), by the Northern Irish novelist Robert McLiam Wilson (b. 1964), has shared with recent Scottish writing a desire to reinvigorate tradition with the language and experience of often disaffected urban life. (Wilson's novel is one of the best to deal with the Belfast of the 'Troubles'.) Kelman's *How Late it Was, How Late* (1994) remains the most celebrated example of such urban writing. Set in and around Glasgow, it is a paean to the possibilities and impossibilities articulated in cursing and swearing. Some critics were shocked when it won the Booker prize and even more shocked by the national and class antagonisms of Kelman's acceptance speech.

America, particularly the 'dirty realist' fiction promoted in Britain by *Granta* magazine, has provided a style for new Celtic writing, and also an audience insofar as Celtic groups in the USA have moved away from a culture of shame in emigration to a more positive self-construction as diaspora. New emigrants mainly congregate in the cities and find that a fiction of alienated urban existence is more congruent with their own experiences in New York or Chicago than a nostalgia for rural life and landscape. The young Dubliners in Alan Parker's film of Roddy Doyle's (b. 1958) *The Commitments* (1990) notoriously claim that 'The Irish are the blacks of Europe', and the Celtic identification with Black Americans, which has a long history given new vigour in the civil rights movements of the 1960s, partly expresses an impulse to move away from essentialist constructions of nationality. *The Adoption Papers* (1991), for instance, by the black Scottish writer Jackie Kay (b. 1961) (whose strategies strongly resemble the 'bio-mythography' of the African-American writer Audre Lorde) is an autobiographical poem in several dialects that achieved the kind of popular readership normally reserved for novels, while Kay has gone on to explore its theme of hybridity and identity crisis in her subsequent novel, *Trumpet* (1998). Doyle and McCabe offer different versions of a form of super-realism in which the ghastly existences of the young and the poor are transformed but not transcended through excursions into the fantastic.

In the 1970s, the radical playwrights John Arden and Margaretta D'Arcy intervened on behalf of the Irish and Welsh and met with fierce resistance from the British establishment. Their work resulted in a libel suit over *The Ballygombeen Bequest* (1972) (later titled *The Little Gray Home in the West*), which accused British businesses of oppressing the Irish rural poor; a conflict with the Royal Shakespeare Company whom they accused of altering their Welsh-centred play, *The Island of the Mighty* (1972), into a defence instead of a critique of imperialism; and a decade of more or less direct censorship after 1978 when Arden was commissioned to write radio drama for the BBC on the condition that he did not treat contemporary themes. In the 1990s, younger Irish, Scots and Welsh writers speak on their own behalf, their iconoclasm extending to a rejection of Heaney or MacDiarmid as establishment figures. Kravitz, writing of the Scottish situation, suggests that the 'berating of Scotland from within shows a new self-confidence' (Kravitz 1997: xxvi). Welsh and Irish writing of the 1990s is also predominantly characterised by such self-berating. Whether the self-confidence extends beyond writers and writing remains to be seen.

Bibliography

Abse, D. (ed.) (1997) *Twentieth Century Anglo-Welsh Poetry*, Bridgend: Seren.

Armitage, S. and Crawford, R. (eds) (1998) *The Penguin Book of Poetry from Britain and Ireland Since 1945*, London: Viking.

Brown, T. (1985) *Ireland: A Social and Cultural History 1922–1985*, London: Fontana.

—— (1991) 'The counter-revival: provincialism and censorship 1930–65', in S. Deane (ed.) *The Field Day Anthology of Irish Writing*, vol. 3, Derry: Field Day.

Cairns, D. and Richards, S. (1988) *Writing Ireland: Colonialism, nationalism and culture*, Manchester: Manchester University Press.

Carlson, J. (1990) *Banned in Ireland: Censorship and the Irish Writer*, London: Routledge.

Carson, C. (1987) *The Irish for No*, Dublin: Gallery Press.

Corcoran, N. (1997) *After Yeats and Joyce: Reading Modern Irish Literature*, Oxford: Oxford University Press.

Crawford, R. (1992) *Devolving English Literature*, Oxford: Clarendon Press.

Crawford, R. and Varty, A. (eds) (1993) *Liz Lochhead's Voices*, Edinburgh: Edinburgh University Press.

Day, G. and Docherty, B. (eds) (1997) *British Poetry from the 1950 to the 1990s: Politics and Art*, Basingstoke: Macmillan.

Deane, S. (1985) *Celtic Revivals: Essays in Modern Irish Literature 1880–1980*, London: Faber and Faber.

—— (1986) *A Short History of Irish Literature*, London: Hutchinson.

—— (ed.) (1991) *The Field Day Anthology of Irish Writing*, 3 vols, Derry: Field Day.

Dunn, D. (1979) *Barbarians*, London: Faber and Faber.
—— (ed.) (1992) *The Faber Book of 20th-Century Scottish Poetry*, London: Faber and Faber.
Eagleton, T. (1995) *Heathcliff and the Great Hunger: Studies in Irish Culture*, London: Verso.
Gibbons, L. (1996) *Transformations in Irish Culture*, Cork: Cork University Press.
Graver, D. (1992) 'John Arden', in *Modern British Writers* Supplement II, New York: Scribners.
Heaney, S. (1980) *Preoccupations: Selected prose 1968–1978*, London: Faber and Faber.
—— (1983) *Field Day Pamphlets 1: An Open Letter*, Derry: Field Day.
Hederman, M. P. and Kearney, R. (1982) *The Crane Bag Book of Irish Studies*, Dublin: Blackwater.
Johnston, D. (1994) *The Literature of Wales*, Cardiff: University of Wales Press.
Jones, D. (1996) '"I failed utterly": Saunders Lewis and the cultural politics of Welsh modernism', *Irish Review* 19: 22–43.
Jones, G. and Elis, I. Ffowc (eds) (1971) *Twenty-Five Welsh Short Stories*, Oxford: Oxford University Press.
Kavanagh, P. (1964) *Collected Poems*, London: Martin Brian and O'Keefe.
—— (1967) *Collected Pruse*, Dublin: MacGibbon and Kee.
Kiberd, D. (1995) *Inventing Ireland: The Literature of the Modern Nation*, London: Cape.
Kravitz, P. (1997) *The Picador Book of Contemporary Scottish Fiction*, London: Picador.
Lloyd, D. (1993) *Anomalous States: Irish Writing and the Post-Colonial Moment*, Dublin: Lilliput.
Longley, E. (1986) *Poetry in the Wars*, Newcastle upon Tyne: Bloodaxe.
—— (1994) *The Living Stream: Literature and Revisionism in Ireland*, Newcastle upon Tyne: Bloodaxe.
MacDiarmid, H. (1973) 'Saunders Lewis and the real thing', *Anglo-Welsh Review* 22: 50 (Autumn): 153–60.
Morrison, B. and Motion, A. (eds) (1982) *The Penguin Book of Contemporary British Poetry*, Harmondsworth: Penguin.
Muldoon, P. (1983) *Quoof*, London: Faber and Faber.
—— (1987) *Meeting the British*, London: Faber and Faber.
—— (1998) *Hay*, London: Faber and Faber.
Murray, C. (1997) *Twentieth-Century Irish Drama: Mirror up to Nation*, Manchester: Manchester University Press.
Paulin, T. (1984) *Ireland and the English Crisis*, Newcastle upon Tyne: Bloodaxe.
Richards, A. (ed.) (1976) *The Penguin Book of Welsh Short Stories*, London: Penguin.
—— (ed.) (1993) *The Second Penguin Book of Welsh Short Stories*, London: Penguin.
Smyth, A. (ed.) (1992) *The Abortion Papers, Ireland*, Dublin: Attic.
Stephen, M. (1986) *The Oxford Companion to the Literature of Wales*, Oxford: Oxford University Press.

Thomas, R. S. (1997) *Autobiographies*, trans. J. W. Davies, London: Phoenix.
Wallace, G. and Stevenson, R. (eds) (1993) *The Scottish Novel Since the Seventies*, Edinburgh: Edinburgh University Press.
Wills, C. (1993) *Improprieties: Politics and Sexuality in Northern Irish Poetry*, Oxford: Oxford University Press.
—— (1998) *Reading Paul Muldoon*, Newcastle upon Tyne: Bloodaxe.

Chapter 2

Migration and mutability

The twice born fiction of Salman Rushdie

Minoli Salgado

If literary modernism is the product of individual exiles and *émigrés* from and within a culturally-dominant Europe (Eagleton 1970: 9), then the development of literary post-modernism can be seen, in part, as directly aligned to the mass migration of peoples from the crumbling British Empire to the colonial centre. The late 1940s, in particular the years 1947–8, mark a cultural watershed. They herald a shift in Britain's perception of itself from being a cultural dominant that gained a precarious stability at the expense of essentialising its colonial subjects, to what Robert Young has described as a post-modern 'self-consciousness about a culture's own historical relativity' (Young 1990: 19).

In 1947 the British Empire began to fall apart with the emergence of India and Pakistan (together the most profitable colonial acquisition) as newly independent nations; and in 1948 postwar migration to Britain began with the arrival of the 'SS *Empire Windrush*' from Jamaica (Gorra 1997: 12). 1948 also marks the publication of G. V. Desani's novel *All About H. Hatterr*. Desani, an Indian writer who wrote his novel in London during the war, parodically recounts a Eurasian's quest for enlightenment in what Anthony Burgess has described as 'gloriously impure' rhetorical English. The novel's pastiche form, its syncretic linguistic play, its focus on the cultural hybridity and fractured subjectivity of an individual (who allies himself with the devil) seem remarkably contemporary post-modernist concerns. Indeed the work of Salman Rushdie, who was himself born just a year before *All About H. Hatterr*'s publication, could be said to be parented by this cultural fusion of the post-modern and the post-colonial.

Locating Salman Rushdie

Salman Rushdie, an Indian-born British writer, has (to date) published seven novels (including one written for children), a volume of short stories, a travelogue, a film study, and a collection of essays, as well as regular contributions to newspapers and international journals. This wide range in the form and content of his work reflects his ability to move between different modes of writing and testifies to the scope of his ideas and interests. His first novel, *Grimus*, was published in 1975. This novel did not enjoy the critical acclaim of later novels such as *Midnight's Children* (1981), *Shame* (1983), *The Satanic Verses* (1988) and *The Moor's Last Sigh* (1995), partly because it strained against the boundaries of the science fiction genre; yet it is possible to identify all Rushdie's major preoccupations even in this early literary 'failure': his examination of such issues as personal and national identity, the experience of exile, cultural diversity and aesthetic unity, the colonial legacy, fantasy and imaginative truth, and the relationship between the past and the present.

In complete contrast to the critical reception of his first novel, Rushdie's second work, *Midnight's Children*, received staggering critical acclaim. It won a host of literary awards, most notably the Booker McConnell Prize, and was later crowned, 'the Booker of Bookers', the most distinguished of all Booker Prize winners in the prize's twenty-five year history. It is arguably the most important text published in the 1980s. It took a date – the midnight of 15 August 1947, when India became independent – and made a British audience aware that from an insider's point of view, this was not so much the moment when the Empire began to unravel but rather the moment of possibility for the creation of a post-imperial identity for those who had lived under the British Empire. The scope and ambition of the novel, charting the history of post-Independence India from the perspective of a boy who has paranormal powers, coupled with the energy of its linguistic and narrative inventiveness, seemed to dwarf home-grown products and convinced many that the future of the British novel – and of the wider British culture – lay with those who wrote from their divided identities: Timothy Mo, Kazuo Ishiguro, Hanif Kureishi, Clive Sinclair, and Caryl Phillips. It resulted in a wider appreciation of the new writing – from Anita Desai to Margaret Atwood, J. M. Coetzee to Peter Carey, Wilson Harris to Alice Munro – being produced throughout the Anglophone post-colonial world. It also led to a largely critical reconsideration of some of the most admired Commonwealth writers such as V. S. Naipaul, Ruth Prawer Jhabvala and Ngugi wa Thiong'o, and it created the context for the belated appreciation of Paul Scott's four-volume *Raj Quartet*

(1969–75), set in the last days of British rule in India, which was turned into an acclaimed television drama under the title *The Jewel in the Crown* in 1984.[1]

Midnight's Children made critics and readers in Britain more attentive to the work of British-born Afro-Caribbean and Asian writers; and it authorised – more so than any other literary text – the birth of post-colonial studies in Britain. With *Midnight's Children* British literary culture had regained, it seemed, much of the panache and daring last seen with the modernists after the First World War.

The Rushdie Affair

After *Midnight's Children*, Rushdie wrote *Shame*, a playful but potent satire that focused on the political history of Pakistan, and followed this with *The Satanic Verses*, a novel which has drawn as much religious censure as it has critical acclaim. Published in 1988, *The Satanic Verses* links the birth of Islam with the birth of migrant, 'mongrel' identities (Cundy 1996: 80), exploring the nature of revelation (is it divine or human?) and of creativity itself. Although its primary concern is with the evaluation and promotion of certain abstract principles – pluralism over singularity, mutability over fixity, doubt over certainty – its exploration of these concerns within, in part, an Islamic frame of reference has resulted in a controversy of spectacular proportions. The satirical debunking of the life and work of the prophet Mohammed, Islam's founder, and his wives, and the questioning of the validity of religious inspiration and of the authority of the Koran, served to rouse the wrath of Muslim people across the world, culminating in the declaration of a *fatwa* on 14 February 1989 by the Ayatollah Khomeini, the spiritual leader of Iran.[2] The Ayatollah's *fatwa*, based on the novel's perceived blasphemy, called for the death of Salman Rushdie and all those involved in its publication.

The *fatwa* divided world opinion: on the one hand, there were those Muslims and governments of Muslim countries who united in their condemnation of the book and the author; on the other, there were those – primarily writers, publishers, booksellers, journalists, trade unions, and human rights groups, as well as 'moderate' Muslims – from across the world who sought to defend both. There were public demonstrations in England, while riots, in which some were killed and many wounded, took place in Pakistan and India. The book was banned in all Muslim countries and removed from the shelves in bookshops worldwide; bookshops in Britain and the United States were bombed;

thousands of literary figures across the world put their names to a statement of protest; the International Rushdie Defence Committee was launched in London; diplomatic relations between Iran and Britain – already strained – broke down; and Rushdie himself went into hiding under the protection of the British government. Two years later the Italian and Japanese translators of the book were attacked – the former seriously hurt, the latter killed – and in 1993 Rushdie's Norwegian publisher was shot and seriously injured.

Although the Ayatollah Khomeini died just four months after issuing the *fatwa*, the controversy continues. In 1998 the Iranian government declared that they would not officially sanction the death sentence, but as a *fatwa* can only be revoked by the *mufti* who issued it (now dead), and because there are still many who share its sentiments, Rushdie remains in hiding with a bounty on his life approximating £2,000,000 (Appignanesi and Maitland 1989; PEN home pages).

Inevitably in Britain, the Rushdie Affair, as it came to be called, has generated considerable debate on a number of issues: racism and the rights of Britain's ethnic minorities, particularly its 1.5 million Muslims; the nature of blasphemy and the laws which are used to control it (highlighted by an unsuccessful legal action taken by Muslim groups); and, in literary circles, artistic licence and freedom of speech. Many Muslims, angry and hurt by what they perceived as Britain's failure to take account of their beliefs and feelings, united in the wake of the affair to form their own action groups including their own political body, the Islamic Party, to focus on Muslim concerns. The media response to their demonstrations, petitions, and public bookburnings (which had in fact begun before the *fatwa* was declared) served to increase the racial tension in the country and a racist backlash ensued, contributing to the development of what is currently known as 'Islamophobia'.[3]

In Britain, and elsewhere in Europe, the Rushdie Affair quickly polarised into an apparent conflict between a pre-modern Islam and a post-modern West. The day after the *fatwa* was announced a group of writers, literary agents and publishers led by Harold Pinter delivered a letter to the then Prime Minister, Mrs Thatcher, expressing their outrage in what appear to be culturally polarised terms:

> A very distinguished writer has used his imagination to write a book and has criticised the religion into which he was born and he has been sentenced to death. . . . It is an intolerable and barbaric

state of affairs. The Government should confront Iran with the consequences of its statement and remind the Muslim community here that it cannot incite people to murder.

(*Guardian*, 16 February 1989)

Other supporters tried to speak across cultures, but found they could only do so by promoting the very principle of free speech that was in dispute. Prominent members of the Asian community in Britain gathered in Rushdie's defence to argue that 'without the right to dissent from established ways of thought and speech, a multi-cultural and free society is an impossibility' (*Independent*, 24 February 1989).[4] As a consequence, responses to Rushdie have become 'a site of political conflict' and the political imperatives informing the Rushdie Affair have redefined the critical reception of Rushdie's work as whole.[5] Rushdie and his fiction are now all too often read along the polarities of 'western' liberal humanism and 'eastern' religious fundamentalism – 'a clash of languages' as Rushdie has called it – affirming the very social and cultural differences that this complex and challenging novel seeks to question. Indeed in the polarised debate on the Rushdie Affair, 'liberal humanism' and 'religious fundamentalism' appear as static absolutes, themselves a kind of metanarrative in the discourse of political conflict.

Rushdie himself has claimed that the novel was written for the migrant communities within Britain, stating that it is mainly those who have experienced post-colonial displacement who will find 'some pleasure and much recognition in its pages' (*Observer*, 22 January 1989).[6] However, if the novel was written for the very people who wished to burn it, it indicates tremendous miscalculation and failure of vision on Rushdie's part: an indication, it might be said, of the extent of his cultural alienation. For Rushdie is in many ways a minority within a minority; not only a member of Britain's community of ethnic minorities but also, in terms of his class affiliations, a member of the elite, revealing how exile and unbelonging, subjects central to his fiction, take varied and complex forms.

In my exploration of Rushdie's fiction I attempt – like Rushdie himself – to move beyond the polarised and conflictual terms of debate foregrounded by the Rushdie Affair, but I do so by positioning his treatment of exile against his own culturally and socially ambivalent status. My reading of migration is in fact a migrant's reading, containing many of the concerns and doubts of one whose mixed cultural affiliations both enable and require the mutability of multiple subject positions, but nevertheless – and perhaps inevitably – one which prioritises a post-colonial concern with the issue of agency. To what extent, I ask, does Rushdie fulfil his own aim of providing a positive, enabling model of identity for those who have migrated from the former Empire?

The Satanic Verses and Shame: testing the boundaries of migrant identity

Rushdie has written and spoken extensively on the subjects of migration, exile and identity. His observations in critical essays such as 'Imaginary homelands', '"Commonwealth literature" does not exist', 'The new empire within Britain' and 'In good faith' (Rushdie 1991: 9–21; 61–70; 129–38; 393–414), as well as his numerous interviews and newspaper articles, have done much to elucidate the discourse of migration to the point where they have entered the critical vocabulary of post-colonial studies.[7] Rushdie's perspective on the migrant condition demarcated in his critical work has remained consistent and covers a range of subjects from language, literature and the arts to national identity, globalisation and the impact of racism. His aim in his essays is threefold: first, to destabilise essentialist notions of what, for example, constitutes the 'English language' and 'India'; second, to give privileged status to the migrant perspective, constructing an alternative discourse on this basis; and finally, to argue against what he sees as pernicious political practices such as the immigration policies of the Thatcher government and the rise of theocratic politics in India and elsewhere.

While the first two of these aims is amply fulfilled in his fiction, the parodic post-modern dialogicality of his fiction (with the notable exception of Shame) works, I believe, to negate any clear political voice in his novels. Indeed the formal and ideological discrepancy between Rushdie's accessibly written and politically charged essays and his dense, clotted and politically allusive fiction should itself alert one to the dangers of accepting Rushdie's own arguments too easily. While his commentaries are certainly valuable in themselves as analyses of the migrant condition – and of course give us access to the world view of the author – it is nevertheless necessary to step outside Rushdie's own terms of reference in order to position him in the global context. As I will show in my brief analysis of The Satanic Verses and Shame, texts which test the translational capacity of contrasting cultures, Rushdie's fiction helps us distinguish between political agency and social praxis, between linguistic potential and social intervention.

As an Indian Muslim educated in the West, Rushdie's exposure to a range of cultures and traditions has fed into the form of his fiction producing a veritable collage of literary allusions and techniques. This is evident in, for example, his borrowings from Indian mythology, *The Arabian Nights* and *Tristram Shandy* in *Midnight's Children*, and his drawing upon Islamic literature and history, Indian popular film and western classical thought to inform the structural and philosophical framework of *The Satanic Verses*. His extravagant word play involves the self-conscious mixing of traditions resulting in a mongrel, hybridised English: in *Shame*, for example, 'Barbs were flung through the same lattice: "Ohe, Madam! Where so you think he gets your grand grand clothes? From handicraft emporia?"' This blending of English and Indian idiom liberates and simultaneously deconstructs standard English, privileging the migrant experience while asserting its alterity.

At the same time, his mixed cultural background also feeds into his understanding of migrant identity which is at once 'plural and partial' (Rushdie 1991: 15), undermining essentialist notions of a fixed and coherent authentic self. It reaches its peak in *The Satanic Verses*, a novel which focuses on displacement in all its forms: the crisis of identity experienced by two Indian migrants in Britain, the unsettling of religious conviction and the displacing of historical certitude. Central to the novel is the dilemma faced by all migrants: the extent to which one should change, and risk loss of faith and identity, to suit one's new environment (Ruthven in Appigananesi and Maitland 1989: 16). The migrant, for Rushdie, is placed in the position of having to choose an identity, of having to create himself anew:

> A man who sets out to make himself up is taking on the Creator's role, according to one way of seeing things; he's unnatural, a blasphemer, an abomination of abominations. From another angle you could see pathos in him, heroism in his struggle, in his willingness to take risk: not all mutants survive. Or consider him sociopolitically: most migrants learn and can become disguises. Our own false descriptions to counter falsehoods invented about us, concealing for reasons of security our secret selves.
>
> (Rushdie, *The Satanic Verses*: 49)

In this passage Rushdie presents us with many possible readings of the migrant condition. While the need to remake oneself in one's new home is shown to be a liberating inevitability, the act of doing so can be interpreted variously as a transgression – what Homi Bhabha refers to as 'heresy' (Bhabha 1994: 225) – heroism or hypocrisy, depending on one's subject position. For Rushdie there are a multiplicity of perspectives from which the migrant may be perceived by the host society and from which, in turn, the exile may see the world. From the 'stereoscopic vision' (Rushdie 1991: 19) of the migrant who has access to and affiliations with two cultures, to the conflict of identity experienced by the fully hybridised individual in a racially-divided nation, Rushdie explores the insider/outsider boundary through focusing on both the experience of exile and its political ramifications.

Of course, an exploration of the migrant experience is central to many other post-colonial texts such as G. V. Desani's *All About H. Hatterr* (1948), George Lamming's *The Emigrants* (1954), Samuel Selvon's *The Lonely Londoners* (1956), Wilson Harris' *The Palace of the Peacock* (1960), V. S. Naipaul's *The Mimic Men* (1967) and *The Enigma of Arrival* (1987), Kamala Markandaya's *The Nowhere Man* (1972), Derek Walcott's 'The schooner Flight' in *The Star-Apple Kingdom* (1980), Janette Turner Hospital's collection of short stories, *Dislocations* (1986), and Jamaica Kincaid's *Lucy* (1991).

What sets Rushdie apart from other writers who focus on cultural hybridity and its repercussions is his attempt both to universalise (rather than simply internationalise) the condition of migrancy and to construct a worldview upon this basis, so that migrancy itself becomes the defining characteristic of the modern age. Whereas writers such as Desani, Selvon, Naipaul and Markandaya present us with highly individual and personalised perceptions of the migrant condition, Rushdie's presentation of it involves an act of deliberate cultural dislocation, a dispersal of the local specificities of his own rootlessness into the abstractions of metaphor such that he can claim in his study of *The Wizard of Oz* that it is not so much that there is 'no place like home' but that 'there is no place *as* home'. Indeed, he claims in *Imaginary Homelands* that:

> The past is a country from which we have all emigrated . . . its loss is part of our common humanity. . . . The writer who is out-of-country and even out-of language may experience this loss in an intensified form. It is made more concrete for him by the physical act of discontinuity, of his present being in a different place from his past, of his being 'elsewhere'. This may enable him to speak properly and concretely on a subject of universal appeal.
>
> (Rushdie 1991: 12)

Rushdie's oft-quoted indictment of 'the folly of trying to contain writers in passports' (Rushdie 1991: 67), and his claim that they are 'citizens of many countries: the finite country of observable reality . . . the bound-less kingdom of the imagination, the half-lost land of memory' (*Times Literary Supplement*, 25 February 1994), extend this idea to its logical conclusion: migration now has an ontological status divorced from the historical and political conditions that gave rise to it. As some analysts have put it, migration, in these terms, is not so much 'a mere interval between fixed points of departure and arrival, but a mode of being. . . . For those who come from elsewhere and cannot go back, perhaps writing becomes a place to live' (King 1995: xv).

Twice born fiction: the privilege of displacement

In my view, this eliding of material conditions can be seen as a product of the specific nature of Rushdie's belonging to an intellectual and aesthetic elite of post-colonials who are variously described as Third World cosmopolitans or internationalists. Born in Bombay, India's most cosmopolitan city, and raised in what he describes as the 'intellectual tradition' of Islam, he was educated first in the Cathedral Boys' High School, an English mission school in Bombay. Then at the age of eleven he was sent to England to study at Rugby, one of Britain's leading public schools, and then on to Cambridge University where he graduated in history. During his teens his family moved to Pakistan, a country he got to know 'in slices' during the intervals afforded by school holidays. After graduating he remained in Britain to work first as an actor and then as an advertising copywriter, both occupations which demand a sophisticated awareness of the linguistic and social nuances of his host culture, depending as they do on an ability to translate cultural codes and practices.

One might say that Rushdie's homelessness is held in tension with what one critic has described as 'an excess of belonging' (Ahmad 1992: 130), with the result that his 'rootlessness' is part and parcel of his self-perception as an internationalist belonging to too many places at once. Indeed he adds a new twist to the meaning of the term 'twice born' which has been used to describe the dual cultural heritage that frames the discursive framework of the Indian writer in English.[8] For it is a term that also has explicit class (and caste) associations. Boys (signifi-cantly, girls are exempt) from the top three castes in the Hindu echelon are considered 'twice born' when they are ceremonially initiated into their responsibilities as Hindus. The term does not contain the notion of rebirth that is implicit in the notion of the 'born again' Christian, but rather of a divided persona – a split subjectivity rather than a renewed one – a point I will come back to later. Needless to say it is also a term weighted with social privilege.[9]

Rushdie's work, it seems to me, both exemplifies and redefines this notion of 'twice born' fiction. For in 'crossing the black water' and becoming a British resident and citizen Rushdie has indeed been born again, his identity created anew in the British Isles. Although not born a Hindu *Brahmin*, his education in the most prestigious British educational establishments places him firmly within the elite of Indian society. If the mixed cultural heritage and elite status (in India) of the Indian novel in English make it 'twice born', then the migrant position of many of its present exponents deepen these cultural markers. 'To be born again,' sings Gibreel Farishta the airborne protagonist of *The Satanic Verses* as he tumbles towards England in the opening to the novel, ' first you have to die' (Rushdie, *The Satanic Verses*: 3).

This redefinition of 'twice born' fiction accommodates two con-trasting notions of individual identity: one of a split subjectivity and the other of a renewed self: both aspects of migrant identity explored by Rushdie, most explicitly in *The Satanic Verses*. It is a redefinition predicated on fundamentally different notions of selfhood: one of a self that is fragmented, divided and inherently unstable (what could be broadly described as a post-modernist conception of identity) and the other, a sense of self that relies on a notion of retrievable essence or authenticity (found in most nativist and nationalist conceptions of post-colonial identity). In *The Satanic Verses*, the figures of Saladin Chamcha and Gibreel Farishta delineate but also disturb these polarised positions: Chamcha, a voice-over *artiste*, is determined to be 'a good and proper Englishman', to use 'paleface masks, clown-masks until he fooled [the English] into thinking he was "okay", he was "people-like-us"' (Rushdie, *The Satanic Verses*: 43); Farishta, an actor in Hindi 'theologicals', holds on to a notion of a continuous, coherent self, evident in his firm belief in reincarnation and sees himself as 'regenerated, a new man with a new life' (ibid.: 31) on arriving in London. Such divergent conceptions are given philosophical form in the novel when 'the mutability of the essence of self' is discussed in relation to Lucretius' view that the challenging of boundaries brings about the death of the old self and to Ovid's diametrically opposed belief in metamorphosis (ibid.: 276).

Both Chamcha and Farishta are impersonators, the 'mimic men' of Naipaul's fiction, but their very different conceptions of selfhood are deliberately doubled, split and inverted by Rushdie. Chamcha (whose name is a Hindi synonym for 'toady') is demonised by British racism, transmogrifies into a goatish devil, gains acceptance on this basis by the black community in London who identify with this demonisation, and finally returns to India. Farishta's monologic perception of self, which is compared to the 'terrifying singularity' of the figure of Mahound he is trying to portray, breaks down into schizophrenia and eventual suicide. The pattern followed by Rushdie is to unify the split persona of Chamcha and split the apparent unity of self embodied by Farishta.

Rushdie and Bhabha: some connections

Rushdie's conceptions of migrant identity have much in common with the theoretical models delineated by the post-structuralist critic Homi Bhabha. The latter has written extensively of the 'splitting and doubling' of the post-colonial subject. Drawing upon the work of the Martiniquan psychiatrist Frantz Fanon, Bhabha argues that the process of colonisation involves the splitting of postcolonial subjectivity so that the colonised wishes to both occupy the position of the coloniser and retain 'the slave's *avenging* anger' (Bhabha 1994: 44).[10] Bhabha extends Fanon's conceptual model to posit the notion that the desire to remain the same but also be like another effectively destabilises the power relationships between the coloniser and the colonised, the metropolitan centre and the migrant community, based as they are on discrimination and difference. In so doing Bhabha stresses the importance of the 'liminal': that which lies 'between fixed identifications' (ibid.: 4).

What is significant to our study of the migrant sensibility in Rushdie's fiction is that Bhabha ascribes an *agency* to the unfixed, liminal position of the migrant so extensively explored by Rushdie (Bhabha 1994: 185). Within this model, Rushdie would not be simply revealing the process of cultural syncretism that social analysts such as Paul Gilroy have argued is the formative experience of post-colonial migration (Gilroy 1987: 155–6), but actively working to undermine the very notions of cultural exclusivity upon which constructions of 'Britain' and 'India' are based. According to Bhabha, it is the '*inter*national dimension both within the margins of the nation-space and in the boundaries *in-between* nations and peoples' that 'carries the burden of meaning of culture' (Bhabha 1990: 4; 1994: 38). The discourse of minority groups such as the migrant community simultaneously marks and destabilises the boundaries of national culture delineating 'the in-between spaces through which the meaning of cultural and political authority are negotiated' (Bhabha 1990: 4). Bhabha's model can of course be applied to literary production. Just as the very marginality and mixed cultural affiliations of migrants work to define the borders of a nation, making them active constituents in the process of national formation, so too, it could be argued, does 'migrant literature' and discourse both define and dis-place the cartography of a 'national literature', breaking down its boundaries to assert the presence of the *inter*national.

How true would it be to say though that the deconstructive drive of Rushdie's post-modernist fiction has post-colonial political power? To what extent is this celebratory play on the mutability and plurality of the migrant subject empowering, providing an enabling model of identity for Britain's migrant and immigrant community? While Rushdie has in interviews and essays acknowledged that he is aware of his socially privileged position, there is no corresponding acknowledgement in his fiction; except that is, in *Shame*. Here the authorial perspective is different from that of Rushdie's other novels. Both *Midnight's Children* and *The Satanic Verses* create an ironic distance between narrator and author; the first by deliberately muddling and distorting historical events, the second by exploring the ethical ambiguity at the heart of artistic inspiration and revelation. *Shame* too has an unreliable narrator. That unreliability, however, is based not on ironic distance, but rather on its absence. *Shame's* unnamed narrator clearly shares Rushdie's own culturally ambiguous position. It is clear that the narrator speaks with Rushdie's voice (Ahmad 1992: 132, 149), having the same relationship to his material as the author himself.

Acknowledging a partial knowledge of a country he has got to know 'in slices' (Rushdie, *Shame*: 69), the narrator, we are told, may not have the right to relate Pakistan's history because of his own outsider status:

> *Outsider! Trespasser! You have no right to this subject!* . . . I know: nobody ever arrested me. Nor are they ever likely to. *Poacher! Pirate! We reject your authority. We know you, with your foreign language wrapped around you like a flag: speaking about us in your forked tongue, what can you tell but lies?* I reply with more questions: is history to be considered the property of the participants solely?

In what courts are such claims staked, what boundary commissions
map out the territories?
Can only the dead speak?

(Rushdie, *Shame*: 28)

There are many claims being made here: from the acknowledgement
(before the Rushdie Affair) of his relatively safe vantage point to a
rhetorical assertion of his equal authority to speak on a nation's history.
It is the self-conscious vantage point of the privileged exile. The very
stridency of this assertion – and it interesting that Rushdie feels the
need for it at all – reveals the ambiguities of his authority and the
uncertainty of displacement more so than his other more nuanced texts
on migrant identity. It is paradoxical that the stark satire of *Shame* registers the inflections of cultural disjunction more clearly than those
texts that seek to celebrate the migrant condition.

Shame is easily Rushdie's most problematic novel to date. In carica-
turing the personal and political lives of two of Pakistan's leaders,
Zulfikar Ali Bhutto and Zia ul-Haq, Rushdie reveals some of his own
limitations. Here we witness the breakdown of the dialogic impulse
evident from the time of his very first novel, *Grimus*, where he explores
the predicament of 'a man rehearsing voices on a cliff top: . . . looking
for a suitable voice to speak in' (Rushdie, *Grimus*: 32). Instead of dialogicality the reader is presented with closure and the monopolising
perspective of a partial but far from peripheral narrator.

In striking contrast to *Midnight's Children* which celebrates multiplicity of perspective and plurality of vision in its treatment of the past, in
Shame historical events are reduced to the lives of two ruling families and
the experience of an entire nation is reduced to the experience of this
elite (Ahmad 1992: 140, 152). The interaction between the Harappa
and Hyder family closely parallels that of Mr Bhutto and General Zia,
and so keen is Rushdie to cement his presentation of the totalitarian and
exclusive nature of Pakistani politics that he links the families together
by marriage in a way that they were never linked in life.

Indeed the novel, as Ahmad has shown, presents a very limited
picture of Pakistan, excluding the voice of the masses and the ordinary
narratives of resistance, oppression and human bonding (Ahmad 1992:
139). The struggle for civil liberty and human rights within Pakistan is
simply not represented, lying as it does beyond the narrator's vision.
These narratives could be seen as the untranslatable chunks in Rushdie's
construction of Pakistan's history; their very absence determining the
borders of Rushdie's cultural affiliations. Migration may be an ontological

condition which translates the unstable, fluid identities of his characters in his other novels, but it is clear that Rushdie's post-modern flexibility and elusiveness give way to the fixity of satiric caricature when confronted with the 'otherness' of Pakistan and its past. Plurality does not lead to multiplicity and openness but is here fully partial.

It is no coincidence that these anxieties of authorship are related to a text that deals with the elite ruling class, for in questioning the validity of their political authority it could be claimed that Rushdie is forced to question his own discursive authority to speak for others. His only recourse here is to appeal to the sympathies of his audience: it is as if Rushdie's 'consistent playful association of Islam with authoritarianism operates in the conviction of writing for an audience that will accept this kind of joke' (Brennan 1989: 127). It is of course precisely this audience that is appealed to in *The Satanic Verses*, an audience of those both familiar enough with Islam to recognise his fabulated critique of it but also detached enough to accept the position of scepticism endorsed by the novel. Yet, of course, Rushdie is not writing simply for those who think and feel as he does. One of his aims – and it is important to bear in mind that Rushdie's stated aims are not always consistent – is to take risks in fiction, challenging the boundaries of what it is acceptable to say and to think.[11] In this context he takes on the role of a literary terrorist who attempts to match linguistic pyrotechnics with political dynamism. What is interesting, however, is the discrepancy between his many stated objectives and the actual outcome, a discrepancy that reveals a potentially liberating enunciative gap when what the author claims he meant and what is in fact understood constitute very different things.

The Rushdie Affair marks the culmination of this discrepancy, but it is evident some six years earlier in 1983 when Rushdie described his aims in the writing of *Shame*. One of his aims in the novel, he claimed, was to empower the Pakistani people to resist authoritarian rule, and another was to urge his British and American readers to protest against their leaders' active support of these corrupt regimes. The very narrowness of *Shame*, he argued, was related to the first of these aims. By depicting Pakistan as an isolated country uninfluenced by Western power brokers, by delineating, in other words, the fixity rather than the permeability of cultural and national borders, he wanted to 'pretend . . . that we did have power over our own lives and that we would assume that the outside influence is minor and that the internal influence is the important thing'. This desire to empower his Pakistani audience, is as Ahmad has shown, unsuccessful. Worse, it served to undermine his second intention. While he wished to get Western readers 'to think about the idea that the freedoms which are so prized in the West are bought at the expense of other people's freedoms', the novel, he found, was instead read by westerners as a fantasy in which the political elements are 'quite subsidiary' (Rushdie 1985: 15–16). *Shame* therefore is qualitatively different from *The Satanic Verses* in that here the inability of the migrant to mediate between different cultures is revealed in the narrative itself and in its critical reception.

This is not to deny the importance of Rushdie's genuine attempt to bridge cultures and his exploration of migrant identity and experience. His fiction gives us valuable access to the intersection between post-modern and post-colonial debates on the construction of the subject, forging a creative link between post-modern ontology and post-colonial hybridity. Yet it could be claimed that the focus on the individual subject is itself a political act. In the words of one political activist, 'the "return" of the subject to the centre of the political stage brings with it, of course, the politics of the subject: individualism, consumption, choice, sexuality, style, pleasure, "international humanism"' (Sivanandan 1990: 45).

Rushdie's critique of racism is correspondingly limited to the level of art and the power of discourse (descriptions determine lived reality in *The Satanic Verses*): that is, to the level of performative potential rather than social praxis. While the celebration of the fluidity of migrant identity is potentially enabling, it is a privilege primarily reserved for an elite minority of the (im)migrant minority who have the option to explore the liberating potential of these liminal identities on a practical as well as an imaginative level (Gorra 1997: 172; also Parnell 1996: 256–7). It is a freedom, it could be said, predicated upon a degree of social mobility denied to those who are bound by class, caste and economic circumstance to the lower echelons of society. As Linda Hutcheon has pointed out, the post-modernist rejection of the coherent subject is something of a 'luxury', given the need of the majority of people from post-colonial countries 'to affirm a denied or alienated subjecivity' (Hutcheon 1991: 168).

Points of departure

It may prove of little comfort to the author himself to know that there have been at least three positive outcomes of the Ayatollah's proclamation: the first is that the politics of critical practice have been brought to the fore in the aftermath of the declaration. The critical reception of Rushdie's work now overtly locates the critic as much as the text. It would be impossible today, for example, to claim of Rushdie's work, as a reviewer for the *New York Times* did in an assessment publicised on the jacketcover of *Midnight's Children*, that it reflects 'a continent finding its voice' (obliterating at a stroke over a century of Indian writing in English). Rushdie clearly does not speak for the Indian people and although he is still accorded the guardianship of the Asian migrant perspective in publishing circles, the indifferent response within India to his editorial reflections in *The Vintage Book of Indian Writing* (1997) reflects the increasing distance between the author and his homeland.[12] This politicising of the critical field helps displace the current tendency in cultural studies to emphasise the mutual and the global with a recognition of both the constructed nature of cultural difference and its materiality, thereby placing these issues at the very centre of literary studies.

A second positive outcome of the Rushdie Affair, related to this denial of (what Bhabha might call) translational fluency and transnational communication, is the corresponding foregrounding of the cultural co-ordinates and class affiliations of Rushdie's own hyphenated identity. Although he periodically appears in the British press as the champion of free speech or the voice of enlightened humanism he is, like all enforced exiles, deeply isolated: banished, it could be claimed, into the only domain to which he can claim full citizenship, that of the imagination.[13] As his fictional world increasingly develops into a veritable Rushdieland – with intertextual cross-referencing and characters migrating between novels – it could be argued that, taken as whole, his novels construct a discrete, self-referential domain that parallels his own paradoxical relationship of isolation and connectedness with the world.

This depiction of Rushdie as an isolated aesthete is, however, undermined by what could be seen as a third positive outcome of the Rushdie Affair: that is, the creation of a space for debate and dissent for those within Islamic communities, both within Britain and elsewhere, who have experienced a fracturing of faith. As the Arab critic Sadik Jalal al-ᶜAzm has pointed out, the Rushdie Affair is just one in a long line of similar cases to be found in the Arab world and coincides with what many 'critically minded Muslims have discussed with each other in private (and often publicly) over the ages' (al-ᶜAzm 1994: 279–80, 289; also *For Rushdie* 1994). From this perspective, the Affair itself marks a crisis of becoming by renegotiating the culture of belonging. Within this frame of reference Rushdie becomes an exemplary iconoclast, his fiction 'an angry and rebellious exploration of very specific inhuman conditions and very concrete wicked social situations and rotten political practices' (al-ᶜAzm

1994: 282), and his desire to 'open the universe a little more' is amply fulfilled (Rushdie 1991: 21).

Notes

1 As Rushdie himself has pointed out, the popularity of Scott's saga was itself part of a 'Raj revival' symptomatic of a post-Falklands-War jingoism that thrived under the Conservative government in Britain during the 1980s. Rushdie was scathing in his criticism of Scott's work, claiming it relegated Indians to 'bit-players in their own history' (Rushdie 1991: 90).

2 A *fatwa* is a statement made by a religious lawyer or *mufti* which is usually used to help settle marriage, inheritance or divorce cases which have been unresolved; its power rests entirely on its acceptance among the people. The Ayatollah's *fatwa* stated,

> I inform the proud Muslim people of the world that the author of *The Satanic Verses*, which is against Islam, the Prophet and the Koran, and all involved in its publication who were aware of its content, are sentenced to death. . . . I call on all zealous Muslims to execute them quickly, wherever they find them . . . whoever is killed on this path will be regarded as a martyr.
>
> (Appignanesi and Maitland 1989: 68)

3 For example, Charles Moore, editor of *The Spectator*, has written in an article entitled 'Time for a more liberal "racist" immigration policy' that

> You can be British without speaking English or being Christian or being white, but nevertheless Britain is basically English-speaking, Christian and white, and if one starts to think that it might become basically Urdu-speaking and Muslim and brown, one gets frightened and angry. . . . Because of our obstinate refusal to have babies, Western European civilisation will start to die at the point when it could have been revived with new blood. Then the hooded hordes will win, and the Koran will be taught, as Gibbon famously imagined, in the schools of Oxford.
>
> (*Spectator*, 19 October 1991)

And Robert Kilroy-Silk, the former Labour MP, wrote of Muslims in the *Daily Express* that 'they are backward and evil, and if it is being racist to say so then racist I must be and happy and proud to be so' (Runnymede Trust 1997: 14).

4 These included I. G. Patel, Director of the London School of Economics, the writer Hanif Kureishi and the cultural critic Homi Bhabha.

5 Tim Parnell has shown how the study of Rushdie's work inevitably locates the critic:

> the western critic who stresses the 'Indianness' of Rushdie's novels is in danger of subscribing to an orientalist notion of otherness. . . . And yet the focus on his transnational or 'cosmopolitan' location has led to criticism of Rushdie for commenting on the postcolonial

subcontinent 'from the comfort of the observation tower'. Short of naively claiming that the novels have nothing to do with the world, there is no meaningful context for [them] which is not also a site of conflict.

(see Parnell 1996: 242)

6 'This is the saddest irony of all,' Rushdie said shortly after the *fatwa*, 'that after working for five years to give voice and fictional flesh to the immigrant culture of which I am myself a member, I should see my book burned . . . by the people it's about' (*Sunday Times*, 19 February 1989).

7 All citations from Rushdie's texts are from the editions listed in the bibliography.

8 To be found in Mukherjee's extensive study of 'twice-born' Indo-English fiction (1971). It is not a recent study but the term itself is, I believe, a useful one and is worth re-evaluating in the light of contemporary debates in post-colonial studies.

9 This privilege has been explicitly contested by Mukherjee (1971), unpaginated Preface.

10 Further explorations on the splitting and doubling of the subject can be found in Bhabha's essay 'Of mimicry and man: the ambivalence of colonial discourse' in Bhabha (1994). Bhabha's essays provide a valuable insight into Rushdie's representations of migrant identity and experience, but they are allusive and opaque. This means that any reading of Bhabha – including mine – is partially subject to personal interpretation. Childs and Williams (1997), Moore-Gilbert (1997) and Young (1990) all discuss Bhabha's main ideas in unambiguous and accessible terms.

11 Rushdie's views on the political role of fiction are outlined in his essay, 'Outside the whale' in *Imaginary Homelands* (1991: 87–101).

12 Rushdie makes a number of contentious claims in his Introduction – for example that the best Indian writing of the last fifty years is written in English, that it takes the form of prose fiction, and that the quality of translations from India is too poor to merit inclusion in the volume – but he has yet to be taken to task for them by critics outside India.

13 For example, in a recent article, Rushdie simultaneously attacks religious 'hypocrites' and appeals to global goodwill in calling for the cancelling of third world debt as a way of marking the new millennium (*Guardian*, 6 January 1999).

Bibliography

Abdallah, A. (ed.) (1994) *For Rushdie: Essays by Arab and Muslim Writers in Defence of Free Speech*, New York: George Braziller.

Ahmad, A. (1992) *In Theory: Classes, Nations, Literatures*, London: Verso.

al-ᶜAzm, S. J. (1994) 'The importance of being earnest about Salman Rushdie', in M. D. Fletcher, *Reading Rushdie*, Amsterdam: Rodopi: 255–92.

Appignanesi, L. and Maitland, S. (1989) (eds) *The Rushdie File*, London: ICA/ Fourth Estate.

Bhabha, H. K. (ed.) (1990) *Nation and Narration*, London: Routledge.

—— (1994) *The Location of Culture*, London: Routledge.

Brennan, T. (1989) *Salman Rushdie and the Third World: Myths of the Nation*, London: Macmillan.

Childs, P. and Williams, P. (1997) *An Introduction to Post-Colonial Theory*, London: Prentice Hall/ Harvester Wheatsheaf.

Cundy, C. (1996) *Salman Rushdie*, Manchester: Manchester University Press.

Eagleton, T. (1970) *Exiles and Émigrés: Studies in Modern Literature*, London: Chatto.

Gilroy, P. (1987) *'There Ain't No Black in the Union Jack': The Cultural Politics of Race and Nation*, London: Hutchinson.

Gorra, M., (1997) *After Empire: Scott, Naipaul, Rushdie*, London: University of Chicago Press.

Hutcheon, L. (1991) '"Circling the downspout of empire"' in I. Adam and H. Tiffin, *Past the Last Post: Theorizing Post-Colonialism and Post-Modernism*, London: Harvester Wheatsheaf.

King, R., Connell, J. and White, P. E. (eds) (1995) *Writing across Worlds: Literature and Migration*, London: Routledge.

Lee, A. R. (1995) *Other Britain, Other British: Contemporary Multicultural Fiction*, London: Pluto.

Moore-Gilbert, B., (1997) *Postcolonial Theory: Contexts, Practices, Politics*, London: Verso.

Mukherjee, M. (1971) *The Twice Born Fiction: Themes and Techniques of the Indian Novel in English*, London: Heinemann.

Parnell, T. (1996) 'Salman Rushdie: from colonial politics to postmodern poetics', in B. Moore-Gilbert, *Writing India 1757–1990: The Literature of British India*, Manchester: Manchester University Press: 236–62.

PEN web pages: www.pen.org/freedom/mideast/rushdie4.html

Runnymede Trust (1997) *Islamophobia: Its Features and Dangers*, London: Runnymede Trust.

Rushdie, S. (1975; 1996) *Grimus*, London: Vintage.

—— (1985) '*Midnight's Children* and *Shame*' (Lecture/Interview given at the University of Aarhus on 7 October 1983), *Kunapipi* 7: (1): 1–19.

—— (1991) *Imaginary Homelands*, London: Granta.

—— (1983) *Shame*, New Delhi: Picador.

—— (1988; 1998) *The Satanic Verses*, London: Vintage.

—— (1992) *The Wizard of Oz: A Short Text About Magic*, BFI Film Classics, London: BFI.

Rushdie, S., and West, E. (eds) (1997) *The Vintage Book of Indian Writing 1947–1997*, London: Vintage.

Sivanandan, A. (1990) *Communities of Resistance: Writings on Black Struggles for Socialism*, London: Verso.

Young, R. (1990) *White Mythologies: Writing History and the West*, London: Routledge.

Part II

From welfare state to free market

The postwar settlement

In July 1945, much to the surprise of many who had voted for it, a Labour Government was elected with a huge parliamentary majority. On reflection, the size of this majority was unsurprising. The Conservative party, which had been the dominant party in government in the inter-war period, was still popularly associated with the sufferings, inequalities and harsh measures of the pre-war depression. At the same time, after six years of war, there was in all sections of society a determination to make a fresh start. Within three years, the new government had done this by laying the basis for what was called the 'welfare state'. It set up a system of social security, providing pensions, sickness and unemployment benefits; it created a free National Health Service; it funded a free and much expanded secondary school system and provided opportunities for those from poor homes to go on to university; and it set in motion extensive plans for housing and re-development. At the same time, on the grounds that this was necessary for the re-vitalisation of the British economy, it also laid the foundations for what was called the 'mixed economy' by taking into public ownership the coal, iron and steel industries, road haulage, the railways and public utilities such as gas and electricity.

When the Conservatives returned to power in 1951, they not only left the welfare state intact but also (with the exception of the iron and steel industries and road haulage, which they returned to private ownership) the mixed economy. Again, on reflection, this decision was unsurprising. On the one hand, the Conservatives wanted to stay in power; on the other hand, there was also, on the postwar right as on the postwar left, a genuine acceptance of the fundamental principles of the postwar settlement. The detailed planning for the welfare state had taken place during the war-time coalition and had involved cross-party co-operation. The report on social welfare had been written by a prominent Liberal, Sir William Beveridge, while reforming legislation on education had been promoted by a prominent Conservative, R. A. Butler. By fostering a sense of national unity and an acceptance of the benefits of centralised control, the Second World War was to change decisively the ideological terrain of postwar politics (Hennessy 1992; Addison 1994).

Indeed, during the next three decades, the Conservative and the Labour parties won elections by persuading the electorate that they were the best equipped to make a success both of the welfare state and of the mixed economy. In the 1950s, Conservative governments (with the benefits of the postwar economic recovery) took credit for increasing levels of social welfare and completing ambitious targets for building council houses, schools and roads; in the 1960s, Labour governments (1964–66; 1966–70) made the modernisation of Britain their focus. Through increased government intervention in the mixed economy, the Labour Prime Minister, Harold Wilson, hoped to create a dynamic, technologically advanced economy; through increased spending on education (new universities, science-based polytechnics, the Open University and the comprehensive school system) he hoped to create a better educated and more egalitarian society. The relative weakness of the British economy not only undermined these plans but also led to the first concerted challenge to the postwar consensus. On the left, some suggested that the welfare state and the mixed economy (what was termed 'welfare-capitalism') mitigated the crisis of capitalism and made revolutionary political and economic changes unlikely (Anderson 1992); on the right, others suggested that the welfare state and the mixed economy misdirected funds from productive investment into unnecessary social expenditure and wasteful state subsidies (Barnett 1986).

Thatcherism and the end of the postwar settlement

Throughout the 1970s, the British economy (which had been the most powerful in Europe at the beginning of the 1960s) went into a rapid and seemingly irreversible decline. Already high inflation was made worse in 1973 by huge increases in the world price of oil. As strikes and industrial conflict became more frequent (in 1974 British industry was forced to adopt a three-day week because of industrial action by coal miners), Conservative and Labour governments tried to defend both the welfare state and the mixed economy through forms of incorporation: of labour by the Conservatives, of business by the Labour Party. Britain's economic difficulties became so severe that in 1976 the Labour government had to approach the International Monetary Fund for emergency loans.

In May 1979, at the end of a decade in which Britain seemed to many increasingly ungovernable, Margaret Thatcher became Prime Minister. She won the election because she seemed, by comparison with the last Labour Prime Minister James Callaghan, reassuringly decisive; but her decisiveness was derived in large part from her undeclared ideological objective to undo the postwar settlement: on the one hand, by moving away from a mixed to a free-market economy; and on the other, by re-organising the National Health Service, the state education system, and the other institutions set up to provide the services of the welfare state on free-market lines.

With the depression of the 1930s in mind, the maintenance of full employment had been the one common objective of all postwar British governments. By withdrawing subsidies from state-controlled industries, reducing public expenditure on capital projects and increasing interest-rates, the Thatcher government created large-scale unemployment as an instrument of policy, with the economic intention of re-structuring the British economy and the political intention of undermining the power of the trades union movement.

During the course of three administrations (1979–83; 1983–87; 1987–90), Mrs Thatcher realised her objectives: first, state-controlled industries and utilities, including those taken into public ownership after 1945, were transferred to private ownership; second, the power of organised labour was severely reduced; third, the economy was re-structured, with the service sector replacing manufacturing as the key to national prosperity; and fourth, the National Health Service and the state education system were re-organised on free-market lines.

For some, Thatcherism (as the neo-liberal doctrine inspiring these changes was termed) was an attempt to return Britain to the pre-war situation (Hall and Jacques 1983); for others, it was a necessary attempt, in radically changed and changing circumstances, not only to find more efficient ways of delivering the objectives of the welfare state but also to generate the prosperity to make the welfare state less necessary (Kavanagh and Seldon 1989).

From neo-liberalism to libertarianism: feminism and queer politics

For most social historians, the lives of both men and women in Britain have been transformed for the better since 1945, with the improvement of health, education and living conditions, the under-mining of traditional social and cultural hierarchies and gender differences, and the extension of personal freedoms (Lewis 1991; Marwick 1996; Obelkevich and Catterall 1994). For some, however, the welfare state has failed to end poverty or overcome inequality because it favours the middle-classes (Le Grand 1982); for others, it has not only failed to ensure equal pay and appropriate levels of child benefit but has also played a major part (after the wartime lib-eration of women) in returning women to a subordinate and domesticated role within patriarchal and familial structures (Wilson 1980, Gilbert and Gubar 1994). In the 1970s and 1980s, these latter arguments were most commonly found on the left, the feminist critique being one aspect of a more general critique of the capitalist division of labour.

Since the 1990s, in America and Britain, avowedly post-modern social historians and critics have begun to advance explicitly liber-tarian views of politics and culture, arguing that to depend upon the state for the provision of services and benefits – in health, educa-tion, social welfare, urban planning or the arts – allows the state an unwarranted control over the lives of individual citizens, not least through its power of description. What they seek is a weakening of the state's powers and a renewal of civic associations, arguing that these twin aims can best be achieved in and through the free-market, with individuals forming identifiable groups by virtue of lifestyle, cultural preferences, sexual choice or new ideals of social citizenship (Marquand 1995). Nowhere have these issues been dis-cussed more fully than in feminist and gay studies, not least in the examination of the links between identity and consumption (Segal 1994; Mort 1996; Segal 1997; Sinfield 1998).

Yet, as some of the most important recent analyses of postwar British politics and culture have shown, the welfare state won assent because it embodied the spirit of modernity, giving new authority to experts – in economics, science, urban planning, education and administration – who defined what they thought were not only the most rational forms of political and social behaviour but also the most rational forms of subjectivity (Conekin *et al.* 1999).

Indeed, the development of the feminist movement in Britain may be counted, overall, as one of the successes for progressive reform in the culture of the postwar. In her essay in this book on the fiction of Pat Barker and Penelope Lively, Margaretta Jolly privileges realism over post-modernism, arguing the case for a feminist culture of commemoration based within a broadly working-class rather than a narrowly middle-class experience of British twentieth-century social history.

By contrast, the situation for lesbians and gay men in postwar British culture has been more uneven. Male homosexual acts were decriminalised in 1967 and many gays 'came out'. Then the AIDS epidemic and government harassment in the 1980s stimulated a new wave of activism. However, eager market-exploitation has in the 1990s overwhelmed traditional ideas about sexuality, as it has other ethical and cultural hierarchies. Crucially, Alan Sinfield argues, in a synoptic reading of gay culture in postwar Britain, pressure from commodification appears to have broken down the distinction between literature and pornography. Exploring changing attitudes to culture and consumption during the postwar period through a comparison of novels by Angus Wilson and Alan Hollinghurst, Sinfield frames concepts of literary writing and sexuality together in terms of the aspirations of welfare-capitalism and the ascendancy of the market.

Bibliography

General studies on the history of the postwar settlement

Addison, P. (1994) *The Road to 1945: British Politics and the Second World War*, rev. edn, London: Pimlico.

Anderson, P. (1992) *English Questions*, London: Verso.

Barnett, C. (1986) *The Audit of War: The Illusion and Reality of Britain as a Great Nation*, London: Macmillan.

Conekin, B., Mort, F. and Waters, C. (eds) (1999) *Moments of Modernity: Reconstructing Britain 1945–1964*, London: Rivers Oram.

Cook, C. and Stevenson, J. (1996) *The Longman Companion to Britain since 1945*, Harlow: Longman.

Digby, A. (1989) *British Welfare Policy: Workhouse to Workfare*, London: Faber.

Gilbert, S. M. and Gubar, S. (1994) *No Man's Land: The Place of the Woman Writer in the Twentieth Century, vol. 3: Letters from the Front*, New Haven: Yale University Press.

Hennessy, P. (1992) *Never Again: Britain 1945–51*, London: Cape.

Kavanagh, D. A. and Morris, P. (1994) *Consensus Politics from Attlee to Major*, 2nd edn, Oxford: Blackwell.

Le Grand, J. (1982) *The Strategy of Equality: Redistribution and the Social Services*, London: Allen and Unwin.

Lewis, J. (1991) *Women in Britain since 1945: Women, Family, Work and the State in the Post-war Years*, Oxford: Blackwell.

Marquand, D. (1995) "How united is the modern United Kingdom?," in A. Grant and K. J. Stringer (eds), *Uniting the Kingdom? The Making of British History*, London: Routledge: 277–91.

Marwick, A. (1996) *British Society since 1945*, 3rd edn, Harmondsworth: Penguin.

Obelkevich, J. and Catterall, P. (eds) (1994) *Understanding Post-War British Society*, London: Routledge.

Wilson, E. (1980) *Only Half-Way to Paradise: Women in Postwar Britain, 1945–68*, London: Tavistock.

General studies on the political effects of Thatcherism

Hall, S. and Jacques, M. (eds) (1983) *The Politics of Thatcherism*, London: Lawrence and Wishart.

Kavanagh, D. A. and Seldon, A. (eds) (1989) *The Thatcher Effect*, Oxford: Oxford University Press.

Mulgan, G. (ed.) (1997) *Life after Politics: New Thinking for the Twenty-First Century*, London: Fontana.

Samuel, R. (1998) "Mrs Thatcher and Victorian values," in *Theatres of Memory, vol. 2: Island Stories: Unravelling Britain*, London: Verso: 330–48.

Wainwright, H. (1994) *Arguments for a New Left: Answering the Free-Market Right*, Oxford: Blackwell.

General studies on gender, sexuality and culture

Baker, N. (1989) *Happily Ever After? Women's Fiction in Postwar Britain, 1945–60*, Basingstoke: Macmillan.

Chapman, R. and Rutherford, J. (eds) (1988) *Male Order: Unwrapping Masculinity*, London: Lawrence and Wishart.

Freeman, S. (1997) *Putting Your Daughters on the Stage: Lesbian Theatre from the 1970s to the 1990s*, London: Cassell.

Kirkham, P. and Thumin, J. (eds) (1993) *You Tarzan: Masculinity, Movies and Men*, London: Lawrence and Wishart.

—— (1995) *Me Jane: Masculinity, Movies and Women*, London: Lawrence and Wishart.

Mort, F. (1996) *Cultures of Consumption: Masculinities and Social Space in Late Twentieth-Century Britain*, London: Routledge.

Segal, L. (1994) *Straight Sex: The Politics of Pleasure*, London: Virago.

—— (ed.) (1997) *New Sexual Agendas*, Basingstoke: Macmillan.

Sinfield, A. (1998) *Gay and After*, London: Serpent's Tail.

—— (1999) *Out on Stage: Lesbian and Gay Theatre in the Twentieth Century*, New Haven: Yale University Press.

Chapter 3

After feminism

Pat Barker, Penelope Lively and the contemporary novel

Margaretta Jolly

It has become a critical *cliché* to state that the British novel since the war has been so diverse as to render futile any generalisation but diversity itself. Yet despite the general acceptance that there have been many lines of fictional development in this period, the legacy of a well-worked canon of largely male, Anglo-British writing continues to dominate.[1]

Attention to women's writing is a crucial element of a more committed attempt to explore the variousness of fiction during the last fifty years. Recent studies of writers from Doris Lessing to Maureen Duffy, Eva Figes to Jeanette Winterson, have shown the range of style *within* women's writing. Often women have different interests and patterns from the male novelists hitherto taken as representative of the period.[2]

While the 'Angry Young Men' were writing about conduct and class, Niamh Baker shows us writers such as Barbara Pym, Pamela Hansford Johnson or Elizabeth Taylor subtly satirising the cult of 1950s domesticity in their superficially romantic novels. The newly populist and 'permissive' 1960s have been well charted in relation to writers such as John Fowles, Kingsley Amis or Angus Wilson. Maggie Humm instead discusses Nell Dunn and Margaret Drabble's fictionalisations of single motherhood from both ends of the class spectrum as a very different inflection of sexual and social swinging. Dunn's aesthetic emerges as quite distinct from either the liberal realist or experimental trends said to characterise the 'British novel' of the period.[3]

Feminism, as a political struggle of particularly cultural proportions, dramatically changed the novel from the 1970s onwards. At the most basic level, it swelled the numbers of women writing and getting published, with its culture of self-expression and the establishment of women's presses. In aesthetic terms, it significantly reshaped *genre* as well as content, most obviously within the previously masculinised formulae of science fiction, crime and thriller, but also in the traditionally feminised genres of the romance, history and, arguably, in the realist novel itself. Writers such as Fay Weldon, Beryl Bainbridge and Molly Keane invert the English comedy of manners into biting satires on the war of the sexes.

The domestic novel has been thoroughly re-visioned by Michèle Roberts, Marina Warner, Verity Bargate and Sara Maitland among many others. Gillian Hanscombe's *Between Friends* revives the epistolary form to discuss feminist political philosophy. Eva Figes, Jeanette Winterson, Maggie Gee and Emma Tennant, pit fantasy against realism to explore new sexual identities. Doris Lessing and Margaret Drabble have produced so-called 'condition of England' novels from women's perspectives, while Buchi Emechta, Merle Collins, and Suniti Namjoshi mix Nigerian, Caribbean and Indian with English cultural forms respectively. Such developments have affected less overtly political writers such as Anita Brookner, A. S. Byatt, Penelope Lively, Margaret Forster or Anita Desai. Male novelists are influenced as well, Hanif Kureishi, Roddy Doyle and Adam Mars-Jones being only some of the more obvious. In the wake of the establishment of the annual Orange Prize for Fiction in 1996, an award specifically celebrating women's writing, it would seem that public attention to women's writing has become relatively mainstream.[4]

In arguing for this more pluralist interpretation of the history of the British novel, I am clearly not suggesting that women writers can themselves be homogenised, nor that there is any consistent separation between men and women writers' literary interests. Iris Murdoch, Angela Carter and A. S. Byatt are three who immediately come to mind as fitting more neatly into this literary epoch as it has been defined around largely male, white English writing, despite their strong interest in topics of gender. In this essay I concentrate on a contemporary woman writer, Pat Barker, who bridges feminist and mainstream literary interests in ways that make her difficult to categorise. On the one hand, she writes from a strongly feminist perspective about the crushing effects of male sexual violence and the sexual division of labour. On the other hand, her later novels have distanced her from her feminist profile through a shift to male protagonists, a favouring of the masculinised spheres of pub, battlefield, hospital or government, and a leaning towards the epic rather than domestic scale. Moreover, while Barker always foregrounds the experience of gender and sexuality in a very political sense, she interrogates some of the conventions within *feminist* theory.

It is precisely Barker's double status as feminist and mainstream writer that makes her novels a good focal point for a discussion of women's writing in the 1990s. She represents both the influence that feminism has had within the literary establishment and the concomitant testing of feminism from within. In particular, her questioning of sisterhood across class difference resonates with historical changes in the position of women in recent years. While many working-class (particularly ethnic minority) women have faced drastic impoverishment and disempowerment with post-industrial decline and high unemployment (whether their own or of dependent men), middle-class women in the same period have been able to take better advantage of the feminisation of the labour market, and the institutionalisation of equal opportunities.

In the first section of this chapter I will explore Barker's treatment of the intersection of class and gender in this context, as an attempt to widen both feminist and socialist perspectives through forcing them into opposition with each other.

Far from being an abandonment of a political vision, however, I go on to suggest that this is part of an attempt in all her work to explain *why* people continue to invest in unjust and limiting identities and systems. For example, her most acclaimed works, *Regeneration* (1991), *The Eye in the Door* (1993) and the Booker prize winner, *The Ghost Road* (1995) (known as the *Regeneration Trilogy*), explore the male psyche and position through writing about the First World War, in which ideas of heroism and invulnerability crumble in the face of scenes of hysterical, disabled, tender and brutal men. Yet what makes the *Regeneration Trilogy* so powerful is precisely her measure of how important and even attractive the war was and still is to both sexes, in different ways. In these respects, her celebrated 'social-realist' style balances critique of social relations as they are with a sympathy for both oppressor and oppressed. Historically, this is an important direction for fiction in the 1990s, so often complacently touted as 'post-feminist'. I bring this point home in the second and third sections of this chapter by comparing her work with the much more superficial reversal of gender roles in Penelope Lively's *Moon Tiger* (1987). Lively's novel, which also won the Booker Prize, parallels Barker's *Liza's England* as a feminisation of twentieth-century English history, and, on a smaller scale, compares to the *Regeneration Trilogy* in its deconstruction of military masculinity. Yet Lively's post-modern style and her explicitly pre-feminist heroine support an individualised vision of gender struggles that ultimately permits the reinstatement of the conventions of both gender and literature in heterosexual romance.

Barker's work then exemplifies the plurality and political liveliness within the postwar novel even outside the dynamism of post-colonial writing or the aesthetic fallout of post-modern theory. Her refining of earlier feminist and socialist novelistic conventions places her as a writer of the 1980s and 1990s. Her reworking of both English history and the social-realist novel though, is a salutary reminder of how diversely these terms have been interpreted in British writing throughout the postwar period.

Mixed motives: class, gender, and the unconscious

Barker's first novel *Union Street* (1982) sets the pattern for all her work in exploring the sarcastic, sexual culture of those close to the margins of survival. Set in an impoverished Northern town, decimated by unemployment, a portrait of a community in crisis is built up through stories of the street's women, progressing in age from thirteen year old Kelly Brown to the elderly Alice Bell. This collective 'life-story' of a working-class woman shows her carrying the burden of poverty but also of caring for male kin, who drink and fight their way through unemployment and illness rather than take domestic responsibility. The women's struggles operate at the most essential level, from the opening chapter, where Kelly is raped, to the last, where Alice decides to die rather than go into a nursing home.[5]

The novel's implicit critique of the power relations in the domestic sphere is of course a central plank of feminist theory, whose most succinct formulation was 'the personal is political'. Yet Barker's concentration on poor women makes this opening out of the domestic painfully and ironically literal. Poverty physically pierces the domestic space within the houses; the window is boarded up with cardboard, the floorboards cave in to trap-like holes. These thin domestic boundaries thus become symbolic of class as well as gender porousness, permitting a punishing regime of neighbourly surveillance. The inhabitants jealously guard their reputations, frightened by the spectre of nearby, half-demolished Wharfe Street, where the abortionist, the homeless and the prostitute women live. From their point of view, survival is as often a question of competition as co-operation. Ian Haywood has convincingly argued that the novel's strange vagueness of time and place, which contributes to the sense

of permanent entrapment, is itself a comment on the cultural disintegration of the north-eastern working-class in the post-industrial
period:

> Unlike *Up the Junction*, which *Union Street* superficially resembles,
> there is no thread of contemporary cultural reference linking the
> stories. What Raymond Williams calls the 'general way of life' is
> almost entirely absent, as each story rarely strays beyond the con-
> sciousness of its benighted and domesticated heroine.[6]
>
> (Haywood 1997: 145)

However, the 'unity' implied by the title is not only an ironic comment
on the proliferating divisions between a people commonly oppressed,
but the recognition of some measure of mutual support within the
women's community, carrying on underneath the redundant struggles
of the male trade unions. The poverty that makes their sufferings so
public also turns the street itself into a kind of domestic space. While
clearly, the 'street' no longer displays the political solidarity of older
working-class communities, the need for a newly *feminist* class struggle
is suggested as the key to change. The formal circularity of the closing
scene, where Kelly meets the dying Alice and takes her hand, clearly
symbolises this immanent recognition within the circle of women.

A similar, though more sinister move is made in her second novel,
Blow Your House Down (1984), which traces a community of prostitutes' reaction to the serial murderer Peter Sutcliffe, known as the
'Yorkshire Ripper'. The title gruesomely calls up the associations of the
children's fable of the wolf at the piglet's frail door. However the novel
demonstrates that the predatory man is not always outside, for the
women know that their punters, any of whom could be the 'Ripper', are
also somebody's husband or son. Even a house made of brick cannot
protect one from an essentially corrupt sexual and economic order. The
women resist not by retreating to their separate houses, but by continuing to work the streets, supporting each other with the hard laughter
of realism.

Barker's metaphorical breaking down of the house, and her exploration of the women's communities of the street or the pub, is one
aspect of her interest in bringing together class and gender. This is
opportune. As the analysis of gender and sexuality has become increasingly refined, understanding of class identity has, conversely, become
clouded, and frequently proclaimed redundant (Gagnier 1998), epitomised in John Major's claim that Britain now represents a 'classless

society'. Barker's novels suggest by contrast, that the class system is still a deep and damaging part of the national psyche. While asserting the vicious material deprivation of the northern towns and estates that characterise the post-industrial period, she also explores the envies, pleasures and performances of class as a subjective and even unconscious identity in the deep sense usually accorded only to gender. Her characters are dynamised by a frightening or pleasurable unconscious that is explicitly linked to experiences of *social* rather than sexual shame or desire. Carolyn Steedman has theorised this in her autobiographical revision of the class biases in Freudian psychoanalysis, *Landscape for a Good Woman* (1986). Steedman's question could be Barker's:

> What becomes of the notion of class-consciousness when it is seen as a structure of feeling that can be learned in childhood, with one of its components a proper envy, the desire of people for the things of the earth[?] Class and gender, and their articulations, are the bits and pieces from which psychological selfhood is made.
>
> (Steedman 1986: 7)

In some ways, this would simply suggest that Barker is simply a 'socialist-feminist', working within the legacy of the white British working-class, who ultimately sees women's suffering as rooted in the effects of their relation to production. There is certainly a sense in which her economic plotting of women's low pay, childcare, disability and sexuality, are the fictional equivalent of this political tradition. It is also worth noting how unusual this is in a fictional movement that has, as Paulina Palmer argues, concentrated on 'radical feminist' themes such as male violence, sexuality, eating and the body, maternity, or lesbianism.[7]

Barker though never sacrifices gender for class. Rather, her exploration of the unconscious of class is always measured against, and entwined with, the relations between the sexes. Palmer comments that

> an interesting feature of [*Blow Your House Down*] is that it succeeds in bringing together both radical feminist and socialist feminist perspectives on prostitution. . . . While Barker's representation of the prostitute's position as victim of male violence is radical or revolutionary feminist in spirit, her analysis of their economic situation is socialist feminist.
>
> (Palmer 1989: 89)

Barker's dialectical synthesising of different feminist analyses is not simply a comment on their false theoretical polarisation, but a reaction to the ironic persistence and even exacerbation of the divisions between women of different classes in the post-industrial economy. Middle-class feminists, often divided from poor or prostitute women in practice if not in theory, face a specific appeal in Barker's novels.[8] A remarkable scene in *Union Street* serves as an example of this dialectical method. Kelly Brown was raped by a stranger who, we are clearly told, is motivated by revenge and disgust for the working-class children that he was protected from in his childhood. Afterwards, in a kind of vengeful trespassing, Kelly steals into a large house whose French windows have been left open. She explores the surfaces and dimensions of its interior, fascinated as an animal at its foreign luxury and the evidence of a girlhood so different from her own:

> The girl's bedroom bored her in the end. Photographs of school – imagine wanting to be reminded of that! Books about ballet, and ponies; lipstick in a drawer. She looked into the garden, so green, so enclosed, so sheltered. She might have pitied or despised the girl who lived in this room, but she would not have known how to envy her.
>
> (Barker, *Union Street*: 52)

So far, the emphasis is on the shaping of gender by class. In the parent's bedroom though a reversal takes place. Suddenly the house is eerily animated as if it were literally a female body. The language, in turn, makes of Kelly a penetrating, even ejaculatory, presence, reversing the class as well as sexual defilement that was practised on her. At first merely plunging her finger into a pot of moisturising cream, her anger becomes more insistent: 'She felt her skin tighten as if at any moment it might split open and deposit her a new seed, on the earth' (Barker, *Union Street*: 53). The ambiguous sense of 'deposit her a new seed', in which she either ejaculates or is ejaculated, suggests the equally ambiguous nature of her desperate pleasure. It is precisely the *envy* Barker says she 'would not have known how to feel' that fuels her contempt. She claws at the flesh-coloured satin skin of the bed, the glossy wood, catches sight of her reflection in the mirror and, seizing some sewing scissors, cuts her hair off. Eventually, she 'slips out' through the French windows (ibid.: 55).

Barker's lurid imagery dramatises more than an action of psychological displacement, in turning Kelly into a kind of 'rapist' of this middle-class bedroom. It suggests that the privatised, feminised domesticity of the middle-class girl and woman can contain a safety and innocence desperately needed. Being raped and the brutal sexualisation Kelly suffers in the prurient or pitying eyes of her community have destroyed a primal sense of her bodily integrity, apparently still preserved for another girl or woman, in these soft, plump, flesh-coloured interiors and the garden, 'so green, so enclosed, so sheltered'. It is not as easy to destroy or criticise the luxury of 'innocence'. This ironises a bedroom scene that is a standard trope of claustrophobia in middle-class women's novels, heightened by the contrast with the earlier description of her own bedroom, pierced by the winds of poverty and maternal negligence. However in a further twist, the very fact of her easy penetration – and its parallel with rape – show the limits that this model of protected femininity affords. Clearly no woman, from whatever class, should be clawed, pierced, cut.

The story of Kelly's rape contains a dual sympathy, for the suffering of the working class and for women of any class, across contradictory allegiances. More challengingly, it points up the mixed motives of both rapist and raped, in which even the male rapist's desire to dominate and destroy involves self-hatred, envy and need. This uncomfortable insistence on the duality or ambiguity in each identity is in fact Barker's key idea. In her heavily Freudian world people do bad things, or accept oppressive systems, because they are attracted to them, or, more precisely, because they fulfil needs. Heterosexuality contains both cruelty and indifference but also intense pleasure and love. War involves physical adventure and a capacity for male caring as well as unparalleled horror and sadism. Doing down your neighbours is part of trying to gain respect in a world where you don't have much status. Wreaking revenge, rape or violence, is, in part, an attempt to gain control over one's life.

We may find this understandable in terms of Kelly's vandalism, even when she smears shit over her school headmaster's office. It is harder to accept when Barker suddenly puts us inside the head of the man who rapes Kelly, or that of the character George Harrison, another inhabitant of the street, as he goes to visit an elderly prostitute. By the time we are made to see through the eyes of the 'Ripper' as he rapes and murders a prostitute in *Blow Your House Down*, what seemed an anomalous switch in sexual focalisation is clearly a deliberate challenge to any simple polarisation of oppressed and oppressor. One of the prostitutes, Jean, offers a *rationale* for 'getting inside his mind', as the means to find and kill him:

It's the only way of finding him: you've got to see what he sees, you've got to know what he would do, and all that time I'd been trying, pushing against the doors of his mind. And then just as I relaxed, just when for once I wasn't thinking about him, the doors swung open, *but from the other side*.

(Barker, *Blow Your Your House Down*: 97)

Jean knows him 'from the other side' because she understands him. She realises his sadism is entwined with envy. Then Barker switches from Jean's perspective to the 'Ripper's' own point of view. He follows, rapes, murders and then plays with the corpse. These five pages must be some of the most uncomfortable for the reader in all Barker's work. They most clearly show her political aesthetic of representing and even identifying with *all* sides of the sexual and class order, as they merge or cross over. The Freudian scenarios that permeate her writing are thus dramatically reworked as social rather than individual pathologies.

In this refined vision of social power, particularly her breaking down of the notion of a monolithic oppressive masculinity, Barker's novels represent the development of feminist thinking in the late 1980s and 1990s. Her dramatisations of differences between women, of masculinities, and of the pleasure as well as pain of identity all find their contemporary theoretical and political counterparts: the evolution of identity politics; the new men's movement and theory; and feminist and queer psychoanalysis. As we have seen, she does not glamorise domination and submission or dissolve struggle into play. It is as if her fiction springs from the need to return to basic questions. Why, despite the impact of feminism, don't women change? Why don't men? Why this poverty and waste, post-welfare and war? Why, don't the poor or the oppressed unite? If not 'why war?', then at least, 'why do men fight?'

The fundamentally idealist impulse behind her meticulously realised grit is summed up in the citation from Nietzsche's *Beyond Good and Evil*, on the flyleaf of *Blow Your House Down*: 'Whoever fights monsters should see to it that in the process he does not become a monster. And when you look long into an abyss the abyss also looks into you'. While Barker never allows the reader to feel safely 'above' the abyss, it is always clear that she is fighting rather than condoning monstrosity. In this sense, her fiction seems not so much simply realist as dystopic and didactic, shadowed by its possible, better alternative.

Barker in the backlash: post-feminist fiction

I have argued that Barker is an important writer in her treatment of the deep influences of class as well as gender, and more generally, her disruption of a simple model of oppressor and oppressed. Yet her dissolution of simple political oppositions is always evoked against a strong note of protest against 'monstrosities' of social injustice, particularly against women. In this sense she represents a maturing, rather than rejection, of the political vision of earlier 'second wave' women novelists. Although she moves away from writing about contemporary women's lives to writing both about the past and from a male perspective in *Liza's England*, *The Man who Wasn't There* and the *Regeneration Trilogy*, her later novels are fuelled by the same protest against the exploitations of class and gender, now more explicitly configured within the peculiarities of white Englishness. This distinction between a *dissolution* and an *extension* of feminist interest is particularly important in the late 1980s and 1990s, as feminist ideas are increasingly appropriated or distorted by writers with other political agendas, and as disillusioned women writers succumb to what has been described as the 'backlash' against feminism (most notoriously Fay Weldon).

A comparison of Barker's third novel, *Liza's England* (1986), with Penelope Lively's *Moon Tiger*, which won the Booker Prize in 1987, points up Barker's unusual mix of general content with feminist analysis, mainstream success with radical allegiances. *Moon Tiger*, by contrast, represents the superficiality of much other mainstream fiction's take-up of feminist plot and aesthetic. Both novels tell the memories of an elderly, dying woman, and use her life story to comment on the last hundred years: 'the century of war' (Lively 1987: 99). In many respects, Lively develops the same feminist themes as Barker. Like Barker, she genders the battlefield, and the writing as well as making of history, in ways that acknowledge the differences between women and the contradictions within masculine stereotypes. Yet where Barker illuminates her characters through the structures of sex, class and nation, Lively suggests that the brilliant individual can transcend such definitions. Ironically, this makes Barker's apparently more tragic version of women's history more open to revision, while Lively's playful style and rejection of the marital plot turn out to be, underneath, the same old romance.

Liza's England (previously titled *The Century's Daughter*), explores the position of working-class women through the century with characteristic symbolism. Liza, born on the stroke of midnight, 1900 and now aged eighty, is provoked into remembering and recounting her past by the visits of a young social worker, Steven, who has been sent to convince her to leave her home for sheltered accommodation. In this way, Liza is set up as the unelected representative of English history, 'the Century's Daughter'. Her final years in a half-demolished street on a violent estate become an implicit comment on the state of England today. If this disabuses us of any facile notion of progress either since the postwar establishment of the welfare state, or its dismantling with Thatcherism, her memories show all too much similarity throughout the century: a devastating cycle of unemployment and war. Liza's extraordinary ability to survive such hardship is established not as exceptional but as only what millions did and do, although often by becoming crueller or more bitter than she. Her own appreciation of her husband's struggle, despite the fact he abandoned her penniless with two children, articulates the positive as well as negative terms of being representative:

> She walked home through the centre of the town, the longest way, but she needed time to prepare herself to meet the children. Day was ebbing in a thin, acid light that couldn't compete with the multi-coloured lights of shop windows, though it etched the faces of the shoppers, making them look thinner and more worried than perhaps they were. Liza carried her pain home with her, carefully, as if it might spill. A tram rattled past and jetted sparks into the dusk. Liza stood on the kerb, one of a crowd of people waiting to cross the road.
>
> Suddenly she started to cry and the tears, once started, streamed down her thin face without stopping. She was crying not for herself but for Frank. It seemed the people hurrying past denied him: his life, his death, the terrible stone-breaking struggle of his final years. She wanted to shout his name, to silence the roar of traffic, so the people who ignored and jostled her would have to stop and listen. She needed words powerful enough to ignite the silence that was densely packed in her, a voice that, fanned by the bellows of her lungs, would stream out of her mouth like a living torch.
>
> The crowd, seeing a gap in the traffic, surged forward, carrying her along with it, and in the struggle to keep her feet she stopped crying, though her eyes still glittered with a hard, brilliant, angry light and her forehead jutted out and gleamed as if it were made of some substance more durable than bone. For one second the chance flare of headlamps caught her and she stood out from the

surrounding darkness. Then the crowd surged forward again and she disappeared into the hurrying, anonymous grey.

(Barker, *Liza's England*: 167)

Just as Frank's life was unacknowledged, Barker dramatises Liza's own 'invisibility', through the metaphor of the crowd. Grief neither distinguishes nor protects her, symbolised in the relentless details of public life: the tram sparks, the shops still trading and the traffic. Yet just as being part of the crowd renders her anonymous, its 'surge' literally forces her to carry on. Unpitied pain transubstantiates her into 'something more durable than bone' in a personification of endurance. In retrospect, Liza's history becomes implicitly her protest, the anger she could not voice, now finally ignited and released by the narrator. Focalised through Steven, who begins to re-evaluate his own family, we realise that Liza possesses a wisdom we need to survive the current depression.

Moon Tiger also makes the elderly woman the embodiment of public history.[9] Claudia, dying from cancer at seventy, lies in her hospital bed. Although the nurses treat her as half-mad, as she mutters to herself, her internal voice glitters with humour and insight, as she informs us that she is going to write 'a history of the world. And in the process, my own' (Lively, *Moon Tiger*: 1). Like *Liza's England*, this involves 'everything and nothing. The history of the world as selected by Claudia: fact and fiction, myth and evidence, images and documents.' Yet in striking contrast, this assertion is Claudia's own, the framework of interpretation included within the text. On one level, this difference is simply between a third-person and first-person narrative, and an upper-middle-class heroine as against a working-class one. On another level, however, it is one aspect of Barker's realism versus Lively's postmodernism.

While *Liza's England* shows a linear unfolding of chronology even as Liza remembers it, *Moon Tiger* uses Claudia's associative thought processes to debate contemporary ideas of history as narrative construct, dissolving any fixed reference as it does so. 'I've always thought a kaleidoscopic view might be an interesting heresy', announces Claudia, before providing us with just such a kaleidoscopic treatment of the Second World War. Both the 'everything and nothing' and the fact of 'selection' therefore, mean very different things than for Barker's common history. In the latter's scenario of the working-class Liza, it is an assertion of the value of the everyday and its embedding in the unofficial records of personal objects, family stories, treasured individual documents. For Claudia, it is an explicit attack on empiricist historiography. 'When you and I', she addresses us with bossy irony,

> talk about history we don't mean what actually happened do we? The cosmic chaos of everywhere, all time? We mean the tidying up of this into books, the concentration of the benign historical eye upon years and places and persons. History unravels; circumstances, following their natural inclination, prefer to remain ravelled.
>
> (Lively, *Moon Tiger*: 9)

It was surely for its stylish animation of these post-modern sensibilities that the novel won the Booker. Yet on another level, the difference in style is also one of social perspective and content. Critics Debrah Raschke and Mary Hurley Moran perceive this fictional mix of autobiography and history, with its interweaving of public and private, as the assertion of a feminist historiography. The defiantly subjective authority of Claudia's account is the stylistic corollary of her pioneering status as a woman war-correspondent in the Second World War and then a professional historian. Always determinedly feminine in glamour, heels, sexuality, she claims to have it all, refusing to choose between desire and achievement, love and work. An unmarried and largely uninterested mother, she candidly admits 'I was not a good mother, in any conventional sense.' The self-consciousness of this rejection of conventional women's roles is underlined by Claudia's triumphant comparisons between herself and her stupid sister-in-law who consoles herself with over-eating for her unhappy marriage and failure to get her English, upper-middle-class house in order. She also compares herself with her mother who spends her time reading the *West Dorset Gazette* and *Country Life* and worrying about her floribunda roses, after her husband was killed in the First World War. As Claudia perceives it, 'History killed Father', and Mother therefore 'retired from history'. In this sense, being a war widow seems merely to exaggerate the secluded but suffocating private sphere of the middle-class woman. By contrast, a war historian and correspondent asserts her right not only to participate in but to define history. Like Liza, she is aware that history is written by the one with the loudest voice. Unlike Liza, she is able to speak loudly without the aid of a narrator.

Moon Tiger is an elegant study in proto-feminism, the professional women who challenged the rules individually but, precisely because she was so successful at doing so, never made common cause with others of her sex. Claudia is explicit about her politics on this matter:

> I was thirty-eight when Lisa was born, and doing nicely. Two books under my belt, some controversial journalism, a reputation for contentious provocative attention-seizing writing. I had something of a name. If feminism had been around then I'd have taken it up, I suppose; it would have needed me. As it was, I never felt its absence; being a woman seemed to me a valuable extra asset. My gender was never an impediment. And I must also reflect, now, that it perhaps saved my life. If I had been a man I might well have died in the war.
>
> (Lively, *Moon Tiger*: 22)

Post-'second-wave' feminism, such insouciance and prickly individuality are refreshingly undidactic and a welcome corrective to earlier idealisations of feminist fiction. However, the explicit rejection of a broader platform of political sympathy makes it puzzling that Raschke (1995) and Moran (1990) have seen this as a particularly feminist novel. For it represents only the narrowest interpretation of women's needs, one of the escape from private to public. Claudia, of course, is neither Lively nor the narrator, and third person narratorial interventions remind us of her contradictions, personal insensitivities and unlikeability. But the power of those checks is weakened by the suggestion that these too are Claudia, in her opening declaration that the history of the world will be her own. The autobiographical mode is thus only superficially allied to the feminist politicising both of the personal and of historiography. It serves instead to conflate the public with the life of an outstanding individual in the most traditional terms of liberal individualism. Raschke points out that in the midst of her deconstruction of time and place, Claudia herself seems 'completely composed', and enjoying her own performance, in a text which abounds with theatrical metaphors. Rather than a post-modern aestheticising of the everyday that Raschke identifies, I would argue that it is the formalising of a disengagement from the politics of individualism that is ostensibly in question.

It is thus unsurprising that the domestic is rejected but not restructured, the opposition between feminine and masculine never really attacked. This leaves the novel with a much more conservative kind of plot than its 'history of the world' originally projects. As the layers of memory and interpretation are peeled away, the 'core' of Claudia's life is revealed as her love affair with Tom Southern, a tank officer in Egypt in the war. This resolves her position as a rebellious woman in personal rather than political terms. In parallel with her rejection of civilian domesticity, he admits fear, confusion, love and doubts about war itself. The fact that we discover this through his diary itself signifies an answering male subjectivity. Heterosexual love between enlightened individuals is suggested as the solution to the conundrums of the binary of gender. Tom, a good British officer with a stiff upper lip, is underneath, a sensitive, vulnerable writer, able to empathise with the acute panic of his new tank gunner Jennings, and to analyse the other men's acute embarrassment as the effect of a repressive code of military masculinity. The more difficult questions of men's power, alongside the power of class, sexuality, nationality, are side-stepped in this strategic confession.

Admittedly, this resolution between the sexes is deferred: the diary is abruptly terminated when Tom is killed by air attack, and much of the poignancy of the novel comes from the belatedness of consummation between the elderly Claudia and her young lover, as she reads these pages for the first time in her dying hours. However, the diary's function as the closing revelation, and only clearly independent voice outside Claudia's, sets up the love between Tom and Claudia as the answer to post-modern fragmentation. History, and the particular question of masculinity, dissolve into romance, a synthesis anticipated in his plea for Claudia to 'make sense' of his experiences for posterity:

> I have put this down – Jennings, my own duel between mind and matter – because one day I am going to want to think about it. This is as it was, raw and untreated. At some point I shall want to make sense of it – if there is sense to be made. C. asked me once – the first time I met her – what it was like out here. I found it hard to explain. Well, at one point it was like this. So this is for her too, perhaps. Maybe one day she will help me make sense of it. She intends to write history books, after all, so it will be within her line of business.
>
> (Lively, *Moon Tiger*: 210–11)

Liza's England is clearly more moralistic in comparison. Paradoxically though, it engages much more directly than *Moon Tiger* with the real conflicts that individuals of any class, gender, nationality or body, experience. Thus, while both Claudia and Liza have disappointingly conventional, dull daughters, Liza understands Eileen's limits, Claudia dismisses Lisa's. Therefore, while for Claudia, male sacrifice and suffering in wartime are the proof of the asset of being female, for Liza they are a profound indictment of the sexual division of labour. Frank's shell-shock from the First World War, and her beloved son's death in the Second World War, only leave her to struggle even more. While Barker's later work sugars such insights with humour, the essential message is that her readers, like her characters, will not be liberated by any simple decision of willpower. The empathy, more than the pessimism which this implies, is surely what appeals so to the 1990s reader, surrounded by calls for personal and economic liberation that, for the most part, are very difficult to fulfil.

War on gender: the *Regeneration Trilogy*

War becomes the central theme of Barker's work after *Liza's England* with *The Man who Wasn't There* and the *Regeneration Trilogy*. In these works, her moralism becomes less obvious, more stringently tested against the investments that people have in the system as it is. For these reasons, they are even more powerful in the context of 'the backlash'. It is impossible to do justice in this short space to the poignant comedy of *The Man who Wasn't There*, and to the immensely complex plot of the *Regeneration Trilogy*, which explores the First World War from the oblique angles of the psychiatric hospital, the Conscientious Objectors' movement and a Polynesian island of head-hunters. Rather than try to do so, I want simply to isolate one further exemplary contrast with *Moon Tiger* to point up their more developed re-visioning of gender. There is an obvious point of comparison, which is that the trilogy also ends with the diary account of a man returning to the front, and in doing so, also confronts the ideals of courage, patriotism, male heroism.

Billy Prior, a man fundamentally 'in-between' the categories of class, gender, region and sexuality, is the quintessential Barker character. From a working-class family, he is nevertheless not exactly one of the 'temporary gentlemen' who gained status as officers in the war, for his corrosive intelligence and bisexuality already put him outside the conventional oppositions. Indeed, in *The Eye in the Door*, he suffers from a literal split in his identity in blackouts of bad conscience he likens to his 'Mr Hyde'. Having suffered from shell-shock, mutism and asthma, he was ironically 'cured' enough to go back, and in a further irony, wished to do so, despite having no illusions about King and Country. This paradox, as we should now expect, is Barker's strategy for exploring not only the cruelty of the war, but precisely the taboos of its attraction, where a man as cynical as Prior finds a kind of fulfilment he never could have by staying in the hide-bound hypocrisy of civilian England. His diary account, like Tom Southern's, exposes the confusion and fear behind the pretence of rationality and bravery in the face of death, but goes far further in revealing the physical excitement of both fighting and living with other men in such existential conditions. While Tom admits to a kind of 'lust' for the chase, likening the feeling to being 'like a pack of hounds', Prior writes of remembering telling his upset doctor that 'the sensation of going over the top was sexy':

> I don't think he believed me, but actually there *was* something in common – blood, risk, physical exposure, a kind of awful *daring* about it. (Obviously I'm not talking about sex in bed.) But I don't feel anything like that now. There's *for me*, a nagging, constant, apprehension, because I'm out in the open and I know I shouldn't be. New kind of war. The trouble is my nerves are the same old nerves. I'd be happier with a ton or two of France on top of my head.
>
> (Barker, *The Ghost Road*: 529)

Prior's mix of lust, sadism, fear, tenderness and insight allows no simple reversal of the macho hero to sensitive writer. Here too, he remains an 'in-between' figure, suspended between moral polarities that refuse to resolve. In stressing the pleasure and pull of the war as part of a masculine experience felt at the most basic level of the body, however, Barker always points up the differences of class, sexuality, place or emotion between men. Prior writes of choosing his 'gentleman's gentleman' (ibid.: 517), who is the only man he ever met who could open doors with his hips; of the cynical, communist Potts who still believes that the war is being fought for a reason; of his joy at the social chaos in what used to be nice bourgeois villages where they are billeted.[10] Most of all, his awareness of men's bodies begins to open up the very connection between male sexuality and violence he insists on making, for here at the front, men find an unparalleled tenderness for each other.

Barker entwines Prior's story with the 'real' histories of the poets Siegfried Sassoon and Wilfred Owen, and their psychoanalytic anthropologist doctor, W. H. R. Rivers. Sassoon and Owen, literary soldiers revolted by the war, have a central place in the dominant discourse about the war since the 1930s, as a tragic national error and waste.

Barker exploits these real histories, however, not simply to confirm the enlightenment of these dissident poets, but to show up how facile this discourse has become in 'Poppy Day' nationalism and enshrinement of these poets as the spokespeople for some kind of literary redemption.[11] Prior's 'anti' anti-heroism forces us to look at not only our continuing cultural investment in war, but also its connections with masculinity. Prior, for example, details in one account his and Owen's inability to stomach the sight of dying insects on a strip of fly-paper and in another, that Owen, 'caped and masked in blood, seize[d] a machine-gun and turn[ed] it on its previous owners at point-blank range. Like killing fish in a bucket' (Barker, *The Ghost Road*: 544).

In this context, Prior's diary itself is problematised as an emblem of the literary war. Like Tom's, it evokes not only the power of an eyewitness document but the implied vulnerability of the first person soldier-writer. Yet Prior refuses to conform to the confessional. While Tom feels 'amazed and ashamed' after his pleasure in 'chase', Prior's first entry begins by parodying the expected war diary:

> 29 August 1918
> Bought this in a stationer's just off Fleet Street. . . . It's a marvellous shop, a real old-fashioned stationer's. Stationer's, second-hand bookshops, ironmongers'. Feel a great need at the moment to concentrate on small pleasures. If the whole of one's life can be summoned up and held in the palm of one hand in the living moment, then time means nothing. World without end, Amen.
> Load of crap. Facts are what we need, man, facts.
> (Barker, *The Ghost Road*: 493)

This is in part the display of a working-class ironic humour, but later, Prior's terse diarising more explicitly investigates the idea of writing as some kind of salvation:

> Saturday, 7 September
> Posted to the 2nd Manchesters. We leave tomorrow.
> It's evening now, and everybody's scribbling away, telling people the news, or as much of the news as we're allowed to tell them. I look up and down the dormitory and there's hardly a sound except for pages being turned, and here and there a pen scratching. It's like this every evening. And not just letters either. Diaries. Poems. At least two would-be poets in this hut alone.
> Why? you have to ask yourself. I think it's a way of claiming

immunity. First-person narrators can't die, so as long as we keep telling the story of our own lives we're safe. Ha bloody fucking Ha.
(Barker, *The Ghost Road*: 497–8)

This is not to say that soldiers didn't write extraordinarily frequently and with existential investment during both the First and Second World Wars.[12] It foregrounds though the civilian reader's own vicarious salvation in reading such a diary. This is underlined by the fact that, unlike Tom's, Prior's diary is not retrieved or read after his death within the narrative. Most particularly, it is not recuperated within a familial or romantic relationship. Although he has a *fiancée*, Prior's diary is counterpointed with the story of his doctor Rivers, who receives his letters while treating the war-wounded in London. While this is a damning enough reminder of the results of the war, Rivers' feverish memories of his time studying a tribe of head-hunters in Polynesia open up further questions about the British cultural investment in war. The British colonialists have banned the horrific practice of head-hunting, which the inhabitants of the tiny island see as essential to the perpetuation of their culture and identity. Yet the hysterical nationalism, punishment of all 'foreigners' and dissidents, and the inescapable parallels between the roles of men as killers, women as nurturers, suggest that the mass slaughter in Europe has equally deep cultural roots and no language as developed as the head-hunters' to talk of the living ghosts it is spawning.

Prior's diary is one small aspect of a whole study not only of a war which exerted a deadly kind of club-membership in cynicism, but of the relationships between men at their most developed and most existential. Masculinity both cuts across and is divided by class, sexuality and nationality (just like femininity in the earlier novels), as relationships of caring and loving develop in this place of ultimate male abuse. By contrast, *Moon Tiger's* focus on the relationships between rather than within the sexes, and the individual rationalisation of the sexual division of labour, loses the clarity of analysis not only of masculinity but of the other social identities manipulated by war. It is true that the culture of the Second World War in relation to the First World War had a much more heterosexual than homosocial character. This has been generally recognised as a complex result of different fighting conditions, as much as cultural context. The Second World War's greater claims to be a 'just' war meant that it did not indict civilian society in the same way. However, in terms of the function of feminist fiction, this might argue even more strongly for a representation of the Second

World War that pulls apart the real conflicts of interest as Barker has done for the First World War.

Conclusion

The comparison between Lively and Barker has shown the much more profound interrogation of social identity that Barker offers, in a more confrontational reflection of current political concerns about gender and history. It has also though suggested that she is less innovative aesthetically. Although most commentators have remarked on her striking symbolism, she clearly writes within a long tradition of social realism.[13] She almost consistently uses the third person omniscient narration, alternating with dialogue and free indirect speech. She never breaks the frame of time or place with meta-fictional commentaries. Even Prior's diary as a rare example of a text within a text provides little writerly 'self-consciousness' of genre, and the 'inter-textuality' of the *Regeneration Trilogy* weaves fact and fiction together so seamlessly such as to increase rather than undermine the realist 'illusion'. Her plots are heavily patterned unities with strong closures that often echo the beginning. *Moon Tiger*'s ending in a petering out of the subjective consciousness, where meaning seeps away, would be unthinkable in a Barker novel where the moral is always brought home.

Barker's literary conservatism, however, as we have seen, is highly effective in representing a vision that continually returns individual pathologies and pleasures to their social context. The third person narration permits the revelation of the social taboos that lie in her characters' unconscious as much as in the belligerent worlds they inhabit. At the same time, we are pulled into strong identifications with them through the continual turn to their inner speech. Barker's favouring of so much free indirect speech, a technique associated with the late-nineteenth-century shift from realism to modernism, is surely because of its inherent mediation between outer and inner worlds.

For a historical novelist, it is striking how little external description of place and habit Barker gives us: what we focus on instead is the psychological face of the social.[14] In Bakhtinian terms, Barker is notably dialogic, for social conflict never implies solipsism or abandoning the attempt to communicate. Her emphasis on both dialogue and dialect clearly underlines this, as does the intercutting of different characters' perspectives, which is always plotted towards eventual rapprochement. Her aesthetic, in sum, is driven by a collective vision on the part of the omniscient narrator, notwithstanding the sense of isolation from which many of her characters suffer. As I have argued, this takes on contemporary resonance as a challenge to the fragmentation of both post-industrial society and post-modern style. It is a point worthy of debate whether Barker's novels are so popular in part because readers still enjoy writing which unifies as well as interrogates historical experience in this way.[15]

Barker is not only an apt prism through which to consider the current interplay between feminism and writing, but a test of the common description of the Anglo-English novel as socially retrospective and formally conservative. In all of her seven novels, she writes of decaying white Anglo-English communities. Her concentration on the two World Wars in five of them clearly marks an interest in national identity extremely common in the postwar novel. Yet her dialectical method of pitting liberal and conservative platitudes against each other renders these well-known literary landscapes almost unrecognisable. Neither the 'Hampstead' novel of manners nor the socialist documentary, Pat Barker's realist novels are a case in point against superficial canonisation.

I will conclude with the reflection that it is precisely because she reworks 'Britishness' from within, in both literary and historical terms, that her work will probably be particularly useful in terms of teaching and researching the English novel of the last fifty years from a more pluralist perspective. For her novels represent an important re-envisioning of that history as the cultural expression of the legacy of the World Wars, white anxieties after decolonisation, the decimation of the working class after Thatcherism, the explosion of the postwar consensus, and, above all, the revolutionary perspectives of feminism on the family and the community. *Regeneration*, which was released as a film in 1997, has already been turned into an education pack for teaching the First World War in schools in ways that raise just these kinds of issues.[16] Ann Ardis has written of an arguably even more challenging didactic use of her writing in discussing prostitution and sexual violence with American undergraduates through reading *Blow Your House Down*.[17] The fact that Barker is both so near and so far from the canon seems to be a fitting development of the method within her fiction.

Notes

1 See Stuart Laing's *Novels and the Novel*, for an excellent, brief discussion of literature in the 1940s, 1950s and 1960s, that avoids the dangers of

homogenising literary movements in this period. Malcolm Bradbury and David Lodge are well-known exponents of the 'variousness' thesis, yet, like Gindin in *Postwar British Fiction*; Massie in *The Novel Today*; Swinden in *The English Novel of History and Society, 1940–80* and many others, they still trace a canonising 'rise and fall' structure in their histories.

2 See for example, Alexander, *Contemporary Women Novelists*; Anderson, *Plotting Change* and *Women and Autobiography in the Twentieth Century*; Baker, *Happily Ever After*; Cosslett, *Women Writing Childbirth*; Gerrard, *Into the Mainstream*; Ezel, *Writing Women's Literary History*; Hartley, *Hearts Undefeated*; Haywood, *Working-Class Fiction*; Kenyon, *Women Novelists Today*; Palmer, *Contemporary Women's Fiction*; Humm, *Border Traffic*; Sage, *Women in the House of Fiction*.

3 Smith's *Lesbian Panic* offers a particularly good re-envisioning of 1960s literature in terms of lesbian writing.

4 Given the enormous influence of American feminism, American women's fiction has also had a strong influence on British writing. The particular canonisation of black American women writers Alice Walker, Toni Morrison, Paule Marshall, Toni Cade Bambara and Ntozake Shange, however, has not been matched by any parallel recognition of black women writers in Britain, although this may be in part due to their concentration on poetry rather than the novel.

5 One story is written from a male character's point of view.

6 Sharon Monteith in 'Warring fictions' tells us that the novel is set in 1971 when unemployment was at its highest since the Second World War, trade unions were in dispute with the Heath government and electricity and water supplies were interrupted in the strikes. However the abstraction from historical markers is striking. Both Monteith and Haywood offer particularly illuminating readings of Barker in the context of working class aesthetic traditions.

7 Palmer's thorough survey of the impact of feminism on North American and British fiction challenges Sara Maitland's essay, 'Futures in feminist fiction' (1989) which claims that the much-vaunted 'feminist novel' seems never to have been written. As Palmer indicates, this interestingly contrasts with the academy, where socialist and psychoanalytic feminisms hold sway.

8 See Jouve's *The Streetcleaner* for a discussion of feminist responses to prostitution in the context of the 'Yorkshire Ripper' manhunt. Jouve alludes to *Blow Your House Down* in describing her personal necessity to confront her fear of male sexual violence in writing a psychoanalytic study of Peter Sutcliffe.

9 Barker and Lively's revisioning and rewriting of history in terms of a political claim has been a popular strategy of women novelists, not only since second wave feminism. Recent examples include Margaret Forster, Jeanette Winterson, Caiea March, Emma Tennant, Sarah Waters and Kate Atkinson.

10 The descriptions of the liberating experiences of walking across the boundaries of private property in the evacuated French villages are a fascinating return of the motif of the broken-in house that we saw in her early novels. See pages 511 and 514–15.

11 See Walter's Introduction to *Rupert Brooke and Wilfred Owen*.
12 See Blythe, *Private Words* and Jolly, 'Everyday letters and literary form' on the diaries and letters of both male and female servicepeople during the Second World War. Fussell's *The Great War and Modern Memory* is still an excellent introduction to First World War writing.
13 See Alexander, *Contemporary Women Novelists*; Anderson, 'Life on the street: Pat Barker's realist fictions'; Ardis, 'Political attentiveness vs political correctness'; Dinnage, 'Death's gray land'; Haywood, *Working-Class Fiction*; Monteith, 'Warring fictions'; Palmer, *Contemporary Women's Fiction*; Sinker, 'Temporary gentlemen, and Pat Barker on the film adaptation of her novel *Regeneration*'; Taylor, *After the War*.
14 Margaret Forster's *Shadow Baby*, which, like *Liza's England*, tells the century through generations of women, exemplifies a much earlier nineteenth century realist style of detailed external description and little idiomatic consciousness.
15 See Gasiorek's *Post-War British Fiction* for a thorough survey of the many kinds of realism in the postwar period. Gasiorek points out that realism is not only heterogeneous but bears no essential relation to any political position.
16 This pack, produced by the charity Film Education, London, in 1998, was designed with an accompanying BBC screening.
17 Ardis's account of their difficulty in identifying with the descriptions of class identity suggests how very much more live the issue would be in a British context.

Bibliography

Alexander, F. (1989) *Contemporary Women Novelists*, London: Edward Arnold.
Anderson, L. (ed.) (1990) *Plotting Change: Contemporary Women's Fiction*, London: Edward Arnold.
—— (1997) *Women and Autobiography in the Twentieth Century: Remembered Futures*, Hemel Hempstead: Prentice Hall/Harvester Wheatsheaf.
Anderson, S. (1994) 'Life on the Street: Pat Barker's Realist Fictions' in G. Wisker (ed.), *It's My Party: Reading Twentieth Century Women's Writing*, London: Pluto.
Ardis, A. (1991) 'Political attentiveness vs political correctness: teaching Pat Barker's "Blow Your House Down"', *College Literature* 18, 3: 44–54.
Baker, N. (1989) *Happily Ever After? Women's Fiction in Postwar Britain 1945–60*, London: Macmillan Education.
Barker, P. (1996) *The Regeneration Trilogy*, London: Viking.
Blythe, R. (ed.) (1993) *Private Words: Letters and Diaries from the Second World War*, London: Penguin.
Bradbury, M. (1987) *No, Not Bloomsbury*, London: Deutsch.
Cosslett, T. (1994) *Women Writing Childbirth: Modern Discourses of Motherhood*, Manchester: Manchester University Press.
Dinnage, R. (1996) 'Death's gray land: review of Pat Barker's *Regeneration*', *New York Review of Books* 43: 19–21.

Ezell, M. (1995) *Writing Women's Literary History*, Baltimore: Johns Hopkins University Press.

Forster, M. (1997) *Shadow Baby*, London: Penguin.

Fussell, P. (1975) *The Great War and Modern Memory*, Oxford: Oxford University Press.

Gagnier, R. (1998) 'The function of class at the present time', unpublished paper, 'At the millennium: interrogating gender', Birkbeck College, University of London.

Gasiorek, A. (1995) *Post-War British Fiction: Realism and After*, London: Edward Arnold.

Gerrard, N. (1989) *Into the Mainstream: How Feminism has Changed Women's Writing*, London: Pandora.

Gindin, J. (1962) *Postwar British Fiction: New Accents and Attitudes*, Westport, Ct.: Greenwood.

Hartley, J. (ed.) (1995) *Hearts Undefeated: Women's Writing of the Second World War*, London: Virago.

Haywood, I. (1997) *Working-Class Fiction: From Chartism to Trainspotting*, London: Northcote House.

Humm, M. (1991) *Border Traffic: Strategies of Contemporary Women Writers*, Manchester: Manchester University Press.

Jolly, M. (1996) 'Everyday letters and literary form: correspondence from the Second World War', unpublished D.Phil. thesis, University of Sussex.

Jouve, N. W. (1986) *The Streetcleaner: The Yorkshire Ripper Case on Trial*, London: Marion Boyars.

Kenyon, O. (1988) *Women Novelists Today: A Survey of English Writing in the Seventies and Eighties*, Brighton: Harvester.

Laing, S. (1983) 'Novels and the novel', in A. Sinfield (ed.), *Society and Literature: 1945–1970*, London: Methuen.

Lively, P. (1987) *Moon Tiger*, London: Deutsch.

Lodge, D. (1996) *The Practice of Writing: Essays, Lectures, Reviews and a Diary*, London: Secker and Warburg.

Maitland, S. (1989) 'Futures in feminist fiction', in H. Carr (ed.), *From My Guy to Sci-Fi*, London: Pandora.

Massie, A. (1990) *The Novel Today: A Critical Guide to the British Novel 1970–1989*, London: Longman.

Monteith, S. (1997) 'Warring fictions: reading Pat Barker', *Moderne Sprak* 91, 1: 124–9.

Moran, M. H. (1990) 'Penelope Lively's *Moon Tiger*: a feminist history of the world', *Frontiers* 9: 89–95.

Palmer, P. (1989) *Contemporary Women's Fiction: Narrative Practice and Theory*, Hemel Hempstead: Harvester.

Raschke, D. (1995) 'Penelope Lively's *Moon Tiger*: re-envisioning a "history of the world"', *Ariel: A Review of International English Literature* 26, 4: 115–32.

Sage, L. (1992) *Women in the House of Fiction: Post-War Women Novelists*, New York: Routledge.

Sinker, M. (1997) 'Temporary gentlemen and Pat Barker on the film adaptation of her novel "Regeneration"', *Sight and Sound* 12: 22–4.

Smith, P. J. (1997) *Lesbian Panic: Homoeroticism in Modern British Women's Fiction*, New York: Columbia University Press.

Steedman, C. (1986) *Landscape for a Good Woman*, London: Virago.

Swinden, P. (1984) *The English Novel of History and Society, 1940–80*, New York: St Martin's.

Taylor, D. J. (1993) *After the War: The Novel and English Society since 1945*, London: Chatto.

Walter, G. (ed.) (1997) 'Introduction', in *Rupert Brooke and Wilfred Owen: Selected Poems*, London: Everyman.

Chapter 4

Culture, consensus and difference

Angus Wilson to Alan Hollinghurst

Alan Sinfield

Culture and the State

In 1946 Cyril Connolly published in the literary magazine *Horizon* (1940–50) the results of a questionnaire to writers on how literary writing should be financed. He concluded:

> with the decline of private incomes and private patrons, the State must do more to help writers, preferably by indirect subsidy. This will not come to pass without much persuasion from the writers themselves, many of whom disapprove of the State and show no inclination to influence it.
>
> (Connolly 1953: 80)

The assumptions here are far removed from those which prevail at the end of the twentieth century. Today, private incomes and private patrons have little immediate relation with literary writing (*Horizon* itself was financed by a wealthy individual, Peter Watson). Novels do well when they are marketed aggressively; poetry, in the main, is either a prestigious loss-leader or a branch of performance art. The State has become crucial: not for the printed book, which is what Connolly had in mind, but through its financing of radio, television, theatre and education; in those media its roles are scarcely questioned by writers today.

Connolly and his circle (people such as Stephen Spender, John Lehmann, George Orwell and T. S. Eliot) didn't want to be involved with the State: they imagined it leading to a Soviet-style control of culture. They didn't know, though, where else to turn. They saw that 'good' culture had depended on a leisured class fraction which, through the successive blows of the First World War, the Depression, the Second World War and the egalitarian mood of 1945, had lost confidence and resources. The State, conversely, appeared unstoppable: it had fought the War through a total mobilisation of human and material resources. Cultural production, also, had been controlled. On the one hand, there was censorship. It was an offence to circulate any report or statement 'likely to cause alarm or despondency'; news stories were suppressed; the communist *Daily Worker* was closed down and the *Daily Mirror* was threatened (Calder 1971). On the other hand, news stories were invented (writers were employed to do this), and organisations were created to cheer people up and get them thinking along the right lines – the Ministry of Information film unit, the Council for the Encouragement of Music and the Arts, the Army Bureau of Current Affairs, Artists for War (Hewison 1995).

To maintain production levels and morale the State had intervened in the dreadful conditions in which very many people lived. Now it was demonstrated, for all to see, that the employment, health, diet and housing of the great majority of people could be improved by State action. Sir William Beveridge believed it was simply a matter of will: 'all men have value when the State sets up unlimited demand for a compelling purpose. By the spectacular achievement of its planned economy war shows also how great is the waste of unemployment' (Beveridge 1944: 29). The 1945 Labour Government was committed to egalitarian reforms which seemed to threaten the class fraction that had sustained literature.

The answer, Connolly and his friends thought, was that the traditional privileges of the leisure-class lifestyle should be maintained for writers alone: the State 'must give young writers scholarships and older writers Sabbatical years; it must, with its official blessing, thrust leisure as well as money on them' (Connolly 1953: 124). Indeed, State support for 'good' culture was firmly on the agenda. The Butler Act of 1944 made secondary education free for everyone up to age fifteen; the Arts Council was formed in 1945 and the BBC Third Programme (forerunner of Radio Three) in 1946; in 1948 councils were empowered to spend money on the arts.

Few people, though, were thinking very deeply about *what kinds of culture* should be subsidised. As with the newly nationalised industries, the new cultural apparatus was dominated by the people who had dominated the old one, so established structures and attitudes persisted. Connolly had feared that the Third Programme, for instance, might promote Soviet-style social realism, or so he said. But as it turned out there was no such tendency. 'The State is ourselves, *l'état c'est toi*', he exulted (Connolly 1953: 135).

Hemlock and After

Angus Wilson wanted to be a writer in the established literary manner and his publishing career began with a story in Connolly's *Horizon*, in November 1947. But he also believed that new times demanded new themes. In his novel *Hemlock and After* (1952: quotes are from the Penguin edition of 1956), set in the late 1940s, Wilson explores the controversy over postwar changes in the cultural apparatus, and, by making the central character homosexual, allows us to see other underlying assumptions about culture and subculture. I will compare a novel that evokes a quite different awareness of both literary writing and minorities in the context of the late 1980s: *The Swimming-Pool Library* by Alan Hollinghurst (1988).

The central character of *Hemlock and After* is Bernard Sands, a successful author. After lobbying the literary and public world – publishers, editors, critics, cultural committees, universities, the Arts Council, Connolly and *Horizon* – he has gained State backing for the development of Vardon Hall as a retreat for young writers. Connolly's sense that the State might be sympathetic to 'good' culture is confirmed in the person of Charles, a senior civil servant and old friend of Bernard, and in the comment of a local man, an Assistant Secretary at the Board of Trade who keeps up with modern poetry: the Vardon Hall project, he says, 'fills the gap we've all been so disturbed about. We can't bring the patrons back; we don't, God knows, want the State; so we have a nice little mixture of the two. The best sort of English compromise' (Wilson, *Hemlock and After*: 23).

Not everyone is enthusiastic, however. The local business-commuting set is suspicious, out of narrowness, snobbery and self-interest, fearing that such a 'socialist' project will exacerbate their sense of insecurity in the face of postwar change. For them Bernard's project is 'the latest symbol of the war they were waging against a changing world' (19); 'many of the most intelligent of these men and women were ready at the slightest crisis to label him, or any other person whom they associated, however vaguely, with their anxieties, as Communist' (25). However, they respect success, so Bernard can manage them easily enough through his authority as man of letters. His principal local opponent, Mrs Curry, is another matter. She is totally unscrupulous, and wants to turn Vardon Hall into a profitable roadhouse, or worse; it transpires that she is a procurer of little girls for paederasts.

Bernard doesn't say how he expects his young writers to write, of course, since the whole point is that they will be free to do as they choose: he has insisted that they should manage Vardon Hall themselves. He thinks of himself as 'an anarchic humanist' (11), rejecting both the ultra-left hostility of his sister and her friend to the United States, and the reactionary Christianity that dominated immediate postwar literary culture, above all through the figure of T. S. Eliot (few of Bernard's middle-class neighbours, it is said, had not visited Eliot's play, *The Cocktail Party*; 25). Bernard views this right-wing religious tendency with special disrespect, regarding attention to 'the endurance of the human spirit' as a displaced social anxiety: 'They would have liked affirmation of their private conviction that the grievances and grudges they felt against a changing social order should be considered the reawakening of spiritual values'. At Vardon Hall 'there would be none of the neo-authoritarianism, none of the imposition of dogmatic spiritual values upon the writers' (14, 17).

Despite this scepticism, Bernard finds himself preoccupied with 'the growing apprehension of evil that had begun, this summer, to disrupt his comprehension of the world', particularly in the person of Mrs Curry (13). In this, Bernard – and Wilson – belongs alongside other emergent writers such as Iris Murdoch, William Golding, Anthony Burgess and Muriel Spark, who were questioning the efficacy of the liberal-humanist tradition that had dominated the English intelligentsia, more or less since Dickens and George Eliot (Davies and Saunders 1983). Often, in the postwar period, this theme was established with reference to Nazism, Stalinism and the threat of nuclear destruction, and took its philosophical basis from French existentialism. Wilson does this up to a point but, also, he locates evil in the heart of the English countryside, in the pretty cottage of the sanctimonious Mrs Curry, and also in the gratuitously malicious theatre critic, Sherman Winter.

Above all – for this is the English novel – evil has to be addressed in the actions, conscience and psyche of Bernard. As a discreet homosexual, he lacks moral confidence and authority; he has contributed to the breakdown of Ella, his wife, and they have 'failed' with their children; his relations with his lovers are somewhat half-hearted, and he is vulnerable to blackmail and squalid intrigue. His anxieties come to a crisis when he witnesses the arrest of a young man for importuning in Leicester Square. To his horror, he experiences 'sadistic excitement' when the young man is held pinioned before him by a policeman: Bernard's anarchic humanism, it seems, affords no protection from his own worst impulses. Indeed, while he experiences a 'hunter's thrill', the detective's attitude is one of 'somewhat officious but routine duty'. The implication is that an impersonal State might be a more secure source of value and fairness than Bernard's ambitious, personal, but insecurely grounded ethical commitments. 'Truly, he thought, he was not at one with those who exercised proper authority. A humanist, it would seem, was more at home with the wielders of the knout and the rubber truncheon' (109). Is Bernard, therefore, the person to give new impetus to culture in the postwar world?

At the opening party for Vardon Hall, Bernard's guests are disconcerted by the camp and aggressive behaviour of some of the guests. However, for Bernard 'it was not an external picture of concerted enemies that he saw, but the reflection of his own guilt' (148). In his speech he dwells upon the doubleness of motive, and makes Freudian slips ('One can pay too dearly for what one picks up in the Charing Cross Road'; 153). His audience are uneasy and alarmed; the afternoon disintegrates. As a consequence, the Vardon Hall project falls under threat.

Charles, alluding to Ibsen's version of the paralysed upper-class intellectual, urges Bernard not to remain buried with guilt 'in that Rosmersholm of yours' (211). Ella is stirred from the abstraction which has followed her breakdown and they decide how to act upon the issues that face them. Already Hubert Rose, the paederast and ultimate figure of corruption, has been warned away from young girls; that much Bernard accomplished even in his immobilisation. Now Mrs Curry must be reported and prosecuted, despite Bernard's qualms about motive and about collaborating with the law that would penalise him also. And Bernard will go to London to talk to the necessary people and save Vardon Hall. However, after writing a letter making personal peace with his left-wing sister, he suffers a heart attack and dies. Insofar as there are new possibilities for personal and public relations, Bernard is not the person to carry them through. Neither though is Ella, who clears up in an excessively brisk and moralistic manner. At Vardon Hall the bureaucrats move in and the writers lose the autonomy and some of the resources that Bernard had planned. But, we are to understand, it is still worthwhile.

Connolly's respondents felt out of place in the postwar world, but Wilson looks forward to new patterns of public and personal relations. He doesn't complain about the prospect of Soviet-style bureaucracy, or about egalitarian aspirations. There is a good chance, he suggests, that the State will support the creativity of a new generation. However, this will take new forms; Wilson doesn't trust the petty and disgruntled middle-classes, or the backward-looking religiose literary scene that has emerged during the war, or Bernard's humanist tradition.

The main danger is represented as coming from those who under-mine cooperation, community and social values through an amoral obsession with personal advancement. If Bernard doesn't attend to Vardon Hall, Charles tells him, it will be 'at the mercy of some careerist charlatan' (211). The danger, in *Hemlock and After*, is that shared social purpose, which had helped to win the war and would be necessary for a just peace, is being undermined by petty corruption and 'spivs' – unscrupulous opportunists who exploited and evaded the web of State regulations that was designed to secure social fairness and the priority of investment and production (Hughes 1964). Bernard observes two groups at a party: survivors from the 1920s, sustaining an 'intricate web of personal values', and young men depending 'upon their wits and their social success to maintain themselves'. Bernard finds in the 'young adventurers a state of moral anaemia' (102). The danger, in other words, is from a *market* view of economic, social and cultural rela-tions. Wilson is anticipating the ethos that was to undermine the postwar settlement in the 1980s.

Consensus and its problems

Presenting Bernard's discreet homosexuality as the ground of his failure of moral authority runs the risk of suggesting that gayness *as such* is a source of 'evil' (as other writers had done). Myself, I would regard the incident in Leicester Square less as a crisis in Bernard's conscience than as a still familiar mode of police harassment. Nevertheless, Wilson's focus upon Bernard and his gay milieu was exceptionally courageous at a time when Cold War paranoia stigmatised homosexuality as treach-ery against the Western Alliance, and gay men were entrapped and prosecuted under the homophobic inspiration of Sir David Maxwell-Fyfe (Home Secretary, 1951–4). Wilson's US publisher declined the book, and some British public libraries would not stock it (Drabble 1995: 179–80). Bernard's lifestyle is offered as decent in its own way, scarcely remarkable among sophisticated people, and linked with Communism and treachery only in the fantasies of his enemies (Wilson, *Hemlock and After*: 149, 191). The young men in Bernard's life, Terence and Eric (the latter especially), are treated sympatheti-cally, are shown to have gained morally during the narrative, and have positive prospects for independence and responsibility at the end. Bernard and his friends are ready to collaborate in a shared community in a benign State; it is the law that compromises their voice and hence deforms public life. It is the need to be covert that causes the problems.

By bracketing the status of literature with the status of homosexuality and focusing on the prospect for new institutional arrangements for the postwar generation, Wilson suggests a package of liberal-democratic reforms; not of the economy, which mainly preoccupied the Labour Government, but of the moral and cultural fabric of the country. He envisages an *inclusive* social ethos in which poverty and prejudice would be dispelled and everyone would contribute. The ideological underpinning for such an ethos seemed to be offered in the postwar settlement.

In the 1930s, with the stock market crash, the slump and the collapse of democratic institutions in many countries, capitalism was widely believed to be in crisis. There had seemed to be three kinds of future: fascism, communism, and welfare-capitalism (or social democracy) – State intervention in capitalism to make it less oppressive. These three fought it out during the Second World War. Welfare-capitalism won in Western Europe: on the right as well as the left, it was agreed that there should be no return to pre-war conditions. Now the State was to ensure for all people a stake in society, an adequate share of its resources as of right: a job, a pension or social security, a roof over your head, healthcare, education. These good things, which had been enjoyed customarily by the leisure classes, were now to be available to everyone. These promises were the pay-off, quite explicitly, for wartime suffering, and they were to be sustained by State management of the economy, in the manner proposed by John Maynard Keynes, to produce (nearly) full employment. The opponents of welfare-capitalism, and some of its proponents, called it 'socialism'. However, actually welfare-capitalism tended to ameliorate and maintain capitalism by protecting against and compensating for its disadvantages. It was endorsed not only by the Labour Party but, broadly, by 'one-nation' Conservatives, who believed that everyone might find a decent place, though not an equal place, in a society that is well run by the well-meaning upper classes.

Within this framework, which prevailed until the end of the 1970s, 'good' culture, which hitherto had been the special prerogative of the leisure classes, was to be available to everyone. To be sure, this was not a high priority; with such huge profits available to the purveyors of commercial culture it could hardly have been otherwise. Nevertheless, art galleries and museums, deriving from an earlier phase of civic pride, became more user-friendly (Wilson worked in the British Museum Library). The State-maintained public service concept in television and radio aspired to make 'the best' generally available (interestingly, it was Conservative governments that set up

BBC 2 and Channel 4). The scope of the Arts Council was extended to include the Royal Shakespeare Company and the National Theatre, new theatres throughout the provinces, and touring companies (Wilson did a stint as chair of the Literature Panel of the Arts Council, and restlessly toured the world under the aegis of the British Council). And the idea that 'good' culture should be shared became dominant in the school system (though it was partly at odds with the progressive, 'child-centred' approach, which tended to validate the student's own culture).

Equality for homosexuals was by no means prominent in the 1950s vision of the good life. Indeed, insofar as the dominant model of the queer represented him as a leisure-class man who depended upon contacts with lower-class young men, it seemed to some a part of the pre-war exploitative society that was to be superseded (Sinfield 1994). Nevertheless, it was in the mid-1950s, partly in reaction to the increase in prosecutions, that a new way of regarding 'gayness' became powerful. Commentators have often observed that during the twentieth century homosexuality came to be considered less an evil or a sin, and more a medical or psychological condition. That is true; but a third model became dominant: homosexuality was regarded as a *social problem*.

The Wolfenden Committee was set up in 1954 to consider homosexual offences, alongside prostitution, after a minister for home affairs declared: 'Quite clearly, this is a problem which calls for very careful consideration on the part of those responsible for the welfare of the nation' (Hyde 1972: 238). Gordon Westwood recalls how in 1952 he conceived an objective: to bring 'the problem of homosexuality . . . out into the open where it can be discussed and reconsidered'. By the end of the decade he felt this had been achieved (Westwood 1960: 93). Many of these considerations applied to lesbians also; my argument focuses upon gay men because their practices were illegal, and because their role in the literary establishment produced prominent writings through which I can frame the literary and social attitudes of the postwar period.

The social problem is a welfare-capitalist formation. It goes back to the nineteenth century, but is central to the postwar period; it accompanies the rise of sociology as an academic discipline, and of social work as a profession. Juvenile delinquency, unmarried mothers, the colour bar, latchkey children and the homeless . . . suddenly in the 1950s there was a swathe of them. The social problem has a standard aetiology: after a period of discussion in the press, the State commissions a report from a committee of the wise and the good, and then passes laws to improve matters. It is the social equivalent of the mixed economy: the State intervenes to smoothe over extreme injustices and secure steady general progress. The historical specificity of this programme becomes apparent when it is opposed, in the 1980s, by Margaret Thatcher and Ronald Reagan: there are no social problems, they declare, only individual and family difficulties; there is no proper role for the State.

The Sexual Offences Act of 1967 put the Wolfenden recommendations of 1957 into effect in England and Wales (the Scottish and Northern Irish laws were changed later). Male homosexuality was legalised within what its sponsors thought were reasonable limits (there should be only two people, they should be in private and over twenty-one; they should not be in sensitive situations like prisons and the armed services). Thus social justice was enhanced, or (depending how you look at it) the problem was contained. Homosexual law reform, like public subsidy for the arts, exemplifies the welfare-capitalist aspiration to hold together the entire political, social and economic structure through consensual advance organised by the State.

Let us be clear. We are talking about an ideology, not an accomplishment; consensus was an aspiration rather than an achievement. Some groups were never really included: sectors of the working-class, people of colour, the unemployed, many of the elderly, lone-parents and their children, Catholics in Ireland, gays and lesbians. Whether welfare-capitalism could have worked, and whether it still might, are questions to ponder. As Beveridge said at the start, popular commitment is crucial. Unless people really believe that co-operation within the system will produce something for everyone, the removal of the traditional threats of unemployment, poverty and stigma leaves labour undisciplined, undermines class deference, and permits lifestyles that may not enable an effective workforce. The crucial point may be this: the system did not change sufficiently to engage most of us to the point where we were prepared to relinquish sectional interests.

Above all, perhaps, welfare-capitalism seemed unable to pay its way. While the postwar/Vietnam War boom continued, and while the oil-rich territories could be dominated, there was usually more money to push round the system, so that diverse interests could be bought off, piecemeal. The boom ended, however, and suddenly the Keynesian mechanisms for holding the national and world economies steady were revealed as the emperor's new clothes. A moment of truth was when Labour chancellor Denis Healey was forced to capitulate to the International Monetary Fund in 1976. This is the flaw: welfare-capitalism raises expectations with a view to maintaining popular endorsement; but only for a while can the system produce enough wealth to keep pace with those expectations. This has occurred even in Scandinavia and New Zealand, where welfare-capitalism had seemed most at home.

The alternative ideology, which became dominant in the 1980s and which in Britain we call 'Thatcherism' and 'the New Right', is the market: individuals, groups and institutions are in conflict and everyone must scrabble for their own bit. This ideology is enforced by powerful brokers of international capital: the International Monetary Fund and the World Bank (the Washington agenda, this is sometimes called). It produces affluence for some, while presenting the exclusion of others as unavoidable, even as a necessary discipline to keep the rest in place. Thus we return, in effect, to the 1930s, and to the conflicts and suffering which the postwar settlement was supposed to dispel. Sometimes this is represented as a withdrawal of the State, but what we actually observe is the State facilitating the unfettered operations of capital, while increasing police and judicial powers to cope with consequent social disruption. The market ethos correlates with increasing centralisation, and with the end of the 'arm's length' principle of finance and management in the arts, education, broadcasting, the police, and other local and semi-official institutions. For the market is not just an economic model: the end of consensus means a licensing of conflict and meanness; which as Wilson saw, had always been likely to undermine shared social purpose. The spiv was not a temporary aberration.

The Swimming-Pool Library

Will Beckwith in Alan Hollinghurst's novel *The Swimming-Pool Library* (1988) is a creature of the 1980s. He belongs to 'that tiny proportion of the population that indeed owns almost everything' (Hollinghurst, *The Swimming-Pool Library*: 3), and hence has nothing to do except wander around picking up young men; when he gets tired of that he can enjoy thrilling sex with one of the two boys who are semi-dependent upon him (Arthur is Black and unemployed, Phil is a hotel porter). Will's privileged situation is thus strikingly like that of Bernard Sands and the rentier class which was fading around him – which Wilson and Connolly had supposed would fade right away. Will, however, does not spend his energy worrying about culture, evil and personal responsibility. He gives little consideration to anything beyond his short-term pleasure. The first-person narrative voice draws us into Will's experience, and his perceptions of people and the world are shrewd and often funny. However, his best friend, James, describes him as brutal and sentimental (5), and the reader, on reflection, may well agree.

This, it is suggested, is how many people are these days. 'Some young thug called me an old wanker the other day', says Charles, Lord Nantwich, who is in his eighties. 'I said I'm way past that, I can assure you. But he didn't smile, you know. It's so terrible when people don't smile. It seems to be a new thing' (72). Nantwich has a good deal in common with Bernard: each believes that his privileged position requires that he help to improve opportunities for others. Nantwich regards his contacts with Black and lower-class people as responsible and altruistic (he was a colonial administrator in the Sudan and now sponsors boys' clubs). Thinking of neo-fascist attacks on Blacks, Nantwich says: 'There are times when I can't think of my country without a kind of despairing shame' (244). We may place him as a one-nation Conservative; Margaret Thatcher had to displace colleagues of this stamp in her own party ('wets' she called them), as much as the Labour Party.

On occasion, Will seems to discover an altruistic impetus in himself: he 'wanted to save Arthur. At least, I think that's what I wanted to do to him. It was a strange conviction I had, that I could somehow make these boys' lives better, as by a kind of patronage'. However, 'it never worked out that way' (284). Spivs rule, OK. Generally, Will behaves as if he were scarcely connected to the rest of society. He doesn't see any common cause with other gay men, and he dissociates himself from other wealthy young men who work in the City – though, like him, they are 'public-school types with peachy complexions and contemptuous eyes'. Up to a point, he is right: 'I was a loafer who had hardly ever actively earned money, and they were the eager initiates, the coiners of the power and the compromise in which I had unthinkingly been raised' (268). But that last clause acknowledges his complicity.

Will finds that, willy nilly, he is involved. First, his wealth and indifference do not protect him from assault by neo-fascist young men. As for Bernard, sadistic violence engenders a vision of evil:

A universal violence had been disclosed to me, and I saw it every-where – in the sudden scatter across the pavement of some quite small boys, in the brief mocking notice taken of me by a couple of

> telephone engineers in a parked van . . . I understood for the first time
> the vulnerability of the old, unfortified by good luck or inexperience.
> (Hollinghurst, *The Swimming-Pool Library*: 176–7)

This moment of general illumination, however, appears not to work
any great transformation in Will. He is stunned, though (and this is the
main action of the novel) when he finds that his life is not independent of history. Nantwich wants Will to write his biography, and his
diaries reveal a sequence of substantial and evocative continuities in
gay experience through the twentieth century. Will thinks at first that
all this has little to do with him:

> Why be encumbered with the furtive peccadilloes of the past, and
> all the courteous artifice of writing them up? I wasn't playing the
> same game as that lot. I looked forward to clear July days, days of
> no secrets, of nothing but exercise and sun.
> (Hollinghurst, *The Swimming-Pool Library*: 189)

He finds though, that Nantwich's journal of life at public school and
Oxford, 'despite its period, spoke for me too, down to the very details
of places and customs' (129). Other occasions in the novel suggest such
continuity. At a performance of *Billy Budd* (the Benjamin Britten and
E. M. Forster opera) Will is moved by the presence of Peter Pears,
Britten's partner and a performer in the initial production of 1951: 'I
felt the whole occasion subtly transform, and the opera whose ambiguity we had carped at take on a kind of heroic or historic character under
the witness of one of its creators' (122). Swimming pools have been
sexy in London, Will discovers, since Roman times (*Hemlock and After*
concludes with an amusing scene in which Eric handles a pick up by a
clergyman at a swimming pool).

Above all, Will discovers eventually that his grandfather was the
law officer who inspired the specially hostile persecution of gay men in
the early 1950s (the moment, of course, of *Hemlock and After*). Lord
Nantwich was a prominent victim (historically, Lord Montagu had
been the most scandalous figure), and Will's family fortunes derive from
his grandfather's homophobic activities. Will is as deeply implicated in
gay history as he can be, therefore; his supposition of autonomy and
lack of responsibility is wrong. Society is more than an agglomeration
of competing individuals; not because of pious hopes but because of
history and social process.

However, this recognition does not, in *The Swimming-Pool Library*, re-legitimate the welfare-capitalist, consensual project. The continuities and coherences that are revealed are internal to the gay milieu, and are informed and validated by the hostility of the larger society. The effect, therefore, is to consolidate gay subculture as the inheritor of a rich and necessarily distinctive tradition, rather than prompt any merging of gays with the mainstream, in the name of a liberal-humanist programme such as Wilson envisaged. Will's brother-in-law supposes, complacently, that the arrest and prosecution of Nantwich occurred in 'another world' (the world, we might say, of Bernard Sands). But Will points out that Nantwich 'was set up by some pretty policeman, and that's really not another world, Gavin, it's going on in London now almost every day' (264–5). The narrative is made to endorse the point: James is similarly entrapped and arrested. His fate, the closing pages suggest, is decided by an establishment that is more corrupt and more out of control than is envisaged in *Hemlock and After*.

Wilson and his protagonist, in the ideological climate of the postwar settlement, think they can make some headway through negotiation with the State. Will finds that all his doings are tangled with the State, but he encounters no model for the inclusion of lesbians and gay men in a more generous social vision. In the 1980s, minorities must grab what space they can. After all, in Margaret Thatcher's view, society does not exist. Correspondingly, 'literature' loses its consensual pretensions and subdivides into women's writing, Black writing, lesbian writing, literatures in English. . . .

The failure of literature

There is no equivalent in *The Swimming-Pool Library* for Bernard's scheme of State support for young writers. Nevertheless, a good deal about the condition of literary institutions may be inferred, and we may observe quite different assumptions from those which Connolly and Wilson were making. They assumed that we all know, pretty much, what literature is and that it commands special respect.

Wilson uses Ibsen as a way of discussing sexual corruption in the midst of bourgeois rectitude, and the scope for the principled intellectual in a bourgeois society. He can rely on literary reference as an authoritative index. Hollinghurst's novel is stuffed with literary allusions, but most of them are purposefully partial, co-opting literary culture for gay purposes – celebrating Ronald Firbank, challenging Evelyn Waugh, commandeering L. P. Hartley and Jean Genet, reinterpreting Wilde and Forster. Sometimes the references are provocatively appropriative: 'The young up one another's arse', for instance (Hollinghurst, *The Swimming-Pool Library*: 165), rewrites Yeats' more 'poetic' line, 'The young in one another's arms'. Will stretches out his limbs in bed 'like one of those queeny Sons of the Morning in a Blake engraving' (14). Nantwich adapts a couplet by Alexander Pope to describe a public lavatory (166–7). And James thinks of Will's cultivation of partially-educated boys as 'raids on the inarticulate' (218), alluding to T. S. Eliot's celebrated evocation of the poetic process in 'East Coker'.

Thus Hollinghurst offers the reader a sense of implication in gay history and culture comparable to that which Will is made to discover in his own life. This is, of course, exciting for the gay reader. The casualty is the coherence and centrality of the literary tradition which has been understood as mainstream, and which Connolly, Wilson and their contemporaries believed to be universal. (The outcome of Will's explorations into Nantwich's past is the loss of a stable position from which he might write a biography.) In this light, Vardon Hall, con-ceived as an opportunity for the whole society to express itself through the transcendent creative efforts of literary artists, becomes a dream. *The Swimming-Pool Library* asserts subcultural history and responsibility, not only against Thatcherite selfishness, but against the consensus that failed to acknowledge gay men. Such dismantling of 'good' culture is of a piece with the effects of feminist writing and of literatures in English from outside the United Kingdom. The alleged universality of 'good' culture has come to appear, in large part, as middle-class, male, Eurocentric presumption.

If *The Swimming-Pool Library* has distinct resonances for gay readers, this does not mean that it amounts to a piece of cheer-leading for gay subculture. On the contrary, gay commentators have been troubled by its deployment of stereotypical images of gay relationships, particularly in respect of Black and lower-class people. It is not pleasant to find that these groups, who figure generally in the western tradition as walk-on parts, appear here as the objects of Will's opportunism, and, hardly more acceptably, as the objects of Nantwich's patronage. What are we to make of this?

Plainly the novel is much concerned with the residues of empire. As Richard Dellamora remarks, the Roman baths may suggest not just a continuity of gay subculture, but a sequence of colonisations. Thus the exuberant sexual images may 'signify not ecstasy but cultural domi-nance' (Dellamora 1994: 89). At a culminating moment, Will allows himself to be sexually assaulted by the son of Nantwich's Sudanese servant/boyfriend. It is as if the oppression of empire is being returned to its point of origin; the empire fucks back. An Argentinian man also adopts a threatening posture but proves ineffectual; I believe this is a joke about how Britain defeated the Argentinian attempt to seize the Falkland/Malvinas Islands in 1982.

But is the novel critiquing or repeating oppressive relations of class and race? David Rees complains that neither of Will's boyfriends 'is conceived as a person with a brain, emotions, interests, idiosyncrasies; they're just cock, tit, arse; wank material' (Rees 1993: 80). Joseph Bristow, however, offers an explanation:

> Although it is tempting to see this work colluding with the 'othering' activity that takes place in stereotyping, it is also exposing these (potentially oppressive, even self-oppressive) images to the scrutiny of history – to consider what life was like in 1983 and whether this portrayal of gay life can be identified with any longer. . . . the stereotype has to be embraced in order to understand how it has arisen.
>
> (Bristow 1989: 77)

The scene presented in the novel has gone. It was, Will says, 'the last summer of its kind there was ever to be' (3) – shortly before the AIDS virus was identified in 1983–4. Like it or mistrust it, Hollinghurst is presenting the world we have lost; hence, Bristow suggests, *The Swimming-Pool Library* may constitute a point from which we may move on. In a later discussion of the novel Bristow places less emphasis on the idea that the stereotypes of gay subculture must be exposed if their presence is to be justified. He remarks that 'nothing about this novel is politically pure'. But still he admires the way 'this narrative positively embraces the stereotypical patterns of gay men's lives to remind us that they now belong to the past' (Bristow 1995: 178).

My own sense is that the received modes of gay fantasy are more entrenched than that interpretation would suggest, and it is rash to suppose that they are on the point of being abandoned. Nevertheless, Bristow's main perception is right: *The Swimming-Pool Library* is certainly available to a reading that sees it as setting up objectified stereotypes so that readers will place them historically and reject them as an infringement of humanity. That would be a characteristically literary-critical reading, securing the text for decency, humanity, literature, beauty and truth (the virtues that were to be sustained by the writers at Vardon Hall). It would be an entirely fair reading of the novel. However, at the same time, an alternative reading is possible. Portions of *The Swimming-Pool Library* may revitalise stereotypical motifs; they may give them new plausibility; they may make them available, in fact, to a pornographic reading. It depends which set of expectations, which reading framework, you deploy; literary, critical or pornographic. The writing admits both.

Appropriately enough, a comparable indeterminacy occurs within the text. Will is divided in his response to a recommended novel; he resents

> its professional neatness and its priapic attempts to win me over. The trouble was that, as attempts, they were half-successful: something in me was pained and removed; but something else, subliterate, responded to the book's bald graffiti. 'Fuck me again, Goldie', the slender, pleading Juan Bautista would cry; and I thought, 'Yeah, give it to him! Give it to him good 'n' hard!'
> (Hollinghurst, *The Swimming-Pool Library*: 268–9)

Will experiences two reading frameworks, and no secure way of ruling out either one of them. Again: Will dresses Phil sexily to visit a photographer acquaintance, but is disconcerted when Phil is persuaded to model. 'That afternoon I had turned him into pornography.' But when they get home Will alters Phil's clothing again, 'restoring his porno image', and they act out a typical scenario (163).

Hemlock and After provoked objections to its treatment of homosexuality; in the years following its publication, the wise and the good pondered how pornography might be banned without interfering with 'good' culture. There were disagreements about whether a text was one or the other (over *Lady Chatterley's Lover* by D. H. Lawrence in 1960 and *Last Exit to Brooklyn* by Hubert Selby, Jr in 1966), and there was always a special space for self-consciously avant-garde writing which proclaimed its own marginality (for instance, Derek Jarman's film *Sebastiane* (1976), which is in Latin with English subtitles). Few doubted, though, that the basic distinction was viable. The customary resolution was that 'good' culture transcends sex and sexuality. Literature is good, pornography is bad, and experts can tell which is which.

The resistance of *The Swimming-Pool Library* to this distinction figures the collapse of the notion of a clear literary register. Even as literary reference fails to signal traditional authority, invoking instead the preoccupations of a stigmatised minority subculture, so 'good' culture is no longer protected, by its very (supposed) nature, from pornographic imputation. Indeed, far more disconcerting sexual images than Hollinghurst's are circulating under the approximate banner of literature and art: Robert Mapplethorpe's, Dennis Cooper's, Del LaGrace Volcano's, Irvine Welsh's. Not only do we no longer know how to draw a secure distinction between the literary and the pornographic, many people no longer consider it important anyway; and that is a measure of how far we have moved from Vardon Hall and the idea of consensual, inclusive cultural authority.

Culture and the market

If *The Swimming-Pool Library* illustrates the collapse of literature and consensus, it can hardly be supposed to be the cause of those changes. I attribute that to the dominance of the market ideology. The superiority of 'good' culture in Europe has always rested on the notion that it needs privileged resourcing, once by princes and prelates, then by the leisure elite, then from State subsidy; that is the point Connolly and Wilson were addressing. The transcendent, universal claims of literature have rested precisely on this: it is above mundane cash considerations. However, New Right enthusiasts for market economics and ethics assert that the market is the best mode of organisation for every aspect of our life: for health, education and basic services (water, power, housing, transport), and for culture as well. Forcing the arts out of the State sector and into the world of commerce is just one part of the New Right assault on welfare-capitalism. Now, 'good' culture must proclaim its dependence on the market, by stating in its publicity its indebtedness to a bank, a brewery or an oil company, by allowing itself to be organised as the 'heritage' industry, and by being aggressively 'marketed'. Increasingly, it is forced to depend on money from the State lottery.

To be sure, 'good' culture can be promoted. Classical music is cheaply available with even more versions to choose from; you can make more money with a successful novel than ever before; and why not benefit from lottery windfalls? But the aura slips away. If literature is just another commodity, what is so special about it? For Angus Wilson, in his later years, all this amounted to 'a new wave of philistinism' and 'the destruction of the remains of his liberal humanism'. Margaret Drabble, Wilson's biographer, endorses his view: 'Publication, once a quiet affair, was becoming in the Thatcherite Eighties an exhausting and vulgar round of interviews and appearances and book signings. Writers had to sell their own books. . . . the word "hype" was on everybody's lips'; 'The new market economy brought with it into the literary world a new wave of malice, competition and distortion' (Drabble 1995: 543, 546–7, 564). Again, spivs rule.

The de-mystifying of 'good' culture may or may not be a good thing. It would be naive to suppose, though, that the outcome will be a magical escape from cultural hierarchy, into a free-ranging democracy where everyone's culture counts the same and we can all just express ourselves. The New Right stokes up conventional prejudices, setting us all at each other's throats and anaesthetising us against the distress of those who lose out and distracting us from its causes.

Gay men and lesbians know there is no level playing field of cultures. The Greater London Council (GLC), working within the welfare-capitalist ethos, set up a Gay Working Party to consult about 'problems' of prejudice and discrimination in many aspects of life and report on 'practical proposals and recommendations for improvement' (Greater London Council 1985: 4–5). Through artistic and other municipal ventures, lesbians and gay men tried to cash, however belatedly, the promise of 1945: we claimed our share of public resources and public legitimation. The Conservatives joined in tabloid newspaper attacks on the GLC, and then abolished it (making London the only capital in the world without a city government). New Right cultivation of divisive prejudice at the expense of consensual inclusion appeared even more directly in the Section 28 legislation of 1988, which makes it illegal for local authorities to spend resources in ways that might 'promote homosexuality'.

Perversely enough, the market is not immediately bad for all minority groups: it allows that they may struggle for advantage. Lesbians and gay men have proved quite good at this, and as consumers they offer a tidy market opportunity. At the moment, indeed, we are being feted – some of us, in some quarters – for stylish clothes, dancing, music (areas, interestingly enough, where Blacks also are allowed to excel). We see here a persistent contradiction in the market ethos: short-term economic gain is pursued at the expense of medium-term ideological consistency.

The scope that the market concedes to lesbians and gay men, and other minority groups, may be double-edged. First, market-oriented identities may be dangerously narrow, especially for groups who are excluded by prejudice and legislation from other modes of self-expression. Lesbians and gay men are learning to create themselves through the exercise of consumer choice; they are teed up as the perfect consuming subjects, innocent of other knowledges and needs (consider Hollinghurst's Will).

Second, out-groups may be coopted into the fantasies of the mainstream. bell hooks explains, in the context of race, how 'the commodification of Otherness' works:

> it is offered as a new delight, more intense, more satisfying than normal ways of doing and feeling. Within commodity culture, ethnicity becomes spice, seasoning that can liven up the dull dish that is mainstream white culture. Cultural taboos around sexuality and desire are transgressed and made explicit. . . . The 'real fun' is to be had by bringing to the surface all those 'nasty' unconscious fantasies and longings about contact with the Other embedded in the secret (not so secret) deep structure of white supremacy.
>
> (hooks 1992: 21–2).

In the light of this analysis, the mainstream success of Suede (say), k.d. lang, Lily Savage, Ellen DeGeneres and Alan Hollinghurst may indicate not that lesbians and gay men are no longer excluded; on the contrary, their outlaw status may be part of the attraction. They may offer an exotic way for straight culture to explore its weirder fantasies.

Welfare-capitalism remains a significant ideological strand in the governing echelons of the European Union and in Tony Blair's 'new' Labour Party. In the absence of a persuasive revolutionary alternative, it seems the only way out of the strains, injustices and humiliations of the spiv economy and culture. It conceded to British lesbians and gay men a lowered age of consent in 1994 and we may expect an equal age in 2000 (that doesn't cost money). It has been reasserted in Will Hutton's bestseller, *The State We're In* (Hutton 1996). Whether it will have another chance, and whether it will work, are questions for another century.

Bibliography

Beveridge, W. (1944) *Full Employment in a Free Society*, London: Allen and Unwin.

Bristow, J. (1989) 'Being gay: politics, identity, pleasure', *New Formations* 9: 61–81.

—— (1995) *Effeminate England*, Buckingham: Open University Press.

Calder, A. (1971) *The People's War*, St Albans: Granada.

Connolly, C. (1953) *Ideas and Places*, London: Weidenfeld.

Cooper, D. (1992) *Frisk*, London: Serpent's Tail.

Davies A. and Saunders P. (1983) 'Literature, politics and society', in A. Sinfield (ed.), *Society and Literature 1945–1970*, London: Methuen.

Dellamora, R. (1994) *Apocalyptic Overtures*, New Brunswick: Rutgers University Press.

Drabble, M. (1995) *Angus Wilson*, London: Secker and Warburg.

Fyrth, J. (ed.) (1995), *Labour's Promised Land?* London: Lawrence and Wishart.

Greater London Council (1985), *Changing the World: A London Charter for Lesbian and Gay Rights*, London: Greater London Council.

Hewison, R. (1995) *Culture and Consensus*, London: Methuen.

Hollinghurst, A. (1988) *The Swimming-Pool Library*, New York: Random House.

hooks, b. (1992) *Black Looks*, London: Turnaround.

Hughes, D. (1964) 'The spivs', in M. Sissons and P. French (eds), *Age of Austerity 1945–1951*, Harmondsworth: Penguin.

Hutton, W. (1996) *The State We're In*, 2nd edn, London: Vintage.

Hyde, H. M. (1972) *The Other Love*, London: Granada.

Marwick, A. (1996) *British Society since 1945*, 3rd edn, Harmondsworth: Penguin.

National Lesbian and Gay Survey (1993) *Proust, Cole Porter, Michelangelo, Marc Almond and Me*, London: Routledge.

Rees, D. (1993) *Words and Music*, Brighton: Millivres.

Sinfield, A. (1994) *The Wilde Century*, London: Cassell; New York: Columbia University Press.

—— (1997) *Literature, Politics and Culture in Postwar Britain*, 2nd edn, London: Athlone.

Smith, A. M. (1994) *New Right Discourse on Race and Sexuality*, Cambridge University Press.

Weeks, J. (1989) *Sex, Politics and Society*, 2nd edn, London: Longman.

Welsh, I. (1993) *Trainspotting*, London: Secker and Warburg.

Westwood, G. (1960) *A Minority*, London: Longmans.

Wilson, A. (1956) *Hemlock and After*, Harmondsworth: Penguin.

Part III

Britain, Europe and Americanisation

America, Europe and the Cold War

From the Marshall Plan (by which the Americans provided free aid for the re-construction along capitalist lines of the nations of western Europe most affected by the war, including Britain) to the establishment of the United Nations, the USA played the leading role in re-shaping the postwar world. At the Bretton Woods conference in America in 1944, it had already proposed fundamental reforms to the management of the world economic system, in the hope of preventing a return to the depression of the 1930s which many in the USA believed had given fascism its opportunity. The USA even offered generous aid for the postwar re-construction of the Soviet Union. The American offer was perhaps more surprising than the Russian refusal, for during the war, the capitalist USA and the communist Soviet Union had been uneasy allies, with the result that the campaign to liberate Europe – by the Americans from the west, the Russians from the east – became as much a race to establish separate spheres of influence in Europe as it was to defeat Nazi Germany.

At the end of the war, with the development of the A-bomb (which the Americans had used to devastating effect on Hiroshima and Nagasaki), the USA had an undoubted advantage; but by 1948, with the Soviet Union's development of its own nuclear weapons and its open destruction of democratic regimes in Eastern Europe, the so-called Cold War began, as the USA and the Soviet Union confronted one another with increasing antagonism across a partitioned Europe. From the 1940s to the late 1980s when the Soviet Union collapsed, European politics and culture were overshadowed by the Cold War (Reynolds 1991). The major countries of western Europe devoted a disproportionate part of their national budgets to military expenditure to counteract what they saw as the military threat from the Soviet Union, while the USA and the Soviet Union spent large sums not simply on maintaining large garrisons in Europe but also on propaganda, promoting their respective ways of life through various cultural organisations. For four decades, Europe was the site – at the level both of high and popular culture – of the struggle for cultural legitimacy (Sinfield 1997).

From anti-Americanism to Americanisation

At the outset of the Cold War, Britain made itself the USA's closest ally in Europe: in part through a continuation of the wartime alliance; in part through self-interest. For those on the New Left, Britain had become an accomplice in the USA's postwar neo-imperialism (Anderson 1992); for other British historians, Britain's active support for NATO (the anti-Russian military alliance of North American and western European states) and the equally active attachment of Labour and Conservative governments to the so-called 'Atlantic Alliance' revealed a shrewd exploitation of Britain's historical and geographical position, linked by language, traditions, and common inheritances with the USA, yet located physically in Europe (Reynolds 1991). Some have even suggested that British politicians did much to intensify American anxieties about the Soviet Union in order to secure Britain's privileged postwar relationship with America (Taylor 1990). In 1948, however, the American ambassador to Britain reported that anti-American sentiments in Britain 'border on the pathological' (Grosser 1980: 72).

Certainly, members of the cultural elite, as we can see most strikingly in George Orwell's *Nineteen Eighty-Four* (1949), were highly critical of what they saw not only as America's military but also as its cultural colonisation of postwar Europe. In Orwell's novel, Britain is Airstrip One, the forward staging post of America's Cold War engagement in Europe. The currency is the dollar, while Americanisms infiltrate the language.

In elite journals and the popular press, American popular culture, ranging from comics to science fiction, magazines to films, was habitually dismissed as vulgar and commercialised (Webster 1988), although an exception was sometimes made for jazz (Godbolt 1989); but such complaints had more to do with the fact that Britain and Europe were no longer the centre of world political or cultural power. (In the 1950s and 1960s, the Campaign for Nuclear Disarmament, combining anti-capitalism and anti-Americanism with a belief in

Britain's distinctive moral role in the postwar world, relied upon the same residual delusion of imperial grandeur.) From the 1940s onwards, American writers, painters, composers, architects and intellectuals were the leading figures of the postwar international *avant-garde*, while American publishers, galleries, theatres, opera houses, concert halls and journals had resources and audiences unknown in Europe (Steiner 1996).

Britain and American culture

In 1952, a number of British artists and intellectuals, the sculptor and painter Eduardo Paolozzi, the architects Peter and Alison Smithson, and the critics Reyner Banham and Lawrence Alloway, began to meet at the Institute of Contemporary Arts (ICA) in London to celebrate American popular visual culture: its artefacts, its cars, its advertising and its cinema. (For a detailed account of the ICA, see Nannette Aldred's essay in this volume.) This formed the springboard for two of the most important artistic movements of the 1950s and early 1960s: the Independent Group and the Pop Art movement (Marwick 1991: 49). Few, however, gave much regard to American painting or sculpture until two exhibitions of American modern art at the Tate Gallery in London – 'Modern Art in the United States' in 1956 and 'The New American Painting' in 1959 – convinced some younger British artists that American artists, particularly the Abstract Expressionists, had a vitality and significance lacking in contemporary European art. Indeed, in 1960 the RBA Galleries staged 'Situation,' an exhibition which showed the positive response of British artists to American art. For others, the exhibitions had the effect of making them define what they found most characteristic and valuable in the European or British traditions, from landscape to figurative painting (Garlake 1998). From the 1960s onwards, such public debates became commonplace in all the arts in Britain, with American counter-culture in the 1960s and American post-modernism in the 1980s having a particular impact on British culture (Massa and Stead 1994). Indeed, since the 1960s, many of the most important British painters, poets, novelists, designers and architects have found explicit inspiration in the work of their American precursors or counterparts.

The Suez crisis in 1956 (when the USA forced Britain to abandon its attack on Egypt) and the war in Vietnam revived anti-Americanism in Britain (although in the latter case, British protesters identified with the much larger counter-cultural movement in

America) (Marwick 1998). However 1956 was also a decisive year in making British attitudes to the USA much more positive for the Soviet Union's military invasion of Hungary – to put down a popular revolt against Russian rule – disillusioned many on the left who had looked to the Soviet Union as an alternative model to the United States. (The situation was repeated in 1968, when the Soviet Union invaded Czechoslovakia.)

For a new generation in Britain, the USA (which had become by far the most important foreign investor in Britain, particularly in the most advanced technological sectors) represented the future, its designs and styles (along with those from France, Italy and Scandinavia) emulated by the young (Hebdige 1988). Pop-artists explored American-style consumer society with ironic fascination, while pop musicians assimilated American popular music, from blues and jazz to rock n' roll. While the New Left and the old right deprecated Americanisation, it became for many others synonymous with the prosperity and modernisation they desired. Indeed, the immense popularity of American cinema and television programmes had much to do with the fact that they projected the fantasy of a classless society untrammelled by British restrictions on opportunity (McKibbin 1998).

Britain, America and Europe

Since the Second World War, politicians in continental Europe have planned moves – first through the Common Market or European Economic Community (1957), then through the European Community (1980) and finally, through the European Union (1994) – towards pan-European political and economic integration. From the outset, there was a clear logic to this plan: to provide an economic and political framework by which Germany might play a full part in postwar Europe without dominating it. After Suez, British politicians on the left and the right conceded that Britain lacked the military and economic power to stand on its own. They believed that the privileged relationship Britain had enjoyed since the Cold War with the USA could be strengthened by joining the European Economic Community, because Britain would gain influence with the Americans by resisting tendencies within the Common Market towards an anti-American political and economic bloc. Indeed, the French government opposed Britain's first application to join the Common Market in 1961 on the grounds that Britain would be an American 'Trojan horse', but in 1973, (as France itself underwent its own belated Americanisation) Britain was finally admitted (Robbins 1998). Ever since, Britain has not only pursued what it has seen as common Anglo-American interests, from defending free trade to opposing restraints in the labour market; it has also opposed European attempts to restrict American domination of Europe's audio-visual culture, particularly cinema and television. Seeking to prevent the development of an exclusive German-American axis, the protection of the so-called 'special relationship' with the USA remains, within Europe, Britain's main foreign policy objective.

Some recent commentators have argued that the postwar American *avant-garde* – from the Abstract Expressionists to Andy Warhol – has merely replicated the achievements of the inter-war European *avant-garde* (Steiner 1996), while others (even while conceding American indebtedness) have found in the postwar American *avant-garde* something which was never achieved in Europe: a genuine democratisation of feeling (Ruland and Bradbury 1991). Questions of priority aside, such arguments acknowledge the common space – at once of shared inheritances and of specific differences – within which postwar American and European cultures have been produced.

With the ending of the Cold War, some scholars have begun to examine the extent of the damage it inflicted on British and European culture (Sinfield 1997); others to explore – particularly in the study of the cinema, poetry and the visual arts – the more positive effects of cultural inter-relationships between America and Europe.

In his essay on postwar British cinema, Alistair Davies suggests (while acknowledging the dominance of Hollywood) that British cinema draws self-consciously upon both American and European cinema in order to establish its distinctive identity as a cinema in-between. In his essay on the postwar career of W. H. Auden, Davies also explores the transnational space of postwar international modernism, locating both Auden and his contemporary admirers within it. In this way, he points to new ways of reading the histories of postwar British film, poetry and postwar British culture.

Bibliography

General studies on Britain's postwar relations with America and Europe

Anderson, P. (1992) *English Questions*, London: Verso.

Grosser, A. (1980) *The Western Alliance: European-American Relations since 1945*, London: Macmillan.

Reynolds, D. (1991) *Britannia Overruled: British Policy and World Power in the Twentieth Century*, Harlow: Longman.
—— (1994) 'Great Britain', in *The Origins of the Cold War in Europe: International Perspectives*, New Haven: Yale University Press: 77–95.
Robbins, K. (1998) 'Fragile bearings 1945–' and 'Losing (domestic) bearings? 1945–' in *Great Britain: Identities, Institutions and the Idea of Britishness*, London: Longman: 297–343.
Taylor, P. J. (1990) *Britain and the Cold War: 1945 as a Geopolitical Transition*, London: Pinter.

General studies on American or European influences on postwar British culture

Blake, A. (1996) 'Re-placing British music', in M. Nava and A. O'Shea (eds), *Modern Times: Reflections on a Century of English Modernity*, London: Routledge: 208–38.
—— (1997) *The Land Without Music: Music, Culture and Society in Twentieth-Century Britain*, Manchester: Manchester University Press.
Conekin, B. (1999) '"Here is the modern world itself": the Festival of Britain's representations of the future,' in B. Conekin, F. Mort and C. Waters (eds), *Moments of Modernity: Reconstructing Britain 1945–1964*, London: Rivers Oram Press: 228–46.
Frith, S. (1988) *Music for Pleasure: Essays in the Sociology of Pop*, Cambridge: Polity.
Garlake, M. (1998) *New Art, New World: British Art in Postwar Society*, New Haven and London: Yale University Press.
Godbolt, J. (1984) *A History of Jazz in Britain, 1919–1950*, London: Quartet.
—— (1989) *A History of Jazz in Britain, 1950 to 1970*, London: Quartet.
Hebdige, D. (1988) *Hiding in the Light: On Images and Things*, London: Comedia/Routledge.
O'Shea, A. (1996) 'English Subjects of Modernity', in M. Nava and A. O'Shea (eds), *Modern Times: Reflections on a Century of English Modernity*, London: Routledge: 7–37.
Mandler, P. (1999) 'New towns for old: the fate of the town centre', in B. Conekin, F. Mort and C. Waters (eds), *Moments of Modernity: Reconstructing Britain 1945–1964*, London: Rivers Oram Press: 208–27.
Marwick, A. (1991) *Culture in Britain since 1945*, Oxford: Blackwell.
—— (1998) *The Sixties: Cultural Revolution in Britain, France, Italy and the United States, c. 1958–c.1974*, Oxford: Oxford University Press.
Massa, A. and Stead, A. (1994) *Forked Tongues: Comparing Twentieth-Century British and American Literature*, Harlow: Longman.
McKibbin, R. (1998) 'The cinema and the English', in *Classes and Cultures: England 1918–51*, Oxford: Oxford University Press: 419–56.
Ruland, R. and Bradbury, M. (1991) *From Puritanism to Postmodernism: A History of American Literature*, London: Routledge.

Sinfield, A. (1997) *Literature, Politics and Culture in Postwar Britain*, 2nd edn, London: Athlone.

Steiner, G. (1996) 'The archives of Eden', in *No Passion Spent: Essays, 1978–1996*, London: Faber: 266–303.

Webster, D. (1988) 'The long reaction: "Americanization" and cultural criticism', in *Looka Yonder! The Imaginary America of Populist Culture*, London: Routledge.

Chapter 5

A cinema in between

Postwar British cinema

Alistair Davies

Hollywood and British cinema

Had matters taken a different course, Brighton and Hove (where some of the earliest British film-makers were based) rather than Hollywood might now be the centre of world cinema. For in the first decade of the century, British directors, like their counterparts elsewhere in Europe, were amongst the most creative and innovative in the world. By unsettling production and distribution, the First World War not only disrupted the impetus of the European cinema but also enabled Hollywood's subsequent domination of world cinema (Caughie 1996: 2). Yet, as Pierre Sorlin notes, there were other important factors. The Americans were the first to think of film as an industrial product, to be manufactured and marketed like any other industrial product. At the same time, they established the narrative conventions, the identifiable *genres*, the standards of production and design and (after the advent of sound in the late 1920s) the levels of technical reproduction necessary to capture and hold on to a large popular audience. Hollywood's 'classical style', Sorlin writes, cannot be easily defined but everyone knows empirically what it is:

> good, sharp pictures, a soundtrack which helps the spectator to follow the plot-line without ever encroaching upon her or his pleasure, audible dialogue, good actors, and, more importantly, a well-defined story, with a situation revealed at the outset, developed logically, and unambiguously closed or solved at the end.
>
> (Sorlin 1991: 1–2)

In short, Hollywood won because it 'was the first to settle the formula and because it was financially stronger than its European competitors' (ibid.: 1–2).

Despite quotas, tariffs, tax advantages and subsidies to domestic producers, European national cinemas have been unable to reverse the domination of Hollywood. In Britain, American films have since the 1920s made up the bulk of annual programming, with the proportion of American films increasing dramatically from the 1950s onwards. If the postwar decline in indigenous production was due to the unwillingness of British financial institutions to risk investment in film production, their prudence was justified for the return on investments had been severely affected during the 1950s by a sharp fall in cinema attendance.

Until the 1950s, cinema-going had been for most British families their favourite form of entertainment, but with the advent of television (Independent Television began to broadcast in 1955) they preferred to stay at home or to spend their disposable income on new consumer goods and on other leisure pursuits. The figures for the period reveal how severe the decline in cinema-going was. Between 1955 and 1963 over two-thirds of the audience and over half the cinemas disappeared (Richards 1997: 149). Since the 1980s, the building of multiplex cinemas has reflected an increase in cinema-going but their principal function has been to provide an outlet for Hollywood productions in the British market. Recent European Union initiatives to support European production and distribution have had negligible effect, even if they have raised awareness amongst European policy-makers of the complex economic, political and cultural issues involved (Finney 1996; Moran 1996).

Nothing provides a more striking illustration of these issues than the British situation in the late 1940s. As a result of direct government subsidies, a degree of centralised planning and reduced American access to the British market, British cinema during the Second World War flourished both critically and commercially (Murphy 1989). Recognising this (and in the hope of reducing the outflow of funds at a time when the British economy was virtually bankrupt), the first postwar Labour government proposed to continue to subsidise British production while imposing an import duty on American films. It was, however, forced to withdraw its proposal to tax American film-imports because of powerful pressure from the American government which recognised the ideological as well as commercial importance of unrestricted access to the British market at the very moment that Britain had moved decisively to the left (Jarvie 1991). Yet this was not the only reason for a change of policy, for the British government also faced public hostility following a prolonged boycott of the British market by American distributors. In the wake of wartime suffering and in the midst of postwar austerity, American cinema provided the glamour absent from everyday-life.

For some, the British public has from the outset been drawn to American cinema because of the absence in American films of the class-ridden structures and the undemocratic values of British society (Swann 1987: 13–29). For others, both at the time and subsequently, the Labour government's humiliating *volte-face* revealed the degree to which postwar Britain from 1945 has been subject to American economic and political hegemony, while the public reaction to the Hollywood boycott showed how easily the British public had consented to Hollywood's desiring-machine (Swann 1987: 105–25; Jarvie 1991; Wollen 1993).

Realism or tinsel?

In the light of American domination, British producers and directors have had two obvious choices. On the one hand, they could compete with Hollywood by copying Hollywood, including (as with pre-war Gaumont-British or postwar Rank) the development of an American-style studio system, a preference for cinematic illusion and spectacle, a heavy expenditure on production values and advertising and the promotion of stars. In the pre-war period, Alexander Korda's London Films had been notably successful in making so-called 'international films' of the kind which sold well both in Britain and America, including *The Private Life of Henry VIII* (1933), *The Scarlet Pimpernel* (1935) and *The Thief of Bagdad* (1940) (Kulik 1990). *The Thief of Bagdad* (which was co-directed by Michael Powell) was at the time unrivalled in its use of colour and of special effects and was clearly designed to appeal to the same family audience as *The Wizard of Oz* (1939). On the other hand, they could compete by stressing British cinema's intrinsic cultural difference (Murphy 1989; Higson 1995). In a pamphlet published in 1944, Michael Balcon (who was running the Ealing Studios) defined what this was by contrasting the 'realism' of the British cinema with the 'tinsel' of Hollywood. Balcon's 'realism' derived from the British documentary tradition of the 1930s, largely associated with John Grierson and the GPO Documentary Unit.

Yet what distinguished British cinema from Hollywood was not simply a question of aesthetics. As we can see most movingly in the wartime drama-documentaries of Humphrey Jennings, *Listen to Britain* (1942), *Fires Were Started* (1943) and *A Diary for Timothy* (1945), the British documentary tradition made the community its subject and celebrated communal rather than individual values. In *Fires Were Started*, we follow a day in the life of a unit of volunteer firemen during the London blitz. We begin with the surprisingly easy assimilation of a middle-class newcomer into the largely working-class unit. (Henry Green's novel *Caught* (1943) gives a very different account of a similar situation, stressing not comradeship but a profound class hostility and distrust.) Then, after a night-time raid, we witness the fighting of a fire in the docks during which one of the firemen is killed. However, his death is not in vain, for the firemen prevent the fire from spreading to a munitions ship moored in the docks. What is shown throughout is the willing self-sacrifice of the one for the many. Indeed, for those who were concerned to define such differences, what underlay the aesthetic difference between American and British cinema was an ideological one. While Hollywood was essentially individualist, British cinema was essentially communitarian (Higson 1995).

Accordingly, for many, postwar British cinema falls readily into two clearly defined traditions. To grasp what these were we need only to contrast the imaginative and often fantastical technicolour films of Korda and Michael Powell and Emeric Pressburger with the realistic black and white films of the Second World War such as David Lean's *In Which We Serve* (1942) (starring Noel Coward), Frank Launder and Sidney Gilliat's *Millions Like Us* (1943) and Anthony Asquith's tribute to the Royal Air Force *The Way to the Stars* (1945); or contrast the late 1940s costume dramas and historical romances of Gainsborough Films with the social problem films and the even more famous comedies of the Ealing Studios; or in the 1950s and 1960s contrast David Lean's *The Bridge on the River Kwai* (1957) and *Lawrence of Arabia* (1962) (with their epic scale and their dramatic use of foreign locations) with the provincial films of the British New Wave.

For those committed to the 'realism' of British cinema, the contrast carried its own implicit evaluation. Yet the fact that Powell and Pressburger were commercially successful and used extravagant effects did not mean that their films were mere entertainments. For during the 1940s, they made some of the intellectually and cinematically most adventurous British films ever made. In *The Life and Death of Colonel Blimp* (1943), they gave sympathetic flesh to a comically reactionary cartoon character, Colonel Blimp. Ranging from the Boer War to the Second World War, they showed in their film how out of touch their Blimpish Major-General Candy (played by Roger Livesey) had become (not least with regard to the changing role of women) in a world in which his military codes of honour no longer had a place. In *A Matter of Life and Death* (1946), their most visually arresting work, they explored both the here and now (in colour) and the afterlife (in black and white); in *Black Narcissus* (1947), the clash between east and west in a convent situated in the Himalayas; and in *The Red Shoes* (1948) (based on the Hans Christian Andersen fairytale about a girl who cannot stop dancing when she wears the red shoes) the destructive power of the artist-figure.

What linked these films was not simply their extraordinary use of staging and of colour but also their exploration of metaphysical themes: time, identity, the relationship between the body and the spirit and (anticipating Powell's later study of cinematic voyeurism, *Peeping Tom*, 1960) the power of the image itself.

At the same time, while Powell and Pressburger were concerned with the tensions caused by the Second World War between the generations, the sexes and even the allies, Lean, Launder, Gilliat and Asquith were content to show how divisions of class and of gender were effortlessly elided under the guise of a common patriotic purpose and a patriotic common bond (Higson 1995). Nor were the Gainsborough films mere entertainments or Lean's cinema (as some have suggested) a grandiose version of a boy's own adventure. Gainsborough's costume dramas – of which Leslie Arliss' *The Wicked Lady* (1945) is the most famous – explored human sexuality at a time when such explorations were heavily censored, while Lean's cinema was multi-valent, the pleasures of spectacle co-existing with an intricate assessment of the British imperial mentality (Richards 1997).

The Ealing films may well have pitched communal values against individualism (Henry Cornelius' *Passport to Pimlico*, 1949) and the life of the community against the external impositions of bureaucracy (Alexander Mackendrick's *Whisky Galore!*,1949) but they remained very heavily indebted to wartime ideals of unity which seemed – to judge from the 'spiv films' of the late 1940s – already out of date when the war had ended.

In the films of the British New Wave (Karel Reisz's *Saturday Night and Sunday Morning*, 1960; Tony Richardson's *The Loneliness of the Long-Distance Runner*, 1962; Lindsay Anderson's *This Sporting Life*, 1963) the idea of a living community provided the grounds for criticising the social and economic tendencies leading to its dissolution, but there was a marked, if understandable anachronism to their complaint. It is perhaps not surprising that at the moment when television was eroding the audience for cinema, these films should be particularly hostile to it and to the new consumerist culture it sustained. In *The*

Loneliness of the Long-Distance Runner, for instance, when Colin Smith's mother squanders on consumer goods the money she has received in compensation for her husband's death, her spending spree is shown in the particular format devised for showing advertisements on commercial television.

Importantly, for its practitioners and its admirers, the realism of postwar British cinema was not simply an aesthetic which reflected the social realities of postwar Britain but was also one designed to elicit from its audience a critical response to them. In the 1950s, the team of director Basil Dearden and producer Michael Relph used the feature film to address specific social problems: juvenile delinquency (*The Blue Lamp*, 1950), racial relations (*Sapphire*, 1959) and the blackmail of male homosexuals (*Victim*, 1961). Dearden's sympathetic treatment of a married barrister (played by Dirk Bogarde) facing blackmail on account of his homosexuality is credited, by some, with changing public attitudes to the legal status of male homosexuality, thereby preparing the way for the liberalising legislation of the 1960s. The directors of the British New Wave were also noted documentarists, while the 'Swinging London' films – Richard Lester's *The Knack . . . and How to Get It* (1965), Lewis Gilbert's *Alfie* (1966) and Silvio Narizzano's *Georgy Girl* (1966) – maintained a critical eye on the social and sexual changes they seemed to celebrate (Murphy 1992).

The high regard in which Ken Loach is held, both in Britain and in Europe, derives from the fact that he is seen to be the major contemporary exponent of the social realist tradition in British film, from his quasi-documentary films made for television *Up the Junction* (1965) and *Cathy Come Home* (1966) to his feature-films *Poor Cow* (1967), *Kes* (1969), *Family Life* (1971), *Fatherland* (1986), *Hidden Agenda* (1990), *Riff-Raff* (1990) and *Raining Stones* (1993). In his films, (including his historical films, *Days of Hope* (1975) regarding the social unrest between the First World War and the collapse of the General Strike in 1926, and *Land and Freedom* (1995) on the Spanish Civil War), Loach has been concerned not only to give expression to working-class figures habitually excluded from cinema but also to respond to the particular injustices – poverty, homelessness, the casualization of employment, state terrorism in Northern Ireland, or unemployment – by which they are trapped. If *Victim* helped to change public attitudes to homosexuality, *Cathy Come Home* (in large measure because it was shown on the BBC) had an even greater impact on changing public attitudes to the shortage of adequate public housing in Britain. Indeed, since the 1960s, social realism has remained the dominant aesthetic of British television drama; but it is a form constantly re-invigorated by cinema itself (Stead 1989: 205).

A multiple cinema or a British national cinema?

Recent historians of postwar British cinema, however, have begun to question such bi-polar readings of postwar British cinema. For some critics, it not only provides a spurious coherence to the fragmentary history of postwar British cinema but it also excludes from account the sheer range of postwar British cinema: thrillers, romances, science-fiction films, comedies, war films, musicals, empire films, action films and the films of the *avant-garde* (Landy 1991; Street 1997). It privileges so-called 'quality' over popular cinema, neglecting many of the com-mercially most successful films of the period: Frank Launder and Sidney Gilliat's *St Trinian's* films (with Margaret Rutherford and Alastair Sim); the *Carry On* and *Doctor at Large* series; the Boulting brothers' *I'm All Right Jack* (1959) and *Heavens Above!* (1963) (both starring Peter Sellers); and the Bond and Hammer Horror films. It underestimates the degree to which British realist cinema defined itself not only against Hollywood but also under Hollywood's omnipotent gaze.

In the Gainsborough films, Stewart Granger was Britain's answer to Errol Flynn, while Richard Burton (in Richardson's *Look Back in Anger*) and Richard Harris (in *This Sporting Life*) were cast because they seemed in their physical directness and emotional intensity the closest British equivalents to Marlon Brando. Above all, it ignores the fact that the nature of cultural difference may reside less in aesthetic and ideological questions than in British cinema's projection of its own native cultural traditions (Barr 1986; Street 1997; Richards 1997).

To what extent have British comedies, for instance, from the Will Hay and Norman Wisdom films to the *Carry On* and *Doctor at Large* series, drawn upon older forms of popular entertainment from the variety show to farce? To what extent has British cinema defined itself through the pictorial and literary traditions of romanticism, not least in its representation of the city and its exploration of deeply repressed passion? Why has British cinema, more so than any other national cinema, been a cinema of adaptation, both of stage plays re-written for the screen and of novels and short stories? Many of the classic films of the 1940s – Thorold Dickinson's *Gaslight* (1940) and *The Queen of Spades* (1949), Laurence Olivier's *Henry V* (1944) and *Hamlet* (1948), David Lean's *Blithe Spirit* (1945), *Brief Encounter* (1945), *Great*

Expectations (1946) and *Oliver Twist* (1948), John Boulting's *Brighton Rock* (1947), Anthony Asquith's *The Winslow Boy* (1948) and Carol Reed's *Odd Man Out* (1947), *The Fallen Idol* (1948) and *The Third Man* (1949) – were adaptations, while all the films associated with the British New Wave – unlike the films of the French New Wave from which the term came – were derived from contemporaneous stage plays, novels or short stories. Indeed, throughout the postwar period, many leading writers have established creative associations with directors: Joyce Cary with Thorold Dickinson, Graham Greene with Carol Reed, Harold Pinter with Joseph Losey and, more recently, Hanif Kureishi with Stephen Frears.

We find similar reservations in recent discussions of a British 'national cinema'. During the 1940s, the volume of high quality British-made films dealing with British history and the British way of life convinced many film-makers and critics that Britain had at last produced its own 'national cinema' (Murphy 1989; Higson 1995). It was for this reason that throughout the postwar period the 1940s has seemed 'the golden age' of British cinema, its achievements setting the measure against which to judge the subsequent failure of British cinema to reach a similar level. With the recent emergence of a regional cinema, queer cinema, black cinema and feminist cinema, some wonder if it is now desirable to aim for a British national cinema when the very notion of a national identity has become problematic? (Higson 1995; Young 1996). Is the nostalgia for the 'golden age' of British cinema not in fact a nostalgia for the images of national continuity and coherence it provided?

For recent critics, the British 'national cinema' of the 1940s did not so much reflect as construct a British national identity with its reassuring stereotypes and situations far distant from the very real political and social tensions of the period. Its dramas of military life portrayed not simply the bravery of British servicemen under fire but also reinforced the class-bound, hierarchical structures of British military and social life, while its dramas of the home-front glossed over the profound disruptions caused by the entry of women both into the workplace and into the services (Lant 1995).

By linking pro-Nazi activity with the traditional figures of authority in a British village, Alberto Cavalcanti's *Went the Day Well?* (1942) (adapted from a short story by Graham Greene) cleverly disrupted many of the expectations of 'patriotic' cinema. Similarly, film historians have begun to re-evaluate the cinema of the 1960s and the 1980s when the globalisation of culture and later the globalisation of the economy disrupted altogether traditional notions of a national identity (Hill 1986; Murphy 1992; Friedman 1993; Richards 1997).

European and British cinema

'We Europeans,' Sorlin writes matter of factly, 'create and see the world through Hollywood's lenses' (Sorlin 1991: 1). The failure of postwar European film-makers to mount an adequate response to Hollywood, he argues, lies in their failure to win audiences for films based on the experiences postwar Europeans have in common: the liberation of Europe and the postwar reconstruction (although as some one concerned with the consumption of images, he also notes the unwillingness of national audiences to give up purely national tastes in cinema.) Yet, from the beginning, European film-makers created modes of narration, framing, editing and characterisation distinctly at odds with the dominant 'classical style': from the German expressionists, the French impressionists and the Soviet constructivists to the Italian neorealists, and the French and German New Waves (Bordwell 1997). One of the more striking aspects of postwar British cinema is the extensive repetition in 'quality' cinema of such European alternative styles. Olivier's *Henry V* (1944), for instance, has been admired for its contribution to Britain's wartime patriotic cinema; but, like his later *Hamlet* (1948), its distinction lies in its aesthetic stylisation: the opening out of a theatrical version of the play staged at the original Globe theatre into a filmic representation of events; the use of a painterly *mise-en-scène* derived from medieval manuscripts; the staging of battle-scenes in the manner of Sergei Eisenstein. The opening aerial shot of the Globe theatre reminded contemporary audiences of the historic London under peril from the blitz; but the European elements of the film's design (for a Shakespearean play in which personal and national reconciliation follows from victory) provided a countervailing discourse to the dominant nationalistic discourse of wartime propaganda.

With their long-duration shots and their deliberate artifice, Dickinson's films of the 1940s, *Gaslight, The Next of Kin* (1942) and *The Queen of Spades* (1949) relied heavily upon the example of pre-war French cinema (Richards 1986), while in the 1940s films of Powell and Pressburger, we find the mixture of artifice in design, of psychological extremism in characterisation and of the symbolic use of lighting present in pre-war German expressionism (Christie 1994).

Even the Ealing films did not escape European influences: the treatment in Charles Crichton's *Hue and Cry* (1947) of a group of children in the derelict spaces of bomb-damaged London recalls the Italian neo-realists (Murphy 1989), while the intricate narrative structure and amoral tone of Robert Hamer's *Kind Hearts and Coronets* (1949) came directly from Sacha Guitry's *The Story of a Cheat* (1936).

The pre-war influx of directors, scriptwriters, designers and cameramen from Nazi persecution in Europe played a major part in this European influence (including Pressburger who scripted Powell's films and Alfred Junge who designed them) (Petrie 1996); but from the 1920s onwards (as recent discussions of Alfred Hitchcock's pre-war work have confirmed) many British directors and cinematographers working in mainstream cinema followed developments in European cinema very closely (Street 1997). We may see the results of this in Carol Reed's extraordinary trilogy of psychological thrillers: *Odd Man Out* (1947) with its sympathetic treatment of an IRA man on the run; *The Fallen Idol* (1948) in which a young boy, believing wrongly that his father's butler is a murderer, implicates him by telling lies to protect him; and *The Third Man* (1949) in which, by contrast, Holly Martins (Joseph Cotten) maintains his belief in the innocence of Harry Lime (Orson Welles) until he has to face up to the fact that his friend is a crook and murderer. All of these films make use of expressionist devices: the striking use of light and shadow; distinctive close-ups and framing; the focus on an increasingly desperate central figure; the use of locations – the backstreets of Belfast, the rooms of a Knightsbridge mansion, the sewers of Vienna – to convey the sense of entrapment. Yet the influences did not simply come from one source. The death of the central male figure in *Odd Man Out*, for instance, closely resembles the death of the central male figure in Julien Duvivier's celebrated *Pépé le Moko* (1936).

Nor were these influences confined to the cinema of the 1940s. In many of the films of the British New Wave, the indebtedness to European film (besides their greater sexual frankness) was clear: the running sequence in *The Loneliness of the Long-Distance Runner* was an obvious homage to Truffaut's *400 Blows* (1959); in *This Sporting Life*, Anderson makes use of flashback in a manner reminiscent of Alain Resnais's *Hiroshima mon Amour* (1959), while John Schlesinger's *Darling* (1963) was an English version of Federico Fellini's *La Dolce Vita* (1960).

In the 1960s and 1970s, in *The Servant* (1963), *Accident* (1967) and *The Go-Between* (1971), the American-born Joseph Losey used the architecture of British houses and institutions to mirror the moribund forms of Britain's class-bound existence, making Losey as stylish an anatomist of the English as Michelangelo Antonioni was of the Italian bourgeoisie. Indeed, during the 1960s, a number of European directors (Antonioni, Roman Polanski, Jean-Luc Godard and François Truffaut) made films in England, while a large number of British directors, as Richard Murphy has shown, drew widely upon European art-house cinema (Murphy 1992).

In the 1970s, Mike Hodges's thriller *Get Carter* (1971) aestheticised violence in the manner of Jean-Pierre Melville's *Le Samourai* (1965), while Bill Douglas's autobiographical films, *My Childhood* (1972), *My Ain Folk* (1974) and *My Way Home* (1979) rendered his upbringing in a deprived, Scottish working-class home with a Bressonian intensity and spareness. Peter Greenaway and Derek Jarman have acknowledged the impact of a wide range of European directors on their work (Hacker and Price 1991), the opulent use of colour and the questioning of the European pictorial tradition in their films emulating Rainer Werner Fassbinder's *The Bitter Tears of Petra von Kant* (1973) and Jean-Luc Godard's *Passion* (1982) (Walsh 1993: 258).

Did mainstream film-makers graft such techniques onto an underlying 'classical style' in order to enhance the cultural value of their films for a postwar British audience increasingly familiar with European cinema? Or were these devices deliberately chosen to subvert the 'classical style': by making characterisation more complex, by adding ambiguity to motive and action, by making place symbolic, and by frustrating the pleasures of a happy ending? In *The Third Man*, for instance, the use of the expressionists' canted style of framing conveyed the strangeness and the menace of postwar Vienna, reduced as it was to rubble and divided up between the allied powers; but it also emphasised the disorientation the American Holly Martins felt in the face of a moral and a political situation he could not understand. Nothing stressed his failure more fully than the film's final scene in which he expects the late Harry Lime's girlfriend (as would be the case in Hollywood cinema) to take his arm and walk off happily ever after. In the event, Reed frustrates expectations; and his departure from the 'classical style' implies a critique of Holly's need to make the world conform to Hollywood's conventions. Certainly, many of the best and most distinctive British films of the postwar period have occupied this space in-between, using European devices to ironise Hollywood's 'classical style' without overthrowing it.

A British avant-garde?

'The British are coming,' declared Colin Welland when receiving his Oscar for writing Hugh Hudson's *Chariots of Fire* (1981). In retrospect, such confidence was misplaced, but during the 1980s and early 1990s, a number of British films, including Marek Kanievska's *Another Country* (1984), David Lean's *A Passage to India* (1985), James Ivory and Ishmail Merchant's *A Room with a View* (1986), *Maurice* (1987), *Howards End* (1992) and *The Remains of the Day* (1993) and Richard Attenborough's *Shadowlands* (1993), all proved highly successful both in the British and American market. At the time and subsequently, they have been dismissed as 'heritage cinema': films providing the compensatory fantasy of a stable and ordered British past at the very moment when the economic and social policies of the Thatcher government were not only eroding stability and order but also utilising a rhetoric of national greatness in order to justify doing so (Elsaesser 1993; Higson 1996). What, however, has concerned some of their critics is that the attention they received in America obscured the broader achievement of recent British cinema: not just films dealing with the effects of Thatcherism – Richard Eyre's *The Ploughman's Lunch* (1983), Stephen Frears' *My Beautiful Laundrette* (1985) and *Sammy and Rosie Get Laid* (1988), Mike Leigh's *High Hopes* (1988) and *Naked* (1993) – but also a cinema of retrospection in which film-makers revisited decades or events in the postwar period with a more critical eye (Wollen 1993).

In the 1930s, Korda, who had himself worked in Hollywood in the 1920s, argued that British film-makers could only compete against Hollywood by providing characters and situations – the gentlemanly aristocratic Englishman in Harold Young's *The Scarlet Pimpernel* or the brave but niggardly Scotsman in René Clair's *The Ghost Goes West* (1936) – easily recognised by the audiences of other countries (Kulik 1990: 96–115). By evoking a world of country houses, upper-class life, social restraint and sexual hypocrisy, the 'heritage cinema' of the 1980s simply provided what was needed for international success in an American-dominated market defined by the competitive circulation of idealised images. Nor were they alone in this. Other successes, from Bill Forsyth's *Local Hero* (1983), which recalls Korda's own film (and Alexander Mackendrick's *The Maggie*, 1954) in the contrast it draws between Scottish islanders and American businessmen, to Charles Crichton's *A Fish Called Wanda* (1988) and Mike Newell's *Four Weddings and a Funeral* (1994), also depended heavily upon the use of national stereotypes.

For others, what was lost amidst the claims of a revival of British cinema was the emergence in the films of Peter Greenaway, Derek Jarman, Sally Potter, Terence Davies, Isaac Julien, Cerith Wyn Williams and John Maybury of a British New Wave worthy of the name (Wollen 1993; Street 1997). While it had its origins in the radical counter-culture of the 1960s – 'the art world, the satire boom, experimental theater and the post-1969 *avant-garde*' (Wollen 1993: 35) – this was a movement in which the visual was predominant. (Maybury's *Love is the Devil* (1998) not only deals with the life of Britain's most celebrated postwar painter Francis Bacon but also emulates his distinctive mode of seeing.)

Noting that the directors of the British New New Wave were the products not of universities or drama schools but of art colleges, commentators have begun to explore the historical links between British cinema and the visual *avant-garde* and to re-write the narrative of British cinema in terms of its visual sense as demonstrated by the films of Powell and Pressburger, Donald Cammell and Nicolas Roeg, Ken Russell, Terry Gilliam, Greenaway and Jarman (Dodd and Christie 1996). Nor, as art historians have recently shown, was this a one-way transaction. From the 1940s onwards, the British visual arts have in turn been profoundly marked by popular and *avant-garde* cinema (Garlake 1998).

Much current discussion of British cinema concerns questions of funding and distribution, particularly in the light of the continued failure of British cinema, even when funded by grants from the European Union and the National Lottery, to counteract the domination of the domestic market by Hollywood. Nevertheless, if recent studies have increased recognition of the accomplishment and complexity of postwar British cinema, the single most important insight of current revisionary readings is that British cinema, positioned between American and European cinemas, has been one of the truly international spaces of postwar British culture where music, literature and the visual arts have been able to combine freely and creatively.

Bibliography

Barr, C. (ed.) (1986) *All Our Yesterdays: 90 Years of British Cinema*, London: British Film Institute.

Bordwell, D. (1997) *On the History of Film Style*, Cambridge, Mass.: Harvard University Press.

Caughie, J. (1996) *The Companion to British and Irish Cinema*, London: Cassell/British Film Institute.

Christie, I. (1994) *Arrows of Desire: The Films of Michael Powell and Emeric Pressburger*, London: Faber.

Dodd, P. and Christie, I. (1996) *Spellbound: Art and Film*, London: Hayward Gallery/BFI Publishing.

Elsaesser, T. (1993) 'Images for sale: the "new" British cinema', in L. Friedman (ed.), *British Cinema and Thatcherism: Fires were Started*, London: UCL Press: 52–69.

Finney, A. (1996) *The State of European Cinema: A New Dose of Reality*, London: Cassell.

Fluegel, J. (ed.) (1984) *Michael Balcon: The Pursuit of British Cinema*, New York: Museum of Modern Art.

Friedman, L. (ed.) (1993) *British Cinema and Thatcherism: Fires Were Started*, London: UCL Press.

Garlake, M. (1998) *New Art, New World: British Art in Postwar Society*, New Haven: Yale University Press.

Hacker, J. and Price, D. (1991) *Take 10: Contemporary British Film Directors*, Oxford: Oxford University Press.

Higson, A. (1995) *Waving the Flag: Constructing A National Cinema in Britain*, Oxford: Blackwell.

—— (ed.) (1996) *Dissolving Views: Key Writings on British Cinema*, London: Cassell.

Hill, J. (1986) *Sex, Class and Realism: British Cinema 1956–63*, London: British Film Institute.

Jarvie, I. (1992) *Hollywood's Overseas Campaign: The North American Movie Trade*, Cambridge: Cambridge University Press.

Kulik, K. (1990) *Alexander Korda: The Man Who Could Work Miracles*, London: Virgin.

Landy, M. (1991) *British Genres: Cinema and Society 1930–60*, Princeton: Princeton University Press.

Lant, A. (1991) *Black Out: Reinventing Women for Wartime British Cinema*, Princeton: Princeton University Press.

Moran, A. (ed.) (1996) *Film Policy; International, National and Regional Perspectives*, London: Routledge.

Murphy, R. (1989) *Realism and Tinsel: Cinema and Society in Britain 1939–1948*, London and New York: Routledge.

—— (1992) *Sixties British Cinema*, London: British Film Institute.

—— (1997) *The British Cinema Book*, London: British Film Institute.

Nowell-Smith, G. and Ricci, S. (1998) *Hollywood and Europe: Economics, Culture and National Identity 1945–95*, London: British Film Institute.

O'Pray, M. (1996) *The British Avant-Garde Film: 1926 to 1995*, Luton: University of Luton Press.

Petrie, D. J. (1996) *The British Cinematographer*, London: British Film Institute.

Richards, J. (1997) *Films and British National Identity: From Dickens to Dad's Army*, Manchester: Manchester University Press.

Sorlin, P. (1991) *European Cinemas: European Societies 1939–1990*, London: Routledge.

Stead, P. (1989) *Film and the Working Class: The Feature Film in British and American Society*, London: Routledge.

Street, S. (1997) *British National Cinema*, London: Routledge.

Swann, P. (1987) *The Hollywood Feature Film in Postwar Britain*, London: Croom Helm.

Walsh, M. (1993) 'Allegories of Thatcherism: the films of Peter Greenaway', in L. Friedman (ed.), *British Cinema and Thatcherism: Fires Were Started*, London: UCL Press: 255–77.

Wollen, P. (1993) 'The last new wave: modernism in the British films of the Thatcher era', in L. Friedman (ed.), *British Cinema and Thatcherism: Fires Were Started*, London: UCL Press: 35–51.

Young, L. (1996) *Fear of the Dark: 'Race', Gender and Sexuality in the Cinema*, London: Routledge.

Chapter 6

Faltering at the line

Auden and postwar British culture

Alistair Davies

On 26 January 1939, W. H. Auden and Christopher Isherwood arrived in New York. Five days later, Auden learned of the death of W. B. Yeats, the poet whose re-invigoration of the traditional lyric had a greater impact upon his own poetic development than the more radical formal innovations of Ezra Pound or T. S. Eliot. Almost at once, he wrote the first of the great elegies, 'In memory of W. B. Yeats', he was to complete during that year:

> He disappeared in the dead of winter:
> The brooks were frozen, the air-ports almost deserted,
> And snow disfigured the public statues;[1]
> (Auden, 'In memory of W. B. Yeats', 1939)

Snowbound New York provided appropriate symbols not only for his feelings of loss but also for the wider emotional and psychological *impasse* in the world at large. Yet Auden's poem was profoundly disconcerting for it seemed to discount many of its author's most celebrated poems of the 1930s. In 'Spain 1937' (1937), written in support of the Republican cause in the Spanish Civil War, Auden had famously sub-ordinated art to revolutionary action; now he maintained that 'poetry makes nothing happen'. It stood apart from the direct concerns and sufferings of everyday life, even if, like a river, it had its own irresistible potency. 'It survives,' he wrote

> In the valley of its saying where executives
> Would never want to tamper; it flows south
> From ranches of isolation and the busy griefs,
> Raw towns that we believe and die in; it survives,
> A way of happening, a mouth.
> (Auden, 'In memory of W. B. Yeats', 1939)

As if to emphasise even further the distancing of poetry from effect, Auden dissolved the particularity both of performance and of place into a purely symbolic geography.

By damning coincidence, the day on which Auden and Isherwood arrived in New York was also the day on which Barcelona, the last stronghold of the Republicans in Spain, fell to the Fascists. Throughout the 1930s, Auden had placed himself at the centre of British left-wing culture by analysing the neuroses of English middle-class life with an insider's compelling interiority but his perspective had become an international one. Writing with direct knowledge of the political situation in Germany, Spain and China, (which he visited with Isherwood in 1938 to report on the continuing Japanese invasion), he drew attention to the global nature of the struggle against Fascism. Nanking, Dachau: these were the places, he wrote in the 'Sonnets from China' (1938), 'where life is evil now'. Indeed, when he and Isherwood set out for China, Auden's fame as a leading member of the European anti-Fascist intelligentsia was already such that their journey made front page news. To leave for America in 1939 as the Republican cause in Spain collapsed and as war in Europe became inevitable, and to remain there throughout the Second World War appeared to those he left behind at best a demoralising act of selfishness, at worst a damaging act of betrayal (Osborne 1980: 187–8). The omission or revision of his most politically charged poetry of the 1930s in his Collected Poems (1945) intensified the bitterness his decision to leave for America in 1939 had caused.[2] It is hardly surprising that Auden's reputation in Britain never recovered from what many took to be an opportunist change of heart.

After the war, Auden remained in America and became in 1946 an American citizen. In range and volume the work of his American career greatly exceeded that of the pre-war years: verse-dramas, libretti, critical essays, a documentary, comic-verse, translations and eight major volumes of poetry, published in England as Another Time (1940), New Year Letter (1941), Nones (1952), The Shield of Achilles (1955), Homage to Clio (1960), About the House (1965), City Without Walls (1969) and Epistle to a Godson (1972). Nevertheless, British poets and critics attributed the most harmful consequences to his decision to leave for America, both for his own development as a poet and for the development of the culture he left behind. In a famously dismissive review, 'What's become of Wystan?' (1960), Philip Larkin declared that in America Auden's poetry had become 'a wilful jumble of Age-of-Plastic nursery rhyme, ballet folk-lore, and Hollywood Lemprière served up with a lisping archness that sets the teeth on edge', while his thought had become a mere verbal playing (Larkin 1983: 418). He had paid too heavy a price for detaching himself from the idioms and the experiences of his native culture. Concluding that Auden had been merely the poet of one decade, Larkin presented himself and the other poets of the Movement as the authentic voice of postwar British verse. British literary and cultural historians have been even more severe in their judgement. Auden's departure for America not only undermined British left-wing culture during the war and during the postwar reconstruction but also created a vacuum filled by the reactionary networks – the neo-Romantics, the Sitwells, the Bloomsbury group – his dominant position within the culture of the 1930s had held in check (Hewison 1977; Hewison 1986; Sinfield 1989). Since 1939, Robert Hewison concludes at the end of an authoritative three-volume history of postwar British culture, something in British culture has gone wrong (Hewison 1986: 265).

Recently, however, British and American critics have begun to challenge this dominant narrative. When Auden left for America, he was not, as Cyril Connolly had argued in *Horizon*, abandoning the sinking ship of European democracy. In one reading, he had done so because he believed that the Munich Agreement had averted war (Osborne 1980: 185); in another because he was convinced that through the Munich Agreement the British government itself had betrayed the anti-Fascist cause (Smith 1985: 118). Nor did his decision to leave for America mark a fundamental break in his poetic undertaking. Re-reading Auden through post-structuralist concepts, British and American critics have argued that in the American as well as the English phase of his career Auden remained a profoundly radical poet, using his poetry either to put the sovereign bourgeois subject under question (Smith 1985) or to undermine all forms of discursive authority, including that of poetry itself (Boly 1991). In such readings 'In Memory of W. B. Yeats' ceases to be an act of political and poetic apostasy. Stan Smith writes (in the most brilliant of the recent revisionary readings of Auden's work) that by linking both the sea's mouth and a human mouth at the end of the poem, the poet returned poetry to the 'sea of public discourse' (Smith 1985: 24), while Marsha Bryant contends that he re-defined poetry as a form of communicative action. It flowed from *coterie* audiences ('ranches of isolation') towards much larger discourse-communities ('raw towns'): a conduit through which collective action ('a way of happening') could take place (Bryant 1997: 4). What had once seemed settled in the narratives of Auden's postwar career, of postwar British poetry, even of postwar British culture is now again open to question.

Nothing, however, reveals the changing status of Auden more fully than the homage paid to him by contemporary British poets: James Fenton, Tom Paulin, Michael Hofmann, Carol Rumens, Blake Morrison and Paul Muldoon (Robinson 1988; Corcoran 1993). In '7 Middagh Street' (1987), for instance, Muldoon even makes Auden's decision to leave for America the subject matter of his poem, presenting Auden's journey to America as a spiritual voyage. Following Isherwood's *Christopher and His Kind* (1977), he assumes that the single most important motive for Auden's emigration was his wish to live openly and in an adult fashion as a gay man. (Within weeks, he had met and set up home with his life-long partner, Chester Kallman.)

In the bohemian menage over which Auden presided at 7 Middagh Street (including Kallman, Salvador Dali, Carson McCullers, Benjamin Britten and Peter Pears, Louis MacNeice and the striptease artist Gypsy Rose Lee, all of whom speak in the poem), Muldoon finds a practical celebration of sexual and cultural difference. Yet what interests him more is the way Auden's journey involved the positive embrace of what we now call the post-modern condition. Uprootedness and dispossession did not bring the losses of which Yeats, Pound and Eliot complained, but provided him with the positive possibility of change. 'The roots by which we were once bound', Muldoon writes assuming Auden's voice but echoing Eliot's, '/are severed here' (Muldoon 1987: 39). The roots that bind, of course, can constrain as well as nurture.[3]

At the time of his departure, many of Auden's British critics labelled him a coward. In re-writing the narrative of Auden's departure, Muldoon echoes later commentators who, exploring his interest in existentialist Christianity, have interpreted it as an existentialist act, a leap into the void (Conrad 1980: 194–235). Were there, at least from Auden's point of view, principled grounds for his decision? Let us return for a moment to 'In memory of W. B. Yeats'. When in the final sequence of the poem, Auden reflected upon the burial of Yeats, he repeated Yeats's faith in the power of poetry to release a 'healing fountain' in the 'deserts of the heart.' It was a power, he suggested, greatly needed as Europe stood on the brink of war – 'In the nightmare of the dark/ All the dogs of Europe bark' – even if it offended his reason that Europe again found itself in such a position: 'Intellectual disgrace/ Stares from every human face.' If (as I think we should) we read the poem as an explicit apologia for his departure, Auden made clear that his reasons for leaving lay in the collective failures of the political systems and cultural traditions of the continent he had left behind. Certainly, it was a view he expressed more fully when in May 1939 he composed his second elegy of the year, this time in commemoration of the radical German playwright Ernst Toller who had recently committed suicide in New York. As members of the anti-Fascist European left (Toller's expressionist dramas had had a direct influence upon the verse-plays Auden and Isherwood had written together during the 1930s), Toller and Auden had shared the same political and cultural allegiances. Why, Auden wondered, had Toller killed himself? Was his action the result of childhood trauma? Or had it another cause? Toller had been badly beaten when imprisoned by the Nazis. Auden explored both physical and psychological explanations but he went further to hint at another possibility:

> Or had the Europe which took refuge in your head
> Already been too injured to get well?
> (Auden, 'In memory of Ernst Toller', 1939)

Had the Europe which took refuge in Toller's head during his arrest, the Europe of his revolutionary imagination, been the cause, the processes of idealisation too damaged and damaging to be the source of health? In the elegy for Yeats, Auden had at least been able to convince himself that the creative gifts Yeats himself embodied would not be lost. In his elegy for Toller, Toller seemed to offer nothing of value beyond his own exemplary self-destruction, the victim of a pathology which affected the whole of European culture.

What differences had saved America from the fate of Europe? What tendencies did the two continents have in common? The immediate success Auden achieved in America owed much to the skill and seriousness with which he pursued these questions. In *New Year Letter* (1941), a verse-letter in rhymed octosyllabic couplets addressed to his fellow European exile Elizabeth Mayer, he presented America as the place in which the machine-age was at its most advanced. Surprisingly, given the poem's neo-Augustan form, he celebrated the beneficial results of this. In America, mechanisation had destroyed 'the local customs we enjoyed,/ Replaced the bonds of blood and nation/ By personal confederation' (*New Year Letter* III: 1528–30); but that destruction had also made possible a democratic politics of difference, a culture of 'pluralist interstices' (ibid.: 1594). By contrast, Europe's holding on to the bonds of blood and nation had resulted in endemic nationalism and racism. (For the Jewish refugees Auden had seen twelve months before in Brussels, Europe was, he wrote in *New Year Letter*, a 'haunted house' (*New Year Letter* I: 19).)

Throughout the 1940s, Auden explored the paradox that the extremity of alienation individuals felt in the New World also provided them with a corresponding impetus to change and renewal. In *The Age of Anxiety* (1946), four characters meet by chance in a New York bar. We learn of each character's hopes and fears; but in the verse-drama's central dreamlike sequences, we also follow their journey towards eventual psychic re-integration. There was in this more than an element of self-dramatisation. The imaginary America Auden created was not simply an aspect of his own private myth-making. It functioned for him (as for Isherwood) as the clarifying instance of what Europe was not: egalitarian rather than hierarchical; forward looking rather than nostalgic; a place of metamorphosis rather than of determination. Recalling his arrival in New York, Isherwood imagined an American chorus waiting to greet him: 'Don't you come snooting us with your European traditions – we know the mess they've got you into. Do things our way or take the next boat back – back to your Europe that's falling apart at the seams' (Isherwood 1977: 251–2).

When Auden returned to Britain in 1945, he was somewhat improbably wearing the uniform of an American army major. Co-opted to the Strategic Bombing Survey because of his knowledge of German and of pre-war Germany, he was *en route* to Germany to examine the psychological effects of mass bombing on the civilian population. His experience of the devastation of the cities of central Europe inspired some of his finest and intellectually most complex postwar poems. In 'The managers' (1948), for instance, he reflected upon the loss of religious ('the last word') and of revolutionary hope ('what is to be done') in the era of technology, a loss made even more frightening by the development of nuclear weapons, while in the explicitly Christian poem 'Memorial for the city' (1950) he suggested that the freedom of fallen mankind lay in the choice to make or destroy the ideal city. In Germany's ruined cities, 'The barbed wire runs through the abolished City', he encountered the most complete repudiation of that ideal.

For his British friends, however, Auden had become merely a propagandist for the American world-view: 'uncle Sam Wystan' in John Lehmann's dismissive phrase (Osborne 1980: 218). His postwar embrace of Christian humanism, no less than his increasing emphasis upon poetry as play, were dismissed as the gestures of a writer anxious not to offend in Cold War America. In 'Fleet visit' (1947), he may have captured the equivocation of America's postwar relationship to its European allies, part imposition, part co-operation; but if he gently satirised the sailors of the American Sixth Fleet in the Mediterranean, his satire gave way at the end to an admiration for their ships as aesthetic objects: 'pure abstract design/ By some master of pattern and line'. Had he not turned himself, as John Fuller suggests, into an apologist for the postwar *pax Americana* (Fuller 1970: 216)?

There is no doubt that Auden's reputation in postwar Britain was profoundly affected by widespread resentment at the unexpected asymmetries of the postwar period as cultural as well as economic and political power shifted from Europe to America.[4] In *Put Out More Flags* (1942), Evelyn Waugh had lampooned Auden and Isherwood for absconding to America; in *The Loved One* (1948) he produced a much less forgiving satire of British expatriates in California, where Isherwood had settled in 1940 to earn his living as a scriptwriter in Hollywood. In one of the first full-length studies of Auden's career (1951), Richard Hoggart (who was later to give cultural studies in Britain an insistently anti-American bias) attributed the failures of his American poetry directly to the pathologies of the American way of life. Yet what is lost in such criticism is the irony at play in Auden's postwar writing. The transformation of the fleet's warships into sublime objects takes place in the imagination of their crew: 'Mild-looking middle class boys' who read the comic strips: 'One baseball game is more/To them than fifty Troys.' What critical charge lies in this description or in the description of Italy as an 'unamerican place'?

Auden was very far from endorsing American hegemony, for what he disliked most about postwar America was what he had disliked about pre-war Britain: its deployment of imperialist power. In September 1939, he wrote the third and final elegy of the year, 'In memory of Sigmund Freud'. Freud, who had died in London in exile from the Nazis, was the only one of his elegiac European subjects from whom he did not distance himself. On the one hand, he expressed his respect for the rational endeavour of one who 'knew it was never enough but/ Hoped to improve a little by living'. On the other hand, he expressed his gratitude for the means Freud had granted to individuals to free themselves from the harmful burden of the past: 'he merely told' (the modesty of the task in inverse proportion to the significance of its outcome):

> The unhappy Present to recite the Past
> Like a poetry lesson till sooner
> Or later it faltered at the line where
> Long ago the accusations had begun,
> > (Auden, 'In memory of Sigmund
> > Freud', 1939)

Given the importance of childhood and school in his poetry of the 1930s, it was not surprising that Auden should make the classroom – 'the poetry lesson' – the place in which the unhappy subject had been constituted or the place in which, through faltering at the line, the possibility of telling things in another way might begin. Here Auden expressed the liberation he felt in America outside the social, cultural, even legal institutions by which his English sense of self had been produced. He also defined the essential procedure of his writing in America: the critical re-writing of the childhood texts – Shakespeare, the Augustans, the Romantics, above all the Latin poet Horace – by which his English identity had been fashioned within Britain's imperialist and class-bound educational system. (In one of his earliest works in America, *The Sea and the Mirror* (1943), he undertook a powerful anti-colonialist critique of *The Tempest*.) If Freud had assumed an autocratic pose, it was quite simply 'a protective imitation/ For one who lived among enemies so long.' Auden alluded here not just to the opponents of psychoanalysis and the anti-semitism that often fuelled them. While Freud had transformed modern civilisation so profoundly that he had become 'a whole climate of opinion,' he had still not been able to transform 'the ancient cultures of conceit' which

> In his technique of unsettlement foresaw
> The fall of princes, the collapse of
> Their lucrative patterns of frustration.
> (Auden, 'In memory of Sigmund Freud',
> > 1939)

What was at play here – and it remained at play throughout the remainder of Auden's work – was the link he was keen to establish between narcissism, violence and hierarchy: the construction of a phantasmal (conceited) self through metaphorical identification (a conceit) with systems of class or racial or national superiority. Most of his left-wing friends and associates had ended up working for the wartime Ministry of Information. Had he left England in order to avoid their fate, reproducing such national conceit through propaganda (and thereby ensuring what some have identified as the principal cause of Britain's postwar cultural failure (Piette 1995))? In faltering at the line, however, Auden would in his postwar writing untie the knot not simply of his identity as an Englishman but also his identity as a European.

In 1948, Auden spent the summer on the island of Ischia in the bay of Naples and returned each summer from New York for the next nine years. Here he re-worked Horace's *Odes*, presenting himself as a modern exile from an imperial centre of cultural and political power ('Ischia', 1948, 'Under Sirius', 1949). Some of his poems ('The love feast', 1948) framed Ischia and its inhabitants through a gay sensibility (Hecht 1993: 325); others ('The epigoni', 1955, 'Limbo culture', 1957) explored the historical analogy which linked his work with that of the most prestigious British and European writers and intellectuals of the 1940s and 1950s: T. S. Eliot, Thomas Mann, Evelyn Waugh, André Malraux and Graham Greene. They were convinced that the era through which they were living – the end of the European empires – could best be grasped by analogy with the decline and fall of the Roman Empire: the era of totalitarianism when language became corrupt, civil life was suspended and respect for the individual was destroyed. As we can see from *For the Time Being* (1943) and 'The fall of Rome' (1948), Auden had long shared similar interests.[5] What he did not share was the profound nostalgia for imperial forms of his contemporaries.

In 'Virgil and the Christian World' (1951), Eliot placed Virgil's *Aeneid* at the centre of the European cultural and political imagination. The postwar reconstruction of Europe, he suggested, should replicate the structures bequeathed by the Roman Empire. 'No, Virgil, no', Auden insisted by way of reply in 'Secondary epic' (1959), linking poetic to political mastery, patriarchal succession to the suppression of the female muse:

> Behind your verse so masterfully made
> We hear the weeping of a Muse betrayed.
> (Auden, 'Secondary epic', 1959)

By identifying himself with Horace, Auden staged a fundamental opposition to the conservative classicism of his European contemporaries, who wished to reconstruct the culture and politics of postwar Europe by retrieving unquestioningly its classical-Christian origins. He also staged an equally fundamental opposition, though, to the use of the classics within schools and universities to reproduce the imperialist values of the European elite. Even Cyril Connolly, who in *The Unquiet Grave* (1944) had used Virgil's *Aeneid* to stage his refusal of an imperial destiny, feared the loss of social and cultural distinctions which would follow from the eclipse of Europe.

In 'The fall of Rome' (dedicated to Connolly), Auden satirised the cultural, linguistic, even physiological binaries – 'cerebrotonic Cato' in opposition to the 'muscle-bound Marines' – within which the European imperial imagination worked, while in 'The shield of Achilles' (1952) he re-visited another canonical text, Homer's *Iliad*. Through the representation of 'iron-hearted man-slaying Achilles' he refused to idealise the systems of psychological as well as physical violence upon which, in his view, classical civilisation was founded.

In 1957, Auden bought a farmhouse at Kirchstetten in Lower Austria. In the Ischian poems, he had criticised both British and American imperialism; now in his Kirchstetten poems, he reflected on the moral and political consequences of the Second World War: the displacement of peoples, the division of Europe, the distrust of ideology. What stood at the centre of his work, though, was his concern with the links between the aesthetic principles of European high art and Europe's history of political atrocity.[6] Why had 'my day turned out torturers', he asked, 'who read *Rilke* in their rest periods' ('Prologue at sixty', 1967)? This had been the question with which he had been preoccupied since the 1940s. In 1949, he had been a member of the jury which gave the Bollingen Prize to Pound's *Pisan Cantos* (1948). Understandably, the award stimulated a heated debate. Could the aesthetic merit of the work, critics wondered, excuse its intolerable political content, while Pound's Fascist sympathies opened up an even wider discussion. Had their single-minded concern with the aesthetic blinded Yeats, Pound and Eliot to the illiberal political consequences their aesthetic views entailed?

Throughout the postwar period, Auden marked his distance from Yeats's concept of the artist; in his religious poetry of the 1940s and 1950s, he emphasised the coexistence of 'eros and dust' in order to counter the punitive rigour of Eliot; in his Ischian poems, he appropriated a very different Italy to that presented by Pound's *Pisan Cantos*.[7] In 'In praise of limestone' (1948) the men whose self-esteem Ischia's maternal landscape nourished walked arm in arm, 'but never, thank God, in step.' Some of his most exquisite postwar lyrics ('We, too, had known golden hours', 1950; '"The truest poetry is the most feigning"', 1953) explored the links between the elitist withdrawal of the modernists from mass culture and the corresponding impoverishment of public speech, while others ('Deftly, admiral, cast your fly' and 'The Emperor's favourite concubine', 1948) described the aesthete's sensibility at the heart of such withdrawal.

In his critical writing from *The Enchafèd Flood* (1950) and *The Dyer's Hand* (1963) to *Forewords and Afterwords* (1973), Auden not only traced the illiberal roots of modernism to Romantic notions of the privileged and transcendental subject, but also provided a critique of the political implications of Romantic-modernist notions of the poem as autonomous form. 'A society which was really like a good poem,' he wrote in *The Dyer's Hand*, 'embodying the aesthetic virtues of beauty, order, economy and subordination of detail to the whole, would be a nightmare of horror' (Auden 1963: 85).

Indeed, as we can see from 'In praise of limestone', Auden's critique of the political entailments of literature was not simply confined to the classical tradition. Although the poem was written in relaxed hexameters adapted from Latin to English measures, the line at which Auden faltered here was the English Romantic tradition. Interpreting place as text, the poem's speaker made sense of Ischia's limestone landscape, but unlike the English Romantic poets (Wordsworth's *Lines Composed Above Tintern Abbey* is the poem's most obvious inter-text), he sought in the landscape neither the secret of origins nor any symbol of transcendence:

> If it form the one landscape that we the inconstant ones
> Are consistently homesick for, this is chiefly
> Because it dissolves in water.
> (Auden, 'In praise of limestone', 1948)

What was reassuring about this 'backward/ And delapidated province' was the literal dissolving of stone. In its 'secret system of caves and conduits', he found, as Hecht (1993) suggests, another image for the human subject: flawed and mortal, unmoved by the desire for the ideal and the visionary, a desire he located as much in the pathologies of Wordsworth's Platonic notion of remembrance as in the pathologies of the northern masculine subject. Here, as in 'Ischia', 'Not in Baedeker' (1949), 'In transit' (1950) and 'Ode to Gaea' (1954) (in which he read the European landscape from an aeroplane), Auden countered the abstraction of space by focusing upon archaeological, linguistic and psychological traces from earlier periods of collective development: reminders of an ecologically sounder, less instrumental relationship to the natural and the human world.[8]

During the postwar period, Auden's collaborations, as translator with Bertolt Brecht or as librettist with Igor Stravinsky (*The Rake's Progress*, 1948) and with Hans Werner Henze (*Elegy for Young Lovers*, 1961), seemed to place him firmly within the tradition of European modernism. However, the greatest achievement – and the greatest legacy – of his postwar work was to provide successive generations of American and British poets from John Ashbery to Geoffrey Hill, Adrienne Rich to Peter Porter, James Fenton to Paul Muldoon, with a dialectical rather than a purely chronological sense of their relationship to the modernists. For his postwar poetry involved a constant faltering at the line of the European literary tradition as he recoiled not only from its complicity with inequality and aggression but also from its rhetorical power to master and subdue.

In the first volume of poems he completed after moving to Austria, *About the House* (1965), he celebrated the rooms of his farmhouse. In Britain, both the subject matter and conversational tone of the volume were much derided but what his critics failed to understand was that in both style and content he was marking the difference between a modernist and post-modernist concept of the poet: Auden's inclusive and democratic habitat was far removed from Yeats's exclusive and anti-democratic tower. Indeed, in his poetry of the postwar period, Auden constantly called his own authority into question by addressing those aspects of everyday experience the modernists disdained. (In one of his most moving poems, 'Old people's home' (1970), he describes his visit to Elizabeth Mayer, now very different from 'the pomp and sumpture of her hey-day'.) At the same time, his postwar persona became an increasingly comic one, his last poems (particularly after he finally left New York for Oxford in 1972) acts of conviviality: gentle farewells, festive utterances and advice to the young.[9]

Auden died suddenly in Vienna in 1973. No other poet in postwar Britain or America had raised such fundamental issues or done so with such philosophical acuity and poetic inventiveness. By dismissing the American Auden as lightweight (as Larkin and the other poets of the Movement had done), British poets and critics not only missed the seriousness, variety and originality of his postwar writing but also evaded the profound challenges it posed to them. Moreover, they ignored the fact that he had become both in his criticism and in his poetry a dissident voice at a time when Romantic-modernist ideals, in the guise of practical criticism or new criticism, were still dominant within British universities and schools. Above all, they insulated themselves both from the transnational and the transatlantic circumstances of the best postwar cultural production.[10] For five decades, the figure of Auden as betrayer has underpinned Britain's dominant cultural narratives of loss and mourning. To grasp the full significance of his postwar achievement, we need to free ourselves from what increasingly appears to be, at least on the cultural level, a national culture of conceit.

Notes

1 Throughout I use the first published version of Auden's poetry.
2 This was a central controversy in Auden studies in the 1940s and 1950s. For a recent consideration of the issue, see Mendelson (1991).
3 In the poem, Muldoon is ultimately more concerned with the role of Louis MacNeice, who returned to Britain in 1941. Yet Auden's seeming repudiation of a political role for poetry in a poem concerned with Yeats has, in the Northern Irish context, given rise to very different emphases by Paulin and Muldoon. See Corcoran (1993).
4 Nor is such resentment a thing of the past. Appleyard (1989) begins his unsympathetic account of Auden in America with the sentence: 'The USA was on the move.'
5 See Auden's recently published essay, 'The fall of Rome' (1966) in Bucknell and Jenkins (1995): 121–37.
6 Here Auden anticipates the reflections of George Steiner in *Bluebeard's Castle* (1972). It is easy to overlook Auden's importance in authorising such critiques of his modernist precursors.
7 Auden's most extended critique of Yeats is to be found in the libretto Auden wrote for Henze's *Elegy for Young Lovers*. The artist-genius Mittenhofer is based on Yeats. For the best discussion of Auden's relation to Yeats, see Callan's 'Disenchantment with Yeats: from singing-master to ogre' (1983): 143–62.
8 These works were indebted to David Jones's *In Parenthesis* (1937) and *The Anathemata* (1952), two works Auden held in the highest regard. In his postwar work, Auden's use of arcane vocabulary – 'osse', 'jussive', 'mornes and motted mamelons', 'fronde', 'cerebrotonic' – and his concern with history as sedimentation followed from Jones's concern with recovering 'the word-hoard' of British and European cultures.
9 Auden had been Oxford Professor of Poetry at Oxford in 1956. His final months there – unsurprisingly, he found Oxford hopelessly provincial – were profoundly unhappy.
10 For the most recent account of this, see Massa and Stead (1994).

Bibliography

Appleyard, B. (1989) *The Pleasures of Peace: Art and Imagination in Post-War Britain*, London: Faber.
Auden, W. H. (1963) *The Dyer's Hand and Other Essays*, London: Faber.

Boly, J. R. (1991) *Reading Auden: The Returns of Caliban*, New York: Cornell University Press.

Bryant, M. (1997) *Auden and Documentary in the 1930s*, Charlottesville: University Press of Virginia.

Bucknell, K. and Jenkins, N. (1995) *'In solitude, for company': W. H. Auden after 1940*, Oxford: Oxford University Press.

Callan, E. (1983) *Auden: A Carnival of Intellect*, New York: Oxford University Press.

Conrad, P. (1980) *Imagining America*, London: Routledge and Kegan Paul.

Corcoran, N. (1993) *English Poetry Since 1940*, London: Longman.

Fuller, J. (1970) *A Reader's Guide to W. H. Auden*, London: Thames and Hudson.

—— (1998) *W. H. Auden: A Commentary*, London: Faber.

Haffenden, J. (1983) *W. H. Auden: The Critical Heritage*, London: Routledge and Kegan Paul.

Hecht, A. (1993) *The Hidden Law: The Poetry of W. H. Auden*, Cambridge, Mass.: Harvard University Press.

Hewison, R. (1977) *Under Siege: Literary Life in London 1939–45*, London: Weidenfeld and Nicolson.

—— (1981) *In Anger: Culture in the Cold War 1945–60*, London: Weidenfeld and Nicolson.

—— (1986) *Too Much: Art and Society in the Sixties, 1960–75*, London: Methuen.

Hoggart, R. (1951) *Auden: An Introductory Essay*, London: Chatto and Windus.

Isherwood, C. (1977) *Christopher and His Kind 1929–1939*, London: Eyre Methuen.

Larkin, P. 'What's become of Wystan?' in J. Haffenden, *W. H. Auden: The Critical Heritage*, London: Routledge and Kegan Paul: 414–19.

Massa, A. and Stead, A. (1994) *Forked Tongues: Comparing Twentieth-Century British and American Literature*, London: Longman.

Mendelson, E. (1991) 'The two Audens and the claims of history', in G. Bornstein, *Representing Modernist Texts: Editing as Interpretation*, Ann Arbor: University of Michigan Press: 157–70.

Muldoon, P. (1987) *Meeting the British: Poems*, London: Faber.

Osborne, C. (1980) *W. H. Auden: The Life of a Poet*, London: Eyre Methuen.

Piette, A. (1995) *Imagination at War: British Fiction and Poetry, 1939–1945*, London: Papermac.

Robinson, A. (1988) *Instabilities in Contemporary British Poetry*, Basingstoke: Macmillan.

Sinfield, A. (1989) *Literature, Politics and Culture in Post-War Britain*, Oxford: Blackwell.

Smith, S. (1985) *W. H. Auden*, Oxford: Blackwell.

—— (1997) *W. H. Auden: Writers and Their Work*, Plymouth: Northcote House.

Taylor, J. R. (1983) *Strangers in Paradise: The Hollywood Emigrés, 1933–1950*, London: Faber.

Underhill, H. (1992) *The Problem of Consciousness in Modern Poetry*, Cambridge: Cambridge University Press.

Part IV

Class, consumption and cultural institutions

Postwar cultural reconstruction

In his essay in this volume, Alan Sinfield gives an account – from 1945 to the present – of changes in the funding and conceptualisation of culture in Britain. During the Second World War, state-funded concerts, theatre tours, exhibitions, film shows and opera and ballet performances played a key part in raising national morale. The first postwar Labour government continued and extended the public funding of the arts, not only by setting up the Arts Council in 1945 to oversee the national provision of the arts, to distribute funds and to promote British achievements in the arts, but also by enabling local authorities to sponsor local cultural activities.

During the 1940s and 1950s, with the help of public funding, many of the key cultural institutions of postwar Britain – from the Royal Opera House to the ICA (Institute of Contemporary Arts), the Edinburgh Festival to the regional theatre and opera movements – were established (Harris 1970; Marwick 1991). Some criticised what they feared would be state control of the arts, suggesting that this was the fate of totalitarian rather than democratic societies (Sinfield 1997); but the tradition of the public funding of museums and art-galleries had been well-established since the Victorian period (Taylor 1999). Indeed, the most authoritative pre-war cultural institution in Britain, the BBC (British Broadcasting Corporation) was also publicly funded. During the postwar period, it has been the single most influential publicly funded institution, supporting from its licence fee a number of major orchestras, sponsoring concert series (including the Proms) and commissioning music, plays and original features from many of the leading composers and writers of the day. The establishment of the Third Programme by the BBC in 1946, with its mixture of classical and *avant-garde* European music and drama, interspersed with talks on highly specialised topics, was at once a confirmation of the BBC's elevated sense of cultural purpose and an indication of a broader shift in the cultural policy of the postwar period from an essentially philanthropic concern with the improvement of the public to the promotion by groups of largely male, middle-class experts of the values of the European modernist movement (Blake 1997; Taylor 1999).

Public-service versus commercial television

The BBC's commitment to the education and moral improvement of the public had been established in the 1920s by its charismatic first Director-General, Sir John (later Lord) Reith. The first major challenge to this view came with the introduction of commercial (or independent) television in 1955, named to emphasise its difference from the publicly funded BBC. Funded exclusively from advertising, commercial television was bitterly opposed by leading figures in the universities, the arts, the churches and the political parties, including the Conservative party. It played a fundamental role in promoting Britain's consumer society, but the programmes it produced, often following formats developed on American commercial television, were judged to be so poor that by the early 1960s the Conservative government was forced to set up an inquiry into its standards (Briggs 1995; Smith and Paterson 1998).

The controversy surrounding commercial television gave a wider relevance to the work of a number of literary and cultural critics – F. R. Leavis, Richard Hoggart and Raymond Williams – who were concerned about the effects of 'commercialised' or 'Americanised' mass culture on older forms of culture, broadly conceived as more deeply rooted modes of expression and ways of life (Dworkin 1997).

The mid-1950s also saw the rise of a new generation of writers, directors, and artists opposed to what they saw as the innate conservatism of the political and cultural establishment (Hewison 1981, 1986; Marwick 1991; Sinfield 1997). There followed inevitable clashes of outlook between the older, patrician generation which controlled the new cultural institutions and a younger, meritocratic one which wished to make use of them for social critique: from the 'Angry Young Men' of the late 1950s to the Oxbridge satirists of the early 1960s, associated with the BBC's late night political cabaret, *That Was The Week That Was*. Paradoxically, these conflicts did much to strengthen the position of the new generation: on the one hand, by forcing the re-statement of the principle of artistic independence; on the other hand, by defining the beneficial effect for the national culture as a whole of antagonistic art, whether it was a novel, or a poem, or a stageplay or a television drama (Briggs 1995).

Thatcherism and the arts

During the 1960s and 1970s, rising prosperity and a growing audience for the arts (created in large part by the expansion in the numbers of those entering higher education) greatly enlarged public interest in and spending on the arts; but it also led to an increasing diversification of interests and tastes in both popular and high culture. The BBC contributed to this by launching BBC2 in 1964. (Channel 4, the equivalent in commercial broadcasting, was launched in 1982, after a long debate about its form and funding and about its contribution to the regions.) During the 1960s and 1970s, the Arts Council made grants to fringe-groups (particularly in the regions) as well as to prestigious institutions, a policy which attracted approval from those who welcomed cultural diversity and democratisation and criticism from those who argued that public funds were often being wasted on left-wing and *avant-garde* activity of little aesthetic merit (Witts 1998).

The election in 1979 of Margaret Thatcher as Prime Minister brought a fundamental change not simply to state funding for the arts (which was not only severely reduced but brought under direct government control) but also to the notion that the arts had anything to contribute to national morale or self-consciousness. In particular, the idea (current since 1945) that the arts provided an indispensable national forum – in which current views of the world could be questioned or contested and through which new views could be disseminated – was rejected as the self-serving justification of a subsidised left-wing elite (Appleyard 1984; Hewison 1995; Sinfield 1997).

The new government suggested that the arts should rely not upon public subsidies but upon market forces. On the one hand, leading institutions should look to corporate sponsorship to compensate for the reduction in public funding; on the other, those who had once relied upon public subsidy to promote experimental work would now have to secure an audience by providing what was popular (Bradley 1998). The National Theatre (which in the 1970s had mounted some of the most adventurous theatre of the postwar period) now staged popular American musicals, while art galleries and museums marketed themselves as 'leisure experiences'. The Victoria and Albert Museum even promoted itself as 'an ace Caff with quite a nice museum attached' (Marwick 1991: 145).

During the 1980s, many new galleries and museums were opened (often with the intention of 're-branding' a city or town), while the numbers of those attending museums, galleries, theatres and the cinema increased, not least because television, newspapers and the radio gave wider coverage to exhibitions, plays and films (Bradley 1998). For some, these changes represented a concerted attack on the moral and critical function of the arts, often in the name of the crudest and most philistine populism (Shaw 1987); for others, they recognised that state funding preserved a narrowly class-based culture far removed either from the diversity of cultural expression or the diversification of audiences. In the 1940s, high culture had largely been the preserve of the cultivated middle-class male; by the 1980s, it was open to a wide audience of critical and well-informed con-sumers seeking recreation as well as information (Marwick 1991; Taylor 1999).

New cultures, new audiences

Often those who otherwise had no sympathy with Thatcherism were unwilling to defend what they saw as the class-based privileges of publicly funded high culture in Britain. Why, some asked, should opera receive state funding when pop music did not? Was not British popular culture – from the Beatles to punk – the distinctive achievement of postwar British culture (Bradley 1998)? The counter-culture of the 1960s had unsettled not only the old hierar-chies between the elite and the popular but also those between the arts themselves, so that photography began to have the same attention paid to it as painting, while painting was challenged by conceptual and performance art. Certainly, the success of the commercial radio stations established under the Thatcher government showed that there was no longer one homogeneous audience satisfied by one or two broadcasting or television channels.

Responding to new technologies, the Thatcher government awarded licences for satellite broadcasting to two commercial com-panies, BSB and Sky-TV (which it later allowed to merge to form

BSkyB in contravention of its own policies) and licensed a third commercial channel, Channel 5. Some had hoped that Channel 5 would be a public service or 'educational channel' attached to the Open University but like BSkyB, it has provided an output made up almost exclusively of American series, American films and sport.

What lay behind the government's support for these new developments was an open hostility to the BBC, which during the 1980s came under sustained pressure from the government, particularly over its treatment of Northern Ireland (Bradley 1998). Through its power to set the level of the licence fee, the government (by reducing its resources) forced the BBC to make fundamental changes to the way it operates, with the result that many programmes are no longer made by the BBC's permanent staff but are commissioned from independent production companies (Smith and Paterson 1998). For the Thatcher government's supporters, the government's approach brought a new efficiency to the BBC; to its detractors, it represented a conscious attempt to dismantle the Corporation, in part to free government from an immensely powerful restraint, in part to make possible the sale of the BBC to commercial organisations sympathetic to the Conservative party.

The election of a Labour government in 1997 has seen an end to the immediate threat to the BBC and an increase in the level of public funding for the arts, but the Labour government, like its predecessor, clearly views the generous proceeds of the National Lottery (established in 1994) as a substitute for rather than a supplement to long-term government funding.

What roles have publicly funded cultural institutions played in the postwar period? Should they be publicly funded or should the market decide? Or has the market always decided, the idea of a national culture or of national cultural institutions hiding this truth? The three final essays in this volume intervene in this debate. In an essay on the ICA, Nannette Aldred examines the history of three exhibitions, tracing the ways in which a key cultural institution has sought to reflect significant changes in postwar British culture. In a survey of postwar British theatre, Drew Milne questions many of the central postwar assumptions about theatre as a cultural institution and drama as a social practice. In an essay on the essentially marginal status of poetry in postwar British culture, Andrew Crozier explores the links between canon-formation and marketing.

Bibliography

General studies on cultural institutions and the postwar settlement

Appleyard, B. (1984) *The Culture Club: Crisis in the Arts*, London: Faber.

Blake, A. (1996) "Re-placing British music," in M. Nava and A. O'Shea (eds), *Modern Times: Reflections on a Century of English Modernity*, London: Routledge: 208–38.

—— (1997) *The Land Without Music: Music, Culture and Society in Twentieth-Century Britain*, Manchester: Manchester University Press.

Bradley, C. H. J. (1998) *Mrs Thatcher's Cultural Policies: 1979–1990. A Comparative Study of the Globalized Cultural System*, New York: Columbia University Press/ Boulder Social Science Monographs.

Briggs, A. (1995) *The History of Broadcasting in the United Kingdom, vol. 5: Competition*, Oxford: Oxford University Press.

Carpenter, H. (1996) *The Envy of the World: Fifty Years of the BBC Third Programme and Radio Three, 1946–1996*, London: Weidenfeld and Nicolson.

Dworkin, D. (1997) *Cultural Marxism in Postwar Britain: History, the New Left and the Origins of Cultural Studies*, Durham N.C. : Duke University Press.

Ford, B. (ed.) (1987) *The Cambridge Guide to the Arts in Britain, vol. 9: Since the Second World War*, Cambridge: Cambridge University Press.

Fyrth, H. J. (ed.) (1995) *Labour's Promised Land? Culture and Society in Labour Britain, 1945–51*, London: Lawrence and Wishart.

Garlake, M. (1998) *New Art, New World: British Art in Postwar Society*, New Haven and London: Yale University Press.

Harris, J. S. (1970) *Government Patronage of the Arts in Great Britain*, Chicago: University of Chicago Press.

Hayes, N. and Hill, J. (eds) (1999) *'Millions Like Us'? British Culture in the Second World War*, Liverpool: Liverpool University Press.

Hewison, R. (1981) *In Anger: Culture in the Cold War, 1945–60*, London: Weidenfeld and Nicolson.

—— (1986) *Too Much: Art and Society in the Sixties, 1960–1975*, London: Methuen.

—— (1995) *Culture and Consensus: England, Art and Politics since 1940*, London: Methuen.

Marwick, A. (1991) *Culture in Britain since 1945*, Oxford: Blackwell.

McKibbin, R. (1998) *Classes and Cultures: England, 1918–51*, Oxford: Oxford University Press.

Minihan, J. (1977) *The Nationalization of Culture: The Development of State Subsidies to theArts in Great Britain*, London: Hamish Hamilton.

Shaw, R. (1987) *The Arts and the People*, London: Jonathan Cape.

Sinclair, A. (1995) *Arts and Cultures: The History of the 50 Years of the Arts Council of Great Britain*, London: Sinclair-Stevenson.

Sinfield, A. (1997) *Literature, Politics and Culture in Postwar Britain*, 2nd edn, London: Athlone.

Smith, A. and Paterson, R. (eds) (1998) *Television: An International History*, 2nd edn, Oxford: Oxford University Press.

Taylor, B. (1999) *Art for the Nation: Exhibitions and the London Public, 1747–2001*, Manchester: Manchester University Press.

Witts, R. (1998) *Artist Unknown: An Alternative History of the Arts Council*, London: Little, Brown.

Chapter 7

Art in postwar Britain
A short history of the ICA

Nannette Aldred

Visual culture holds an ambiguous place in British life. It is everywhere but we don't like talking about it, we are suspicious of it and yet at times it has epitomised British success and confidence. (Especially Pop Art in Harold Wilson's sixties, the significance of the Saatchis as collectors in the 'Thatcher years' and the recent rise of artists who have used the notion of 'enterprise culture' to promote their work through well publicised events like the warehouse shows associated with young artists from Goldsmiths' College in the late 1980s, and who have subsequently been associated with the establishment of BritArt as a popular cultural force). Often its success or notoriety runs alongside pop music and youth culture and provides a similar focus for 'moral panic': here I am thinking of Peter Blake's cover for the Beatles' 'LSD' *Sergeant Pepper* album, Jamie Reid's work with the Sex Pistols and the rise of a 'star' like Damien Hirst, a sort of Jarvis Cocker with dead cows. We do not like discussing art, but the British art college system as implemented following the Coldstream Report of 1960, coinciding with the opening up of higher education, has provided an opportunity for creative work that has not, until recently, been bound by specific 'learning outcomes'.

As I am writing this piece, an enormously successful 'blockbuster' exhibition of Cézanne's paintings sells tickets through theatre booking agencies. It is interesting to remind ourselves that a Cézanne exhibition would still have been controversial in the popular press at the end of the war. Architecture, design and the built environment became part of the *inter bellum* dialogue about the quality of life, and the place of modernism was debated within discourses about public health. Those discussions coincided with the immense rise of popular visual experience in the cinema. More recently advertising, the relation between word and image, medium and message has been identified in popular

Plate 7.1   *40,000 Years of Modern Art,* December 1948 exhibition in the
basement of the Academy Cinema, Oxford Street, London.
The highlight of the show, which juxtaposed work mainly
from the Anthropological Collection of Brighton Museum
and Art Gallery with work from the twentieth century, was
'Les Demoiselles d'Avignon' which Alfred Barr had lent to
his friend Roland Penrose from the Museum of Modern Art
in New York.
Reproduced courtesy of the *Architectural Review*

cultural analysis as something that the British are 'good at'. It is generally accepted that the second half of the twentieth century has seen the
rise of the visual at the expense of the verbal and the charting of that
rise has often expressed iconophobia: anxiety about the power of the
image and its accessibility as part of 'mass' culture.

This short essay will concentrate on the history of the ICA (The
Institute of Contemporary Arts) in London as a way of focusing on a
number of diverse issues in visual art of the postwar period. I intend to
consider the ICA's role in postwar Britain not because it has necessarily been at the centre, although I would argue it often has, but because
it allows me to consider art works and events in a theoretical context
at some key moments in British visual culture. The ICA was committed to the contemporary and to contextualising art in terms of ideas,
and so served to focus debates about art and could be seen as a cultural

project aimed at breaking down the fact that we don't like talking about 'visual culture'.[1]

> We wanted a sort of a cross between the Museum of Modern Art in New York and the café life in Paris with all its loose connections. I was surprised at how insular Britain had become after the war, especially in the visual arts.[2]

The ICA was an educational charity whose aim was to support contemporary art and artists. Established in 1947, it fulfilled a long-term aim of one of its founders, Herbert Read the critic and curator. Read's idea for an arts centre was revived after the war through discussions with Roland Penrose, the son of an industrialist, who had enjoyed an avant garde lifestyle in pre-war Paris, hanging about with members of the surrealist group, occasionally producing pieces of his own and buying the work of others associated with the movement. Penrose had enjoyed Paris 'café society' in the 1930s and recognised the importance of an informal meeting place for the development of a critical understanding of new ideas in art. I shall consider the Institution's self-identification as a space dedicated to the professional development of the artist working in postwar Britain and the artist's relationship with work produced in other centres like Paris and New York.

In what follows I indicate some of the areas of cultural debate and artistic innovation in which the ICA has been involved. I give particular attention to three events, not necessarily the biggest, best received or best attended exhibitions, but events that span thirty-five years of art in postwar Britain and which seem to have some purchase on current debates and subsequent work. They are the commission for the Memorial to the Unknown Political Prisoner and the exhibitions *When Attitude becomes Form* and *The Thin Black Line*.

In the introduction to the catalogue of a 1950 exhibition, *Aspects of British Art*, Peter Watson wrote:

> A mixed exhibition in a country where there is no state direction of the arts is likely to give an impression, if not of chaos, of a frivolous lack of conformity. The national traditions of some fifty years ago have given way to a virtually world-wide vocabulary comprising, in addition to all the publicised art movements of the first half of the century and the more important influences of the great individual artists, the whole range of world culture from cave to Sung painting, from primitive to contemporary tropical

Plate 7.2 ICA installation shot of the members' room showing (right)
        'Abstract 1950' by Victor Pasmore and (left) 'Roman
        Window' (1950) by Michael Ayrton
Reproduced courtesy of the *Architectural Review*

cultures; together with microscopy, kinetics, crystallography,
automatism, child art, the art of the insane, the cosmology of the
physicists. In each country this common extension of sources has
stimulated a dozen or so lively tendencies, all justifiably claiming
to be modern and all more or less mutually antagonistic and
mutually stimulating – one aspect of our present society. . . . Here

is a stimulating and valuable comparison between personalities, styles and generations: a kind of token in miniature of the intentions of the ICA.

(Watson, *Aspects of British Art*, 1950)

This statement seems to set the debate over postwar British visual culture: the change from a class-based cultural economy, the breakdown of hegemonic modernism (if it ever existed), consensus and an academic hierarchy, the awareness of a range of different voices and cultures, the place of art in education and the unconscious life, and the relationship between culture and the state. It also suggests the complexity of an association between nation, land and culture which had been marked in neo-Romanticism[3] during the war and which was being promoted as the theme of the forthcoming Festival of Britain. It was, in fact, written for the opening of the ICA's first exhibition in its gallery in the original premises in Dover St, London (although it had held regular shows in the basement of the Academy Cinema in Oxford Street since 1947). (See Plates 7.1–7.3)

Watson was one of the last of the prewar personal patrons of the arts; a significant figure in the current art world, he was also on the committee of the ICA. In discussions about the role of art and visual culture in the years following the depression and the disappearance of traditional patronage, Herbert Read along with so many other commentators in the 1930s had been exercised by fundamental questions about the role of culture in society. There was a consensus that art was 'civilising' in some way and that it should be supported in a modern society. During the 1930s art also seemed to offer an opportunity for a radical intervention into the social. Penrose owned the London Gallery and had worked with Read on the 1936 *International Exhibition of Surrealist Art.*[4]

Surrealism as a theoretical practice (as opposed to a style as it was often discussed and considered) argued for the power of culture to change society through questioning ideas of 'common sense', encouraging practitioners and consumers alike to reconsider cultural practice, art as ritual, and art in its relation to sexuality, to society, to the production of objects and the significance of theory. It also considered art at the limits of physical endurance, as an expression of the unconscious and as just good fun, not merely as pleasant objects on gallery walls. Surrealism's radicalism was evidenced in a 1938 performance in Hyde Park by Penrose, Julian Trevelyan and others wearing masks of Joseph Chamberlain made by F. E. McWilliam.

Plate 7.3 Installation of an ICA exhibition in Dover Street, showing a domestic scale of display and the characteristic juxtaposition of a range of different objects. The large painting on the right is a version of 'The Conflict' by Merlyn Evans
Reproduced courtesy of the *Architectural Review*

I start with the surrealist 'revolution' and its manifestation in London not only to set the scene for postwar art but also to attempt to draw out its implications for the subsequent work for which the ICA has been (in)famous. Other ongoing formations like the social realists, the Artists International Association and workers' painting groups had emerged alongside similar groupings within other cultural forms including film and photography, architecture and design. Was art to educate, inform, entertain or revolutionise? What was socially relevant? The war interrupted rather than resolved these issues. Read wanted to ensure that British art should have the advantage of being part of this debate.

The end of the war saw the airing of another important debate, in various sites, about the appropriate interaction between art, the market and the state. As an anarchist, Read was concerned about the increased intervention from the state that came with 'welfare' culture although he promoted the importance of art for members of that state. The ICA relied on sponsorship from wealthy individuals like Watson, Penrose and E. C. (Peter) Gregory, the printer and publisher. Money from the recently formed Arts Council was available but not sufficient and the ICA always relied on members' subscriptions and other forms of private support. They wanted to complement State provision, to be more daring and innovative, avoid the vagaries of the free market and negotiate a space between the two. Read was aware of the significance of these debates in a larger economic sphere.

In a 1961 proposal for *A Festival of Contemporary Art*, Read put forward a paper on the economic significance of cultural tourism (by that time a growth industry) but which he argued should be 'a pilgrimage of grace' rather than 'an undisciplined scramble', a humanist activity rather than merely an opportunity to 'consume' culture. He was one of many to be concerned with the future role of Britain (specifically in the cultural field) in the postwar settlement.

It was the avant garde, the cutting edge of art practice that interested Read. Berlin and Paris were the two centres before the war and the arrival of European modernist artists into Britain (particularly Hampstead where Read lived) suggested that London would inherit this role.[5] Apart from their practice there was significance in the cultural theories that came with them, particularly artists and teachers from the Bauhaus. As we have seen, before the war modernism had been considered a radical political statement as well as an artistic practice, but with architecture as with painting, modernism was taken up by the Establishment as a style rather than a political practice. The Arts Council promoted its own version of English modernism, for instance in its support for visual art during the Festival of Britain but that event had not attracted the international interest that was first anticipated.

One way of ensuring visibility for London as the new cultural centre was to hold an international competition for a memorial sculpture suitable for the postwar world. Such a piece would be monumental in scale and intention and accordingly a competition was organised under the auspices of the ICA. The idea reflected the significance of British sculpture; of all the artists who had achieved prominence during the war and in the immediate postwar period, Henry Moore was probably the most notable. Read had known Moore in Yorkshire and had become a significant commentator on his work. A particular interest in British sculpture was also nurtured by the highly successful shows of sculpture in the open air seen in the Festival and organised by the London County Council, subsequently by other local authorities, and held in local parks.

Apart from the significance of Moore through his work and radio interviews, debates about sculpture were held in public discussions, broadcasts and publications.[6] The LCC organised well-attended

Plate 7.4 Photograph of the Festival of Britain show 1941–51. Works include Henry Moore's maquette for 'Upright Internal and External Forms' (1951), Francis Bacon's 'Head VI' of 1949, Keith Vaughan's 'Interior with Nude Figures' (1949) and work by John Minton and John Craxton
Reproduced courtesy of the *Architectural Review*

debates at County Hall on the South Bank to consider the role of sculpture within the contemporary built environment. Public art was associated (not always favourably) with the postwar reconstruction of the civic spaces of Britain, often as a way of disguising shoddy materials and compromised architecture but sometimes as an urban spatial event in its own right as well as being the subject of popular interest.

Considering Read's involvement with the ICA and his being associated internationally with successful British art, it was appropriate that the international competition for a monument to 'The Unknown Political Prisoner' would be organised from there. The more surprising aspect of the event was the scale of its ambition given the meagre and irregular resources that were coming into the ICA. The money for such a large scale sculpture competition was always the subject of some controversy and it now seems clear that it was financed by the CIA under its policy of cultural imperialism through the Congress for Cultural Freedom.[7]

The competition attracted the attention of next-generation sculptors, some of whom had represented Britain in the Venice Biennale of the same year. Read had dubbed the work the 'geometry of fear' in its use of 'modern' industrial materials, iron and steel scaffolding, and its move away from Moore's humanism. It also seemed to articulate the angst of the postwar existential moment. The competition was immensely successful and the shortlisted maquettes were shown at the Tate Gallery in March 1953. The winner was Reg Butler whose work evoked Calvary in its organisation of space and its depiction of the instruments of torture and incarceration. Its monumentality lay in its scale, the human figures dwarfed by the ruined tower of steel girders with its tallest tower still able to suggest a soaring human spirit against inhuman experiences. Unsurprisingly given the theme and proposed siting (see Plate 7.5), the Russians refused to take part in the competition and, whilst on display, Butler's maquette was vandalised. This incident seemed to epitomise worry about US involvement in contemporary British culture to such an extent that Alfred Barr from MoMA (the Museum of Modern Art in New York) who had come to London to judge the competition thought better of giving a lecture on 'Art under Nazi and Soviet Dictatorships'.[8] The monument to 'The Unknown Political Prisoner' was never built due to lack of finance and loss of political will during the Cold War, despite quite detailed discussions about its proposed siting next to the new wall and overlooking East Berlin.[9]

The event offers a way of identifying the position of London in relation to the international art world in the early 1950s. The competition attracted a total of 3,500 artists from fifty-seven countries but the covert funding was from the US; Britain seemed to have a place on the international art stage, and, not for the last time, its press seemed unsupportive. Alfred Barr wrote to *The Times*:

> Wake up, Englishmen! For the first time in your history you have a group of young sculptors who have won international recognition, first, informally at the Venice Biennale last summer, now in London. . . .
>
> Whether these sculptors flourish or wither will depend in large part on the encouragement, understanding and patronage afforded them by the British people and their privileged leaders.
>
> (*The Times*, 23 March 1953)

The Board of the ICA addressed the issue of funding at a time when American capital was flooding the markets. Some members of the management of the ICA wanted to distance it from too close an association

Plate 7.5 Reg Butler, photomontage showing working model for a monument to 'The Unknown Political Prisoner' on the proposed site, the Humboldt Höhe, West Berlin

Reproduced courtesy of Rosemary Butler

with the Americans and the Congress for Cultural Freedom; minutes of ICA meetings show concern about the ethics of accepting badly needed support from the USA, and about how closely they should follow the model of MoMA, New York in their organisation. They show a real tension between the ICA wanting to continue to support radical European modernism and the move towards a reliance on corporate sponsorship, especially after the appointment of Anthony Kloman as Director of Public Relations. Kloman had been the USA cultural attaché in Europe.

The ICA modelled its fundraising activities on the highly successful Museum of Modern Art although it could not rely on trading hard currency for cultural capital in the same way.[10] Read's commitment was to the idea of a national culture, which in his opinion had to be informed by knowledge of and an engagement with larger, transnational debates. The ICA aimed to be internationalist, to bring the best of contemporary art to a British (that is, London) audience and to not exclude the recently formed New Commonwealth from this internationalism. The ICA also directly addressed the question of what was taste in the postwar democratic consensus of Labourite Britain and at a time when mass or popular increasingly meant 'Americanisation' (meaning, in fact, from the USA).

In the early 1950s there was a general concern about the infiltration of American goods, especially cultural products whether art, music, film or comics. For many commentators, British culture expressed civilisation in its humanism and respect for tradition. Anxieties about changing values and the democratisation of culture were played out through references to Americanisation. British sculptors had been acclaimed at Venice (which was highly significant in the European art world) and Read had an international reputation as an art commentator and critic. Partly through its identification with the new Commonwealth and an alternative market, Britain was redefining itself before the cultural significance of the USA was wholly apparent. Younger critics associated with the ICA included David Sylvester, John Berger, Richard Hamilton, John McHale and others writers and artists associated with the IG (Independent Group) who were beginning to make a reputation for themselves as commentators on contemporary issues in art.[11]

It has been argued that the art movement, 'Pop', for which British art became famous in the sixties, originated at the ICA through its young 'Independent' Group.[12] Members of the IG were also at the forefront of debates about the relationship between art, design, advertising

Plate 7.6 Installation shot of Victor Burgin's 'Photopath' in the exhibition *When Attitudes become Form: Live in your Head*, ICA 1969

Photograph courtesy of Simon Wilson, Tate Gallery (ICA Archives)

and architecture; about issues around the teaching of art; they engaged with the popular and mass forms of culture and had an early awareness of the new American painting, Abstract Expressionism, that would be so influential in postwar painting. These were artists and critics who finally recognised and celebrated the energy they associated with 'Americanisation' and popular culture, and who were engaged with what they considered to be a continuum of culture (rather than the more traditional view of a pyramid with 'sweetness and light' shining from the top); they provided an intellectual and aesthetic justification for the expanded iconography available to artists associated with 'Pop'.

Although Read and Penrose remained supporters of the European traditions of modernism, the IG was using the ICA in the way in which they had intended, a place to meet other cultural producers, discuss new ideas and have a platform to present them to the public.[13] The group consisted of art critics and historians, architects and planners as well as painters and sculptors. Recent work (Thistlewood 1992: 152–68) has argued that this group of 'rebels' from the original ICA (which included Richard Hamilton and Victor Pasmore who, with others, developed the implications of some of Read's theories of art and its social effect) were responsible for the significant changes in art teaching that influenced not only art but also a more extensive popular cultural scene in the 1960s.[14]

Hamilton was responsible for the exhibition *A Parallel between Art and Life* in 1953, which included photographs of footballers alongside Leonardo's drawings from the Royal Collection; and with Pasmore he organised *An Event*, a 1957 exhibition that relied on games theory to encourage the viewers to participate in the temporal and spatial experience of the exhibition governed by certain game rules and to consider conditions of spectatorship and location, rather than be passive observers of art on walls. In an exhibition of their teaching practice called *The Developing Process* in April–May 1959, they illustrated their attempt to develop a rigorous art training suitable for contemporary theories of art. The process encouraged the student to start with the two-dimensionality of the line, explore further lines to make planes and suggest depth and move into three dimensions through sculpture. The process also allowed for movement into the fourth dimension and so performance. This, combined with an understanding of action painting as process in which the artist's body is an important feature, would provide an aspect of the philosophic underpinning of the next development in sculpture, the use of the artist's own body as sculptural material and the validation of the conceptualisation of the process over the final product.

Since 1950 the ICA had been one site in which it had been possible to combine different art forms (by the late 1960s, when the ICA moved to Carlton House Terrace, the idea that the arts should be brought together in the same venue was the accepted norm with the growth of Arts Labs and Arts Centres), so that, for instance, Pink Floyd could play there with visuals by Mark Boyle, artists and independent film could be combined with performance (or 'happenings' as they were known earlier in the decade) and, later, new video art. There were opportunities for artists and musicians to work together; for the showing of art films by makers like Max Ernst, Hans Richter and Kenneth Anger and happenings orchestrated by Jean Tinguely and Josef Beuys which did seem to fulfil the original aims of the Institute as a meeting place where artists and other cultural workers could exchange ideas.

The early ICA ensured that its exhibitions were put into context by the accompanying symposia or lectures. The influential DIAS (*Destruction in Art* symposium) of 1966 included performances by the Situationist International Group (Blazwick 1989) and the first showing of Yoko Ono's *Number 4* of 1966–7 (the 'bottoms' film) while organiser Gustave Metz was a teacher at Ealing Art School whose students included Pete Townshend (Mellor 1993).

A new art, conceptualism, with its new forms including text and image, its use of the actual, rather than represented, body and landscape and of non-traditional materials was the subject of the 1969 exhibition shown at the ICA, *When Attitudes Become Form: Live in your Head*. Despite the fact that the exhibition did not show objects that could be easily bought and sold and deliberately attempted to combat the use of art as a commodity (in response to the growth of the art market in London in the late 1950s and throughout the west by the 1960s) the exhibition, which was curated in Berne, also relied on extra funding; in this case it came from Philip Morris (Europe) and brought to Britain some of the most interesting artists working in the movement, for instance Josef Beuys from Germany and Robert Smithson from the USA.[15] The exhibition (see Plate 7.6) provided a space for artists working within conceptualism; it brought an international perspective to art being produced in London; and it epitomised a contemporary conflict within the dominant theories of art, particularly between Minimalism and other versions of Modernism, in Europe and the USA. For once London had a place in that debate through the London showing of the exhibition and through commentaries in the serious art press.

At the ICA, the exhibition, which was also informed by a growing interest in ecology and radical politics, included the land artist Richard Long (the only British artist in the Berne show), performance artists Bruce McLean and Gilbert and George, and photographer-theorist Victor Burgin. Charles Harrison, an art historian, critic and future member of the conceptual art producers *Art &*

Language curated *When Attitudes Become Form* in its British manifesta-tion.[16] It was appropriate that the exhibition took place at the ICA. It was a ruthlessly avant-garde show; often refusing easy visual pleasure to its audience but presenting a serious and rigorous investigation of art as idea and process. It included works, concepts, processes, situations and information:

> The effect of work like this is to stretch the range of our imagina-tion and our conceptions. . . . We have to leave our options open, to pose questions to which the answers are not always predictable, to which answers may come from a different language . . . sug-gesting a different grammar – a different system, a changed consciousness.
>
> (Harrison, *When Attitudes Become Form*, 1969: Introduction)

To a certain extent conceptualism also offered a place for women to develop their own language of art. As Griselda Pollock and Roszika Parker argued when talking about traditional art school training and the definition of art, art itself needed to be redefined in order to accom-modate women's concerns.[17] Although *When Attitudes Become Form* was still predominantly a male art show, the media that it included were those taken up later by artists attempting to work in non-sexist practices. The validation of photography and video as artistic media encouraged the use of alternative practices that did not have the same history associated with more traditional materials, forms of representa-tion and their associated regimes of power.

It seemed that art would become less concerned with individuals and style and more with theories of representation. One such example was Mary Kelly's epic work *Post Partum Document* which was an imag-inative and radical attempt to represent the mother and child relationship informed by Lacanian theories of the subject.

It was not only women's maternal desire that was investigated during the 1970s (coinciding with a decision to publish a series of the-oretical *Readers*) but also the place of desire in the social world (harking back to those original Surrealist investigations). Mary Kelly's exhibition had caused an outcry in the popular press ('After the Tate's bricks on show at the ICA . . . dirty nappies' was the *Evening Standard* headline for 14 October 1976, the bricks referring to Carl André's *Equivalent VIII*). The following exhibition, *Prostitution* (organised by Cosey Fanni Tutti and Genesis P. Orridge) led to questions in the House, a call by Nicholas Fairbairn MP for the Arts Council to be 'wound up forthwith', and an article in the *Guardian* was also concerned with the use of public money:

> Now we are getting the lid off the maggot factory. Here at the expense of the taxpayer, the British Council apparently sends these spurious and bogus destroyers around Europe to destroy the values of Western civilisation.[18]
>
> (*Guardian*, 21 October 1976)

Only Emmanuel Cooper in the *Morning Star* and Caroline Tisdall in the more specialist arts pages of the *Guardian* seriously engaged with the debate that the exhibition was designed to encourage. Tisdall put the show into a European context and used it to demonstrate the refusal of the British critical establishment, the popular press and the public to engage seriously with issues within the avant garde and around sexuality, the body, performance, art and commerce that the exhibition addressed. For her it seemed to prove that the British press was becoming more isolated from critical cultural issues and often using such issues to construct an idea of 'Britishness' that was different from this sort of thing. Once again the discussion (as Tisdall pointed out) became far more pressing when it seemed that public money had been used to fund the event.

> Shocking and mocking [two aspects of the anti-avant garde syndrome] are both quickly linked up to the trump card, and that of course is the taxpayer's money that prevented the nappy incident, also at the ICA, hitting the headlines last week. Mary Kelly's serious and non-publicity seeking investigation of her child's development . . . was modest in scale and not obviously financed by public or state bodies, [so] there was no fury to be unleashed. Otherwise the treatment she got was much the same on a smaller scale. She had touched a taboo subject: shit, like sex, is still not acceptable in the visual arts.
>
> (*Arts Guardian*, undated in ICA archive)

Equally distasteful to the popular press was the idea of the then Director-General of the Arts Council, Roy Shaw, who 'mingled among young men wearing lipstick, multicoloured hair and nail varnish at the elegant ICA gallery' (*Daily Mail*, 19 October 1976). When the ICA invited an established artist, Allen Jones to exhibit his reproductions of women's contorted bodies made into 'furniture' in 1978, it was the feminist movement that was outraged. As usual a symposium took place to discuss the controversy and in 1978 *Sexism in the Arts* was followed by a series of talks on *Women as Artists* with critics like Lisa Tickner, Judith Williamson, Germaine Greer, Jo Spence and Eva Figes. In response to the issues raised by a major photographic exhibition *Camerawork* on the theme of 'Woman' a show called *Women's Images of Men* (1980–1) was produced by women artists.[19] The ICA had also been the first major institution to show photography,[20] including the controversial Robert Mapplethorpe show in 1983.

In contrast to the other exhibitions and events I have discussed, *The Thin Black Line* was literally marginal (it was hung along the wall of the café), not a high profile, international event but an event whose importance was recognised both at the time and subsequently. The exhibition was curated by a young black artist, Lubaina Himid, who had recently completed her M.A., *Young Black Artists in Britain Today*,[21] and had subsequently been involved in a number of events whose aim was to raise the profile of and develop a critical language to discuss contemporary British black art.

Since its early days the ICA had aimed to support Commonwealth artists although it wasn't until *The Thin Black Line* (1985) that it actively engaged with the specific issues of ethnicity. Non-European art was regularly included in the programme, for at least two reasons. One was the significance that the newly formed Commonwealth seemed to hold for the postwar settlement. It provided a ready made and familiar market network and as Rasheed Araeen demonstrates it was identified as offering future developments drawing on a sense of internationalism in postwar Britain:

> London had never been an international art market like Paris. It was this consciousness of marginality and the hope that London would develop into an international cultural centre within the independent Commonwealth that created a euphoric spirit among a section of British society that welcomed the arrival in England of artists from abroad.[22]
>
> (Araeen 1989: 12)

The other reason was that the roots of Modernism and Surrealism lay in notions of the 'primitive'. This created a conflict in the way in which non-European became confused with notions of the 'primitive' at the same time Commonwealth artists came to London after the war to work in a centre where they expected to be taken seriously as contemporary artists. However, as Araeen has shown (Araeen 1989) they often found it difficult to break into the London art establishment, and even those that did found their progress blocked by the early 1960s. Read had encouraged a view of art that would transcend difference and lead to peace and lack of conflict.[23]

Colin MacInnes was a member of the ICA who often gave talks there and his enthusiasm for the new cultural experiences offered by the recent black communities as evoked in his books, could offer an insight into the cultural diversity that the ICA seemed to encompass in the early years. In fact his books suggest the energy that the ICA attracted, as the early notes in the archive show. Its talks and events provided a critical platform for a wide cultural analysis as well as reflecting the interest that the members had in 'other' cultures. However, it could be said that the avant garde used other cultures to mark their difference, achieving their avant garde status through that difference.

While an upwardly mobile British working class was moving into model new towns like Harlow (famous for its postwar commissioning of sculpture and other forms of public art), most newly arrived Black British citizens were moving into the poorest accommodation in the inner cities that it had left. Whatever the earlier postwar liberal attitude to Commonwealth artists and Black British citizens, it is clear that by the mid-1960s racist structures could be identified in cultural and social frameworks, and artists who had grown up in Britain were aware of their specific concerns as Black artists.

Young artists Eddie Chambers and Keith Piper, culturally formed in part at least by their experience of the English educational system, curated The *Pan-African Connection* in 1983, and the following year the first national exhibition of Black art was held in Sheffield. Himid's exhibition concentrated on the work of Black (including Afro-Caribbean and Asian, declaring Blackness a political category) women artists: 'We are claiming what is ours and making ourselves visible. We are eleven of the hundreds of creative Black Women in Britain. We are here to stay.'[24] The exhibition covered work in a range of different media including Sonia Boyce working in oil, Brenda Asgard with photography and Himid's witty recycling of Picasso's images appropriating the 'primitive'. The same year saw the publication of a report by the Commission for Racial Equality on *The Arts of Ethnic Minorities*, there were conferences in London and Birmingham and the following year a series of workshops and seminars on 'The black experience' were organised by the Black

Visual Arts Forum. *The Other Story*, curated by Araeen, opened at the Hayward Gallery and toured to Wolverhampton and Manchester from 1989 to 1990.

As Araeen has shown, there are different versions of the story of art in postwar Britain; most would mention figures like Francis Bacon and Lucien Freud as immensely significant British artists. Their work could epitomise discussions about the relationship between abstraction and figuration and between realism and painterly surface, highly significant issues in art since the war. Concentrating on the ICA and the place of the avant garde has allowed me to discuss British art and its theories in relation to the art promoted in other centres like New York and Paris, rather than attempt to construct some underlying notion of 'Britishness'. Serious art offers a place for cultures and nations to artic-ulate a sense of identity but it needs larger cultural support (for instance through media coverage); there are dangers of not engaging with the contemporary and by looking backwards, as Read and Penrose were aware, of being marginalised, provincial and conservative in outlook. This is an account of the attempt to give art significance in national culture.

In the early days, the ICA maintained links with Europe; later, it was a place that engaged with the new cultures associated in particular with the USA (with the scale of its painting and the popular appeal of its culture). More recently, the ICA has held exhibitions and conferences and produced publications that have discussed Britain's contemporary cultural identity in a post-modern world. In a culture whose national identity seems to be defined through its close relationship to the written or performed word, the ICA has attempted to position itself between the word and image and encourage the use of a critical language about the latter. It established itself as the 'other' to dominant British culture.

Notes

1 See Araeen (1989), Royal Academy of Arts (1987), Whitechapel Art Gallery (1981) and the period and movement-based works like Mellor (1987, 1993).
2 Roland Penrose interviewed about the aims of the ICA in the archives, dated 1977.
3 See Mellor (1987) for the fullest account of this movement.
4 Read had argued that the roots of Surrealism lay in a British tradition that included William Blake and Lewis Carroll.
5 Harrison (1981).
6 For a fuller discussion see Richard Calvocoressi, 'Public sculpture in the 1950s', in Whitechapel Art Gallery (1981).

7 See Burstow (1989) and (1997) and the interview between Dorothy
Morland and Joan Edwards in the transcription of a tape in the ICA
archives, where it was clear that very few of those involved with the ICA
knew about this until much later. Penrose probably knew at the time as he
had personal links with MoMA, partly through his American wife, Lee
Miller.

This is not the place for a full discussion of the involvement of the CIA
in funding cultural events that articulated concepts like liberalism, nation
and cultural identity, but Britain was targeted in the early fifties. The
country had turned to the Right after its immediate postwar flirtation with
Socialism, which had established the Arts Council of Great Britain as well
as National Insurance and health schemes. For further information see
Burstow's (1997) very full and fascinating account.

8 See the ICA archives in the Dorothy Morland papers: Box 19 (1952–55).
A letter from Alfred Barr suggests that it would have been interpreted as
more American anti-Communist propaganda 'although it would have
been fun to give this talk, especially if the New Statesman and Nation
crowd could be there. I am still eager for a crack at them, but not under
these circumstances.'

9 Since I first wrote this essay Robert Burstow (1997) has produced a fascinating account of the whole incident, I am indebted to Peter Mills for drawing
it to my attention and to Robert Burstow for discussion on his research.

10 In a letter from Read to fund-raiser, Lady Norton, in the ICA Archives
(1958):

> I think we have a totally different social set-up, and will have to use
> entirely different methods. In the States they have a snobbery of
> wealth which really does not exist here and I cannot imagine rich
> English people paying large sums merely to be called vice-presidents,
> or other honorific titles. I think our policy in respect of membership
> should be to get the widest possible number with an egalitarian basis.

11 Sylvester had been in Paris between 1947–50 exploring existential theory
as a writer about art. He acted as a direct link between recent French
painting and the pre-war work that was more familiar to the older
members of the ICA committee. That awareness informed his significant
writing on Francis Bacon.

Berger resigned from the Board after a disagreement about the status of
social realism as the most appropriate form of socially committed (or political) art. The debate about realisms, and abstraction versus figurative have
been the underlying tensions between much of twentieth century art (in
Britain and elsewhere). He later made the immensely influential Ways of
Seeing in 1972 for BBC television and produced the associated book.

12 As my space is so limited in this account I have chosen not to focus on
Pop, although for many that would be seen as the British (English)
movement in postwar British art. There are many commentators on the
movement: see for example RA (1991), Melly (1970), Lippard (1970).
The ICA was also invited to select a show of contemporary British artists
for the Great British Art Show at Macey's department store in 1968.

13 See ICA (1990).

14 See Frith and Horne (1987) and Walker (1987).
15 They argued in their introduction to the catalogue that new ideas were also the province of corporate business and distanced themselves from the idea of art as investment.
16 For a fuller account of the group see Harrison (1991). Harrison was then deputy editor of *Studio International* and aimed to make it a publication that would take its place within an international framework. He later designed an immensely influential series of accounts of twentieth-century art for Open University courses including *Modern Art and Modernism*.
17 Parker and Pollock (1981). Their argument was in response to the challenge issued by Germaine Greer (1979) in *The Obstacle Race* whereby she accused art historians of refusing to consider women artists seriously. Parker and Pollock's fuller analysis discussed art as an institution and included the education of artists, the critical establishment and the gallery system as items for serious scrutiny and argued that merely finding a few forgotten women artists would not be sufficient for a feminist account of art and its history.
18 'It was revealed today that Orridge was given £52.50 in 1974 by the British Council for a show in Germany', *Evening Standard*, 20 October 1976.
19 Interestingly, part of the associated programme of events to coincide with this exhibition with work by Avedon, Penn and Snowden among others, was a showing of Antonioni's film *Blow Up* and Michael Powell's *Peeping Tom*. Theorists in discussions of the power relations and the gaze; voyeurism, eroticism and violence have subsequently used both films. The show also featured recorded music by Billie Holliday, Kathleen Ferrier, Aretha Franklin, Juliette Greco and Edith Piaf.
20 Sue Butler who later established the Photographer's Gallery was largely responsible (I am grateful to David Mellor for pointing this out). There had also been a tradition at the ICA for taking up photographic exhibitions from MoMA which had had a photographic department since 1940.
21 In the cultural history department of the Royal College of Art.
22 Araeen (1989: 12). Araeen charts the fall in fortune of Commonwealth artists who were welcomed and advanced their careers within the British art establishment from the late 1940s to a state of being virtually ignored during the 1960s when Britain became culturally and economically dominated by the USA.
23 An unfinished and unacknowledged history in the ICA archives suggests that 'the interchange of the arts and cultural activities has been one of the first concerns of the ICA, since it is realised that, particularly at the present time, this is one of the most powerful means of understanding throughout the world'.
24 Unpaginated catalogue for *The Thin Black Line* exhibition.

Bibliography

Araeen, R. (1989) *The Other Story: Afro-Asian Artists in Post-war Britain*, catalogue for a travelling exhibition, November 1989–June 1990, originating from the Hayward Gallery, South Bank Centre, London.

Agard, B. (1989) *The Thin Black Line*, Hebden Bridge: Urban Fox Press.

Blazwick, I. (ed.) (1989) *A Situationist Scrapbook: An Endless Passion . . . and Endless Banquet*, London: ICA.

Burstow, R. (1989) 'Butler's competition project for a monument to *The Unknown Political Prisoner*: abstraction and cold war politics', *Art History* 12: 4.

—— (1997) 'The limits of modernist art as a weapon of the cold war: reassessing the unknown patron of the *Monument to the Unknown Political Prisoner'*, *Oxford Art Journal* 20: 1.

Coldstream Report (1960) *First Report of the National Advisory Council on Art Education by William M. Coldstream*, London: HMSO.

Commission for Racial Equality (1985) *The Arts of Ethnic Minorities: Status and Funding: A Research Report*, London, Commission for Racial Equality (Ctrl. no. 0907920519).

Frith, S. and Horne, H. (1987) *Art into Pop*, London: Methuen.

Greer, G. (1979) *The Obstacle Race: The Fortunes of Women Painters and their Work*, London: Secker.

Guilbaut, S. (1983) *How New York Stole the Idea of Modern Art: Abstract Expressionism, Freedom and the Cold War*, Chicago: University of Chicago Press.

Harrison, C. (1981) *English art and modernism 1900–1939*, London: Allen Lane.

—— (1991) *Essays on Art and Language*, Oxford: Blackwell.

Hopkins, H. (1964) *The New Look: A Social History of the Forties and Fifties in Britain*, London: Secker/ Readers' Union.

Institute of Contemporary Arts (1961) *A Festival of Contemporary Art*, in ICA documents, Tate Gallery Archives.

—— (1969) *When Attitudes become Form: Works, Concepts, Processes, Situations, Information*, catalogue of an exhibition 28 September–27 October 1969, ed. C. Harrison, London: ICA.

—— (1990) *The Independent Group: Postwar Britain and the Aesthetics of Plenty*, catalogue of a travelling exhibition, February 1990–August 1991 originating at the Institute, ed. D. Robbins, London: ICA.

King, J. (1990) *The Last Modern: A Life of Herbert Read*, London: Weidenfeld and Nicolson.

Lippard, L. (ed.) (1970) *Pop Art*, London: Thames and Hudson.

MacInnes, C. (1985) *The Colin MacInnes Omnibus (contains City of Spades: Absolute Beginners: Mr Love and Justice)*, London: Allison and Busby.

Massey, A. (1995) *The Independent Group: Modernism and Mass Culture in Britain, 1945–1959*, Manchester: Manchester University Press.

Mayor Gallery (1986) *British Surrealism: 50 Years On*, exhibition held in London, March–April.

Mellor, D. A. (ed.) (1987) *A Paradise Lost: The NeoRomantic Imagination in Britain 1935–55*, catalogue of an exhibition at the gallery, London: Barbican Art Gallery/Lund Humphries.

—— (1993) *The Sixties Art Scene in London*, catalogue of an exhibition at the gallery, 11 March–13 June 1993, London: Barbican Art Gallery/ Phaidon.

Melly, G. (1970) *Revolt into Style: The Pop Arts in Britain*, London: Allen Lane.

Parker, P. and Pollock, P. (1981) *Old Mistresses: Women, Art and Ideology*, London: Routledge.

Penrose, R. (1981) *Scrapbook 1900–1981*, London: Thames and Hudson.

Read, B. and Thistlewood, D. (eds) (1993) *Herbert Read: A British vision of World Art*, catalogue of an exhibition in the galleries, 25 November 1993–5 February 1994, Leeds: Leeds City Art Gallery/ Henry Moore Foundation.

Royal Academy of Arts (1987) *British Art in the Twentieth Century*, exhibition catalogue, ed. S. Compton, London: Royal Academy/Prestel.

—— (1991) *Pop Art*, catalogue for a travelling exhibition, 13 September 1991–14 September: Royal Academy/Weidenfeld.

Sinfield, A. (1989) *Literature, Politics and Culture in Postwar Britain*, Oxford: Blackwell.

Spalding, F. (1986) *British Art since 1900*, London: Thames and Hudson.

Thistlewood, D. (ed.) (1992) *Histories of Art and Design Education: Cole to Coldstream*, Harlow: Longman with the National Society for Education in Art and Design.

Walker, J. A. (1987) *Cross-Overs: Art into Pop/Pop into Art*, London: Comedia.

Watson, P. (1950) 'Introduction', in *Aspects of British Art*, in ICA documents, Tate Gallery Archives.

Whitechapel Art Gallery (1981) *British Sculpture in the Twentieth Century*, catalogue for an exhibition at the Whitechapel Gallery, London, September 1981–January 1982, ed. S. Nairne and N. Serota, London: Whitechapel Art Gallery.

Chapter 8

Drama in the culture industry

British theatre after 1945

Drew Milne

Introduction: the ancient scenery of British theatre

> The conservative essence of the British political drama occupies a
> smaller and smaller stage, and goes on in an ever-dimmer light. In
> the declining spiral each new repetition of the play, although
> advertized by the players as the same, has a new note of hollowness
> or approaching night. Each time the forces capable of extinguish-
> ing the performance move a little closer to the actors and the
> ancient scenery, and loom more noticeably over events.
>
> (Nairn 1981: 58–9)

Tom Nairn's analysis of the twilight of the British State after 1945
involves no reference to modern drama as a literary form. His metaphor
can nevertheless be read as an allegory of the illusions and politics of
contemporary British theatre. Nairn's political and economic analysis
suggests the diminishing relevance of a Shakespearean dramatisation of
the stage of British politics, and suggests the difficulty of applying historical metaphors to contemporary conditions. If the forces
extinguishing performance are off-stage, can the forces of global capitalism be dramatised in terms of protagonists, courtiers, spear-bearers
and grave-diggers? Who are the scriptwriters? Modern British drama
has often been seen as a golden age of playwrighting comparable to
Elizabethan and Jacobean drama. Shakespeare nevertheless remains
the most performed if not most contemporary playwright (Holland
1997). The conflict between dramatic idiom and society takes shape in
British drama amid ongoing funding crises, and through struggles to
transform the theatrical legacies of Shakespeare and the British state.

The failure of British politics to free itself from a Shakespearian imagination of crown and nation finds its most dramatic symptom in the farcical repetition of the British state's ancient scenery. The 1953 coronation of Elizabeth II provided a pageant of neo-Elizabethan pomp and circumstance. Shown on television, the event also marked the market penetration of television as a 'mass' medium, politically central in the dramatisation of state, church and society as a theatrical spectacle. For the first time a British audience watched itself as an imaginary nation and 'mass' (Williams 1983). By the 1990s this unholy alliance of ancient scenery and modern media had elevated the royal family to a soap opera. The domestic tragedies of the House of Windsor may reflect broader social changes, but they are significant primarily as an index of the powerlessness of individuals to resist the domination of mediation by 'the culture industry' (Adorno 1991). Aristocratic protagonists might yet be written out of the nation's script, if only to improve the viewing figures, but many theatres remain 'royal'. Parliament itself was not televised until the 1980s, but similar rhythms in the media spectacle of politics can be discerned. Margaret Thatcher's rise and fall might have been scripted as a Hollywood remake of *Antony and Cleopatra*, co-starring Ronald Reagan, with scenes from the lives of Queens Elizabeth and Victoria. Stage-managed politics and elections are widely felt to be hollow.

A selection of historic and dramatic events reflected in plays suggests a broader picture. The shadow of the Second World War on civilian life is dramatised in Terence Rattigan's *The Deep Blue Sea* (1952), Howard Brenton's *Hitler Dances* (1972) and David Hare's *Plenty* (1978). India's independence (1947–8) and the relation between racism and colonial history form the historical context of David Edgar's *Destiny* (1976) and David Hare's *A Map of the World* (1983). The 1956 Suez fiasco provides a backdrop for John Osborne's *The Entertainer* (1957), and more obliquely in *West of Suez* (1971). The Vietnam War was attacked in the Royal Shakespeare Company's *US* (1966), directed by Peter Brook. Bloody Sunday in Derry and the subsequent cover-up are dramatised in Brian Friel's *The Freedom of the City* (1973) and haunt Frank McGuiness's play *Carthaginians* (1988). 'Scottish' oil and nationalism form the historical canvas for John McGrath's *The Cheviot, The Stag and the Black, Black Oil* (1973). Steven Berkoff's *Sink the Belgrano* (1986) satirises government lies in the Falklands war of 1982, while Trevor Griffiths's *The Gulf Between Us* (1992) explores the Gulf War. The economic and ideological impact of Thatcherism can be traced from Kay Adshead's *Thatcher's Women* (1987) to Trevor Griffiths' *Thatcher's Children* (1993).

This survey begins to suggest the difficulty of summarising dramatic representation over fifty years. Politics cannot easily be dramatised. Modernity and capitalism, not least the deep social penetration of commodification and information technology, resist literal description, despite the dominance of naturalist representation. Simplification colours both the supposedly objective drama of television 'news' and the aesthetic license of theatrical fictions. Unsurprisingly, then, dramatised documentaries, such as Ken Loach's *Cathy Come Home* (1966) or Jimmy McGovern's *Hillsborough* (1996) have been sites of political conflict between objective representation and imaginative dramatisation. Although dramatised documentaries often generate immediate political controversy, they confirm and reproduce the media information conventions which have undermined the credibility of fictional drama as a representation of reality.

The attempt, however, to hold direct mirrors up to politics or to integrate new technological media has been comparatively rare in political theatre. If theatre can only react to history it confirms the retrospective pull of British imperial decline, looking back in anger or nostalgia rather than forwards. A singular emphasis on the critical relation between theatre and political events distorts both the events themselves and the history of British theatre. Theatre often dramatises state, nation and society through domestic situations which mystify the mediating relations. The difficulty, then, is to dramatise the relation between the widespread experience of powerlessness and the structures of feeling through which power is articulated. Feminist drama and criticism have been particularly important in opening up discussion of the personal as a microcosm of the political.

Many of the most significant plays to shape the cultural imagination dramatise ideological internalisation, legitimation and individuation, rather than immediate political contexts. More oblique dramatisations of society, such as the plays of Samuel Beckett, Harold Pinter or Howard Barker, cannot easily be related to specific political contexts. Beyond the surface of political events, moreover, the catastrophes of modernity, such as the holocaust or Hiroshima, may be impossible to dramatise in terms of individual agency. In short, conventional dramatic idioms provide inadequate modes of political representation. Explicitly political theatre often reduces events to cartoon caricatures to make them dramatically intelligible, thus reproducing the reduction of humans to puppets of historical forces. Understanding such forces requires analysis of the deeper historical transformations.

Theatre and drama in a dramatised society

The decisive question for modern theatre is whether theatre can play an active part in understanding and shaping these transformations. Modern theatre emerged through the struggle for autonomy from state power, religion and the economic structures of civil society. In the process, theatre forged many of the structures of feeling associated with music, narrative and entertainment now dominant in the culture industry. Raymond Williams observes a further dimension. Drama, through television, radio and film, is now a rhythm of everyday life:

> What we now have is drama as habitual experience: more in a week, in many cases, than most human beings would previously have seen in a lifetime. . . . The slice of life, once a project of naturalist drama, is now a voluntary, habitual, internal rhythm; the flow of action and acting, of representation and performance, raised to a new convention, that of a basic need.
>
> (Williams 1983: 12–13)

The concept of 'drama' needs to be rethought accordingly. The development of what Williams calls 'drama in a dramatised society' threatens to marginalise modern theatre. The specific class status of theatre is marked, economically and politically. Alan Sinfield suggests, for example, that theatre between 1956 and 1970 deserves particular attention because although 'patronized by only about 2 per cent of the population it was in this period the particular form within which a new, growing and ultimately influential section of the middle class discovered itself' (Sinfield 1983: 173). Theatre, in this sense, is a minority form. Plays, however, are disseminated in book form, through other media, through amateur theatrical productions, and through the teaching of literature and drama. Even if British television soap operas regularly reach millions of viewers, the dissemination, discussion and study of stage drama cannot be reduced to the size, wallet or class backgrounds of bums on seats.

British theatre has responded to these different conditions by seeking new audiences, performance contexts and theatrical idioms. An exceptional diversity of plays has been produced, from stage plays to television and film adaptations. The range cannot easily be summarised or surveyed (Berney 1994). Traditional approaches combining theatre history with a history of important plays fail to capture theatre's interaction with society. Perhaps more important for theatre's place in the culture industry is theatre's need to define itself against other media. Trying to do what film and television cannot brings a new emphasis on live spectacle and stage presence, often conceived as a revolt against the supposedly traditional dominance of literary text, though such conceptions frequently mistake the history of playscripts for the history of theatre. At the same time theatre is exploited by the culture industry as a research and development sector, providing performers and scripts for film and television 'spinoffs', particularly for television comedy. Emphasis on adapting theatre to other media mitigates the stress on theatricality. Theatre in turn often relies on media 'tie-ins' and the box office charms of television performers and 'personalities'. Boxers and cricketers become pantomime stars and soap stars with dubious stage skills fill up many a provincial theatre.

These historically unusual developments are now second nature, reducing most theatre to a show business which reflects the specific economic and ideological purposes of capitalism. The careers of most actors are orientated towards screen acting rather than stage acting. The screen's emphasis on naturalist acting creates conflicts of convention regarding the transferability of acting skills and audience expectations. Habituation to the mediating distances between camera and performer transforms perceptions of public speaking and rhetoric (Benjamin 1992). Audiences used to film and television often find theatre embarrassingly overstated and overacted. The lure, moreover, of screen adaptation means that plays, like novels, are often written with film in mind or are best known through screen versions. This has direct and subtle effects on playwrighting. Film and television, particularly with the advent of video, have changed the way stage plays are seen, remembered and studied. Previously the most important record of drama was the playscript. Now the living memory of theatre is mediated by new technologies.

Theatre, acting and the culture industry: Laurence Olivier

General tendencies shaping theatre amid the culture industry can be illustrated by the career of Laurence Olivier, often 'billed' as the most important actor in British theatre after 1945 (Olivier 1982). Olivier's reputation was forged by his patriotic film of Shakespeare's *Henry V* (1944), and secured by a series of Shakespeare roles. His stage performances can be glimpsed in his films *Hamlet* (1948) and *Richard III* (1955), but the strain between stage and film is evident. Olivier's slide towards dull respectability is represented by his hammy performance with Marilyn Monroe in *The Prince and the Showgirl* (1957), and Olivier's film of Terence Rattigan's play *The Sleeping Prince*. Olivier then shifted towards the radical drama associated with the Royal Court, performing the role of Archie Rice in Osborne's *The Entertainer* (1957). Archie's sordid affairs echo those of the British state: both have disastrous consequences. Enough of Olivier's performance as a seedy music-hall comic survives in the 1959 film version to suggest an eloquent allegory of England's decline.

This polemical mix of music-hall and naturalism helped establish Osborne's reputation and reinvented Olivier's. A patriot, Shakespearean, film star, director and producer, Olivier also seemed capable of working with new movements in British theatre. In 1962 he was appointed actor-manager of the newly formed National Theatre, a post he held until 1973. The National suffered the ignominy of becoming 'Royal' in 1988, but, along with the Royal Shakespeare Company, became one of the two main institutions of British theatre. Olivier's last significant stage role was as the Marxist John Tagg in Trevor Griffiths's play *The Party* (1973). Screen performances of note survive, but Olivier's performances as a member of the House of Lords confirmed the unholy alliance of show business and the ancient scenery of the British state.

Olivier's career combined money and social status with a specific commitment to British theatre. Awkward shifts between Shakespeare, radical drama and cinema make Olivier emblematic of the social contradictions in theatre's struggle for independence as a significant cultural form. The power of Olivier's example can be gauged by its diminished echoes in the career of Kenneth Branagh, notably in Branagh's films of *Henry V* (1989) and *Hamlet* (1996). The confused populism of Branagh's attempt to finesse the differences of stage acting and film is symptomatic of an increasing gulf between the residual formations of serious bourgeois theatre and the aesthetics of the cinema box office.

The mediation of theatrical forms by the culture industry shapes the context in which particular plays need to be analysed. Films simultaneously shape and obscure the history of acting in relation to which plays are written and performed. The theatricality of society, particularly the dramatic and internalised structures of capitalist naturalism, renders the simple juxtaposition of society and representation naive. Perhaps the hardest relation to discern is the link between the details of social imitation and the reproduction of social processes of action and cognition in performance. Performance skills and self-presentation are central to the social and economic power of individuals. Performance criteria are socially mediated and commodified, from desire and sexual action through labour organisation to political and managerial control. Acting is further mediated by the different demands of stage, television and film acting. The technological archives of performance, from text to screen, reveal a shifting history of performance as a social activity. New plays have nevertheless been catalysts for developments in British theatre, providing some resistance to the prevailing hymn-sheets of show business.

1956 and all that: playwrights and plays

Despite ongoing controversy about the history and future of British theatre, there is surprising unanimity about a critical narrative centred on the supposedly radical impact of John Osborne's *Look Back in Anger* (1956). This play, along with the first production of Samuel Beckett's *Waiting for Godot* (1955) and the visit of Bertolt Brecht's Berliner Ensemble (1956), is often cited as marking British theatre's move from the slumbers of West End bourgeois drama towards serious and innovative new drama (Taylor 1969). This shift is generally associated with London's unfortunately named Royal Court Theatre. *Look Back in Anger*'s importance as a social and media event did not reflect the play's quality. Despite its new tone and attitude, the traditional structure is wooden in construction, and overly dependent on its protagonist's tirades. These weaknesses recur in Osborne's later plays, even if critically foregrounded in *The Entertainer* (1957), *Inadmissible Evidence* (1965), and in the more Chekhovian ensemble of decline in *West of Suez* (1971).

Other notable Royal Court playwrights, such as John Arden, Arnold Wesker and Edward Bond, shared a background shaped by the social reforms of the 1945 Labour government and were hostile to the tottering state of the British establishment. There are marked differences though between their theatrical idioms and the political and sexual sensibilities revealed by their plays. Subsequent socialist and feminist playwrights and critics have observed that the so-called Angry Young Men expressed not the birth pangs of new political articulations but dramatic structures of misogynistic spleen and confused class resentment (Wandor 1986; Segal 1988; McGrath 1981).

What of the earlier theatre *Look Back in Anger* displaced (Chothia 1996)? Noel Coward, J. B. Priestley and Terence Rattigan have been maligned for theatrical and political conservatism, but their modernised 'well-made' plays are more critical than their reputation suggests. Coward's most interesting plays predate the Second World War, but his work remains effective in stage revivals and has continuing influence. Priestley's *An Inspector Calls* (1946) uses a thriller plot to explore political contrasts between the eve of the First World War and the emergent welfare state, contrasts still pertinent when the play was revived in 1997. The contemporary re-evaluation of Rattigan is perhaps even more revealing. In 1950 Rattigan argued against a theatre of ideas in favour of a theatre suitable for Aunt Ednas bored by propaganda. Plays such as *The Winslow Boy* (1946), *The Browning Version* (1948) and *The Deep Blue Sea* (1952) nevertheless dramatise resistances to establishment prejudices and values. Shaw was still alive in 1950 to argue against Rattigan, but Rattigan's plays are closer to Ibsen's critical bourgeois drama than the more brittle Ibsenite posturing of Shaw. Ironically, Shaw's 'Theatre of Ideas' received its comeuppance through the adaptation of *Pygmalion* (1914) into the stage and film musical *My Fair Lady* (1964). T. S. Eliot's modernism was similarly mocked by the success of the West End musical *Cats* based on Eliot's poems for children. This movement from ideas to musical purgatory shaped London theatre through the 1970s and 1980s. Even the Royal Court contributed with Richard O'Brien's camp rock musical *The Rocky Horror Show* (1973), subsequently a West End hit and 'cult' film.

Stage revivals have been kinder to Rattigan's plays, and increasing awareness of gay subtexts in his work has enhanced his reputation. Rattigan was also important as a foil for other writers: *The Deep Blue Sea* (1952) and *Separate Tables* (1954) share significant aspects of dramatic structure with *Look Back in Anger*; Shelagh Delaney's *A Taste of Honey* (1958) was written against Rattigan's *Variation on a Theme* (1958); and John Arden and Margaretta D'Arcy's *The Hero Rises Up* (1968) was written against Rattigan's *Nelson* (1966). Rattigan's use of the well-made play to dramatise individual experience and moral conscience also remains a technique of more overtly left-wing plays. By comparison with Rattigan's best plays, David Hare's state of the nation trilogy, *Racing Demon* (1990), *Murmuring Judges* (1991) and *The Absence of War* (1993) is literal-minded, and represents a regression rather than a consolidation of intervening dramatic experiments.

Important continuities persist, then, from the immediate post-war plays to the 1990s. The situation of British theatre is further complicated by looking beyond the West End to London theatres such as the Communist Party's Unity Theatre and Joan Littlewood's Theatre

Workshop. Theatre Workshop settled in London's East End in 1953 after years of touring (Chambers 1989; Goorney 1981). Innovative productions of new plays, notably Brendan Behan's *The Quare Fellow* (1956) and Shelagh Delaney's *A Taste of Honey* (1958), embodied an influential new mode of radical popular theatre. Films of these plays, however, obscure Theatre Workshop's distinctive theatricality and audience dynamics. Once transferred to the West End or film, a similar fate met the politics of music-hall in Littlewood's *Oh,What a Lovely War* (1963), a fate mitigated by the National's 1998 revival of the play at the Roundhouse.

Outside London, important regional developments include the formation of the Bristol Old Vic Company in 1946 and the Glasgow Citizens' Theatre, which moved to the Gorbals in 1945. The stirrings of an independent Scottish theatre also included Glasgow Unity Theatre's productions of Robert McLeish's *The Gorbals Story* (1946) and Ena Lamont Stewart's socialist-feminist working-class drama, *Men Should Weep* (1947), plays later successfully revived by '7:84 Scotland'. The Edinburgh International Festival, founded in 1947, has brought important international theatre groups to Britain and spawned a diverse fringe theatre, becoming the largest theatre festival in the world. Its most notable Scottish production was David Lindsay's renaissance play *Ane Satyre of the Thrie Estaites* (1948), a focus for calls for a Scottish national theatre (Stevenson and Wallace 1996), and an influence on John Arden's *Armstrong's Last Goodnight* (1965) and John McGrath's *A Satire of the Four Estates* (1996). Notable 'regional' developments also include Field Day Theatre Company's attempt to establish a new kind of Irish theatre in conjunction with the playwright Brian Friel (Pine 1990). London theatre history is often mistaken for British theatre history, but these state subsidised, anti-state and independent regional developments suggest a wider picture (Hughes 1996; Shank 1996).

Beyond naturalism: from T. S. Eliot to the Royal Court dramatists

Attempts to reinvent verse drama after 1945 have also been important and given impetus by the ongoing importance of Shakespeare. The recent history of British Shakespeare productions cannot be sketched briefly. Shakespeare remains integral to the commercial repertory of many touring companies and regional theatres. Major professional productions of Shakespeare are reviewed in the journals *Shakespeare Quarterly* and *Shakespeare Survey*, but the history of productions in regional theatres such as the Glasgow Citizens' Theatre and the Nottingham Playhouse is largely unwritten. Shakespeare's aesthetic and economic importance for contemporary theatre practice and audience experience also works through education and numerous radio, film and television versions. Given Shakespeare's literary and theatrical popularity, the reinvention of modern verse drama has been a persistent project. Even a self-styled theatrical rebel such as Steven Berkoff draws on Shakespearean idiom in plays such as *East* (1975). The critical and theatrical reinvention of Shakespeare can also be traced through plays such as Edward Bond's *Lear* (1971), the Women's Theatre Group's *Lear's Daughters* (1987) and Howard Barker's *Seven Lears* (1987) (Bennett 1996).

T. S. Eliot was particularly interested in the dramatic and poetic problem of moving beyond the anxiety of Shakespearean influence. However, his awkward juxtaposition of tragic myth and contemporary naturalism in the *The Cocktail Party* (1949), *The Confidential Clerk* (1953) and *The Elder Statesman* (1958) was ultimately unsuccessful in reinventing viable modes of poetic drama. Fry's verse comedies were more successful within more modest ambitions, but similarly fruitless. Sean O'Casey continued to write plays with Shakespearean echoes, notably *Red Roses for Me* (1943), *Cock-a-Doodle Dandy* (1949), and *The Bishop's Bonfire* (1955). His synthesis of poetic prose with music and expressionism can also be seen as a Brechtian prototype, foreshadowing many subsequent left-wing forms. With the exception of John Arden, however, O'Casey's direct influence remains marginal.

The postwar vogue for poetic drama was unable to rework the poetic prose developed by O'Casey and other Irish dramatists. This in part reflects continuing tensions between the prosaic power of standard English versus non-metropolitan idioms and class registers. Stage representations of any language other than bourgeois prose can seem paternalistic, patronising or simply inarticulate. The historical power of English poetic drama can also make verse seem archaic, appropriate only for heritage industry costume dramas. Symptomatically, Raymond Williams's *Drama from Ibsen to Eliot* (1952) became *Drama from Ibsen to Brecht* when republished in 1968. The search for literary drama comparable to Elizabethan and Jacobean drama has, moreover, been confused with the struggle to develop theatre's autonomy from text-based drama and from cinematic naturalism. Compromises in films of Shakespeare provide an index of this confusion. Non-Shakespearean cinematic conventions offset naturalist speech and action with different visual and musical counterpoints. Such counterpoints produce significant new non-naturalist dramatic syntheses, but appear clumsy if transferred to a theatrical stage.

Modern theatre has continued to attempt to move beyond the conventions of spoken naturalism to combine language with theatrical action in new ways, but few of the attempts to reinvent verse drama have been more than historical curios. The contradictions are more than merely formal. With the decline of verse drama in favour of prose drama, the social significance of verse has changed profoundly. Conventions which emphasise silence and the gap between visible behaviour and everyday speech have become dominant, though many recent plays contrast prose naturalism with more expressionist poetics of spoken idiom. The analytic language forensics of detective work and legal examination have found popular resonances in police drama, crime thrillers and courtroom drama, particularly on television. Modes of understanding sub-texts beneath what is said have predominated as a form of scepticism about the power of language to disguise and legitimate the unspeakable. Many of the poetic and rhetorical resources of language have been discredited or appropriated by capitalist advertising and political propaganda. Dramatic understatement has seemed more significant than the hypocrisy or theatricality of heightened poetic speech which attempts to soar above the surface of visible action.

Notable examples of verse drama from this period such as Louis MacNiece's radio play *The Dark Tower* (1946) and Dylan Thomas's play for voices *Under Milk Wood* (1953) require no visible action. The BBC's Third Programme, subsequently Radio Three, has been one of the most important forms for radio performances of canonical plays, and also for the encouragement, guided by Martin Esslin, of new writing by a wide range of playwrights including Samuel Beckett and Caryl Churchill (Drakakis 1981; Shank 1996). For many theatre practitioners, however, the gulf between literary script and theatrical embodiment exemplified by radio is part of the problem rather than the solution.

Resources for moving beyond naturalism came from modernist poetics of prose drama and performance art, notably from Samuel Beckett, Antonin Artaud and Bertolt Brecht. *Waiting for Godot* revealed a radically new dramatic imagination, further developed by Beckett's subsequent plays. Beckett's integration of language, dramatic action and theatrical image has provided a model for a wide range of forms, but direct imitation has usually been unsuccessful, and his work has remained an isolated oeuvre. Beckett highlights the aesthetic and formal possibilities of dramatic idioms, including radio, television and film. His work bridges the false polarisation of so-called high and low art forms, combining aspects of music-hall and film with a poetic sense of the depths of everyday speech. Beckett reveals the resistance of British theatre to European modernist traditions, both literary and dramatic, a resistance symbolically confirmed by the voluntary Parisian exile of the influential director Peter Brook.

Artaud's influence has been similarly pervasive and indirect, a theoretical reference for anti-literary theatre and experiments with rituals of the body and performance (Innes 1993). Contradictions in the reception of Artaud's somewhat incoherent theoretical writings were evident in the 1964 *Theatre of Cruelty* season directed by Peter Brook and Charles Marowitz. Their productions of Jean Genet's *The Screens* and Peter Weiss's *The Marat/Sade* took Artaud to legitimate experimentations in theatrical stylisation. Such stylisation undermined the political coherence of the plays, a trend particularly evident in the confused reception, influence and production of Brecht's theories and plays.

The mediation of political theory and theatrical practice through reductive stylisation has been a defining feature of British theatre's intellectual weakness. Cold war ideology deliberately sought to sever the relation between theory and practice in Brecht's political theatre, resulting in an English tradition of anti-Brechtian productions of Brecht's plays. Principal confusions involve the division of Brecht's dialectical presentation of staged conflict into propaganda versus narrative, and widespread misunderstanding of Brecht's conceptions of 'alienation' and epic theatre. Brechtian dramatists such as Edward Bond, Howard Barker, John McGrath and Caryl Churchill, have often retreated ideologically to polemical provocations or to theatre which cheers up the converted, alienating its audience in manners very different from those envisaged by Brecht.

Beckett, Artaud and Brecht, however, have been more discussed than assimilated. The Royal Court's range of plays stretches from Brechtian modes to what has become known through Martin Esslin as 'absurdist' theatre (Esslin 1980). The Royal Court however never successfully synthesised a house style, remaining primarily a playwright's theatre for new literary drama. The tone was set by Osborne's mix of naturalism and radical polemic. The mistaken popular reputation for 'kitchen-sink drama' perhaps owes more to the title of Arnold Wesker's play *The Kitchen* (1959), and the series of grey and white British films which included not only *Look Back in Anger* (1959), but also *Saturday Night and Sunday Morning* (1960), *A Kind of Loving* (1962) and *Billy Liar* (1963). These plays and films helped to fund and popularise a so-called 'new wave' in British drama (Hill 1986; Lacey 1995).

Perhaps the most striking beneficiary of the emerging relation between stage, radio, television and film was Harold Pinter, who was only tangentially associated with the Royal Court. Pinter's reputation as one of the most important postwar dramatists was forged through successful television and stage productions. Pinter also wrote screenplays for the Joseph Losey films *The Servant* (1963), *Accident* (1967) and *The Go-Between* (1970) which are notable for their awkward class and gender dynamics. A new structure of feeling involving shifts in class mobility, linguistic power and sexual politics is given symptomatically anxious shape in Pinter's plays *The Birthday Party* (1957), *The Caretaker* (1959) and *The Homecoming* (1964), a shape whose subverted naturalism belies Pinter's association with absurdist drama. Pinter's subverted naturalism finds an engaging and transformed mode in Joe Orton's farces. Distant echoes of Pinter's understated and imploding class idioms can also be discerned in the peculiarly British television plays of David Mercer, Alan Bennett, Mike Leigh, Alan Bleasdale, Dennis Potter and John Byrne (Brandt 1981, 1993; Nelson 1997).

The parallel history of British television drama is difficult to summarise succinctly, however. The complexity of television drama incorporates not just single plays, but serial forms such as soap operas, crime drama, situation comedies and costume dramas, notably the dramatisations of novels such as *Pride and Prejudice, I Claudius* and *Brideshead Revisited*. Television and film have remained within the terms of serialised realism established by the nineteenth-century novel, and the ideological impact of television serialisation has often swamped attempts to work critically with the medium. Playwrights who have achieved recognition for plays written specifically for television represent only a small portion of the often anonymous dramatic writing for television. Despite attempts to develop the single play as a popular and critical form, notably the BBC's 1970s *Play for Today* series, television drama has been dominated by modes of comic or light naturalism. Even when dramatising the life and death tragedies which are the staples of crime and soap opera, such modes domesticate and neutralise the issues they reflect.

The most significant Royal Court plays were written against the emergent structure of film and television naturalism. The focus of the most important of these Royal Court dramatists – Arnold Wesker, John Arden and Edward Bond – has been restricted to theatre. Wesker's autobiographical trilogy, *Chicken Soup with Barley* (1958), *Roots* (1959) and *I'm Talking about Jerusalem* (1960), exemplifies the limits of the stylised naturalism associated with the Royal Court. The trilogy is torn between naturalist representation of individuals in a social setting and implied generalisations about the fate of socialism and communism. Similar tensions between dramatised individuality and ambiguous political commitment inform David Edgar's comparable play *Maydays* (1983). Wesker's trilogy remains a notable achievement, but his subsequent plays and projects reflect the general failure of socialist culture.

After the contemporary naturalism of his early play *Live Like Pigs* (1957) Arden's characteristic mode of poetic realism, influenced by Brecht, eschews naturalism in favour of experiments with the relations between verse, song and prose. *Sergeant Musgrave's Dance* (1959) develops this into what the play's subtitle calls an 'un-historical parable', a description also appropriate for *The Workhouse Donkey* (1963), *Armstrong's Last Goodnight* (1964) and *The Island of the Mighty* (1972). In 1968, Raymond Williams declared Arden 'the most genuinely innovating of the generation of young English dramatists of the fifties' (Williams 1973: 378). However, the historical and linguistic depth of Arden's work is achieved at the cost of some folksy sermonising and Brechtian 'crude thinking'. These tensions are perhaps most pointed in the epic mixture of verse and dialogue in *The Non-Stop Connolly Show* (1975), written with Margaretta D'Arcy. Arden's attempts to move beyond naturalism, like those of Wesker, foundered on formal problems and frustration with the politics of professional theatre.

Bond succeeded with the modified polemical naturalism of *The Pope's Wedding* (1962) and *Saved* (1965), but later experienced similar difficulties. Despite a series of inventive non-naturalistic plays, such as *Early Morning* (1968), *Lear* (1972), *The Woman* (1978), and *War Plays* (1985), Bond's work has struggled to move beyond naturalism. It often seems torn between didactic and allegorical politics, with ambiguously presented images of violence and inarticulacy standing in for radical protest, social theory and political re-articulation.

Political drama after 1968: from Brecht's babies to Thatcher's children

The difficulty of moving beyond the formal and political contradictions of Bond's work has shaped a generation of political dramatists such as Howard Brenton, David Edgar, David Hare, Trevor Griffiths and Caryl Churchill. Theatre history tends to emphasise 1968 as the landmark date of the abolition of explicit theatre censorship, but the political events in Paris and Prague dramatised in Griffiths' *The Party* (1973), the civil rights movements, Vietnam, student protest and the New Left were more significant influences. These writers were part of a rapid expansion of alternative theatre groups and touring companies such as Red Ladder, Welfare State, the Pip Simmons Theatre Group, 7:84 Theatre Company, Joint Stock Theatre Group, Monstrous Regiment, Women's Theatre Group and Gay Sweatshop. The dramatic forms ranged from agit-prop and performance art through to more conventional stage plays, many of which transferred to larger public stages, television and film.

Argument ranged widely about the most effective use of left-wing theatre as a mode of social intervention, particularly concerning left-wing drama's relation to the predominantly bourgeois theatre audience as opposed to the 'mass' audiences of film and television (Itzin 1980). Reflecting this contradiction, left-wing theatre often directed representations of violence at its audience, as though this might disrupt the smooth running of bourgeois ideology. Brenton's *Magnificence* (1973) for example, collapses the critique of the society of the spectacle associated with situationism into a confused juxtaposition of theatrical image and inarticulate radical protest. The contradictions and naivety of adolescent revolutionaries are criticised by Griffiths' *Real Dreams* (1984). His play *Comedians* (1975), by contrast, dramatises political differences between revolution and reformism through the assimilation of working-class protest into comedy. The concluding image of the disenchanted working-class performer echoes the muted music hall protests of Osborne's *The Entertainer* and, more distantly, the defiant performers of Beckett's *Endgame* (1957), *Happy Days* (1961) and *Catastrophe* (1982).

Griffiths has continued to produce intelligent plays, but his left-wing approach has suffered from shifts to the right in capitalism and culture after 1979. Considered formally, the technical merits of Griffiths' plays exemplify the compound of Ibsenite problem play and Chekhovian group dynamics which could be traced back to Harley

Granville-Barker's *Waste* and George Bernard Shaw's *Heartbreak House*. By contrast, Brenton's *The Romans in Britain* (1980) uses simulated buggery to suggest a parallel between the Roman imperial occupation of Britain and the British imperial occupation of Northern Ireland, exemplifying the structural failure of left-wing allegorical dramatisation to move beyond provocation.

The confused use of sexual politics to develop a more extended political analysis also vitiates Caryl Churchill's plays *Cloud Nine* (1979) and *Top Girls* (1982). Churchill, unlike many of these dramatists, did not reproduce the structure of male anger and violence which persists from the tirades of Osborne. Symptomatic of the difficulty facing radical drama in the theatre was the fate of Churchill's *Serious Money* (1987), which deployed doggerel to attack London's financial traders only to find them an appreciative audience for such knockabout. Churchill's work, however, also needs to be understood in relation to the emerging feminist drama of the 1980s. As well as re-examining the work of earlier women playwrights such as Ena Lamont Stewart, Shelagh Delaney, Ann Jellicoe, Joan Littlewood, Margaretta D'Arcy and Pam Gems, feminist drama and criticism have produced a wide range of plays, exemplified by the series *Plays by Women* initially edited by Michelene Wandor.

Collectively devised drama by groups such as Monstrous Regiment (Hanna 1991) and Women's Theatre Group has been particularly productive if conflictual, not least around tensions between race and class, and differences between heterosexual and lesbian drama (Goodman 1993, Freeman 1997). Numerous women playwrights have achieved prominence, notably Sarah Daniels, Angela Carter, Liz Lochhead, Charlotte Keatley, Louise Page and Timberlake Wertenbaker, but stage plays by women have rarely transferred to the male-dominated major theatres, television or film. There have also been significant contributions by women performers, directors and experimental playwrights (Levy 1992). Churchill, however, has become established as the most innovative and influential feminist playwright. Recent works such as *The Skriker* (1994) and *Blue Heart* (1997) continue her wide-ranging investigation into the politics of theatricality.

David Hare argued against the radical experiments of the early 1970s, suggesting that political theatre had been unsuccessful in effecting change, and that theatre should instead function as a forum for historical and contemporary reflection rather than direct protest. By comparison with other political dramatists of the 1970s, Hare has developed a relatively comfortable relation with the mainstream drama of the National Theatre, television and film, producing earnestly dull and formally conventional plays.

David Edgar, like David Hare, moved from radical experiments to mainstream drama, a trajectory which saw his anti-fascist play *Destiny* (1976) transfer from the Royal Shakespeare Company's experimental small stage to the West End and then to television. Edgar, however, has retained distinctive interests in theatricality, notably in his stage adaptation *Nicholas Nickleby* (1980) which borrowed performance art techniques, and *Entertaining Strangers* (1985), which used Ann Jellicoe's form of community play (Jellicoe 1987; Edgar 1988). 'Community', however, is an unstable term for any critical sociology of contemporary theatre. Definitions of community can be developed out of regional or geographical identity, but 'community' is more often defined by social dynamics within metropolitan and national structures. Identifications of gender, race, sexuality and class are such that one individual might 'belong' to a whole series of overlapping communities. Community theatre is based, then, on politically constructed fictions of identity.

The Conservative government in power from 1979–97 effectively destroyed the basis for radical community theatre by reorganising the local government structures and arts funding on which so much radical theatre depended. This shift affected the confidence and viability of all serious theatre after 1979, but can be traced with particular poignancy in John McGrath's attempts to redefine the cultural possibilities of theatre as a social form (McGrath 1981, 1990, 1996).

Howard Barker's prolific range of plays reveal Barker as the contemporary playwright who has perhaps learnt most from the contradictions of naturalism and political theatre in Bond's work. Barker's theatre of 'catastrophe' has an almost Jacobean idiom of sexual violence, linguistic spleen and political ambiguity (Barker 1989). Comparable theatrical idioms can be seen in many contemporary fringe plays which combine a modified prose naturalism with modes of historical allegory and dream play forms which could be traced back to the late chamber plays of Strindberg. Barker's plays, however, like many interesting hybrid forms have remained on the fringe.

Alan Ayckbourn's plays are better known. The formal dexterity of his reworking of the well-made play is evident in *The Norman Conquests* (1973). His plays use the comforting closure of form to enable an often bleak analysis of the moral hypocrisy of the English middle classes, notably in *Absurd Person Singular* (1972). In 1974

Michael Billington suggested that Ayckbourn was a left-wing writer using right-wing forms (Billington 1990), but Ayckbourn could also be seen as part of the soulless and peculiarly English domestication of Chekhov. Although Ayckbourn can be considered as a popular political dramatist capable of producing stage plays which reflect contemporary society, his theatrical domestication of social conflict parallels the neutralising formalism of much popular television naturalism. The message within the medium leaves the formal sophistication some way short of critical expression.

Tom Stoppard's work is more intellectually ambitious, and has a more secure critical and academic reputation, partly as a supposedly apolitical antidote to the socialist politics prevalent in British theatre since the 1960s. Stoppard established his reputation with *Rosencrantz and Guildenstern Are Dead* (1966/7), a play which flatters its audience that they can join nodding familiarity with *Hamlet* to a nonchalantly reductive 'absurdism'. Stoppard's work is often called brilliant and dazzling, but might also be described as too clever by half. In *Jumpers* (1972) and *Travesties* (1974), Stoppard toys with abstract and philosophical questions, such as temporal relativity and logical positivism, but the exploration of such questions is subservient to theatrical effects and stage business. Stoppard's work invites comparison with Beckett and Pinter, but lacks the depth which sustains their different levels of artifice. Differences are highlighted by comparing Stoppard's explicitly political plays, such as *Every Good Boy Deserves Favour* (1977) and *Professional Foul* (1978), with Beckett's *Catastrophe* (1982) and Pinter's *One for the Road* (1984) and *Party Time* (1991). Beckett and Pinter give the lie to their status as apolitical playwrights with an uncomfortably reflexive theatrical dissidence, whereas Stoppard writes plays about dissidence which comfort their audience with the illusions of theatricality. Stoppard's *The Real Thing* (1982), for example, maps a play about adultery and the self-deluding mirrors inhabited by actors and playwrights onto a reductive polemic against socialist drama. Stoppard's combination of cleverness and fudged political allegory is perhaps best known through his screenplay for the Terry Gillam film *Brazil* (1985). Subsequent plays by Stoppard, such as *Arcadia* (1993), return to Stoppard's exploration of the theatrical possibilities of scientific, historical and philosophical analogies, part of a recent trend for plays exploring science. Set against Beckett and Pinter, Stoppard's formal and intellectual ingenuity lacks emotional or political substance.

Conclusion: old problems and new labours

The Thatcher administration of the 1980s led to the disintegration of theatre funding and the decline of the predominantly left-wing theatre of the 1970s. The Royal Shakespeare Company and the (Royal) National Theatre have since become associated as much with spectacular stage adaptations and musicals as with serious drama. While both these institutions have staged landmark productions of classic drama, they have failed to develop a critical role within the culture. The tension between state funding of the 'arts' and commercial values prefigures a long-term legitimation crisis. Developments in feminist, gay and black theatre have nevertheless continued to emerge, but such developments have rarely transferred to larger public stages, television or film without the attenuation of their theatrical impact.

Contemporary playwrights often achieve recognition and new audiences through television and film rather than through theatre, a development exemplified by the careers of Ken Loach, Dennis Potter, Mike Leigh and Jimmy McGovern. Numerous new playwrights have consolidated reputations since the 1970s, among them Frank McGuinness, Hanif Kureishi, Winsome Pinnock, Nick Ward, Timberlake Wertenbaker, Charlotte Keatley and Jonathan Harvey, but this list is selective and there is little consensus as to the most significant plays or playwrights. Several new playwrights have also emerged in the 1990s, often through studiedly lurid media sensationalism. Plays such as the late Sarah Kane's *Blasted* (1995), Jez Butterworth's *Mojo* (1995), Mark Ravenhill's *Shopping and Fucking* (1996) and Patrick Marber's *Closer* (1997) reveal a new accommodation with the media's exploitation of sex and violence, using soundbites, punchlines and advertising hype.

Traditional lines of transfer between avant-garde playwrighting and more public and commercial forms still persist, but appear ever more subservient to the interests of capitalism. Publishers, notably Penguin, Faber and Methuen, provide one index of contemporary critical reputations, but the processes by which theatre playwrights establish critical reputations have become increasingly diffuse and insecure in relation to the different interests of audiences, theatre practitioners, journalists, arts funding and administration bodies, drama teachers and academics. Regional variation and the diversity of fringe and semi-professional theatre also make generalisation difficult. There are signs, moreover, that the reputation of many apparently well-established playwrights may not be secure. Significant developments in recent theatre practice have also involved a shift away from stage plays and dramatic texts towards devised theatre and performance art practices associated with groups such as Theatre de Complicite, Kick Theatre, Adventures in Motion Pictures, DV8 and Forced Entertainment, often through interaction with international theatrical avant-gardes (Shank 1996).

British theatre since 1945 has sustained a lively and eclectic range of contemporary plays and performance styles, a range unequalled by American or continental European theatre. British actors and directors command international respect, not least through the visibility of their work in film. Hopes for a specifically British culture of drama and theatre have not, however, confirmed the promise of the developments between 1956 and 1979. The comparison with the energy and range of contemporary British popular music and television is striking. The work of Mike Leigh, Dennis Potter and recent television serials such as Peter Flannery's *Our Friends in the North* (1996) show that serious, popular television drama can still be produced, compensating for the production lines of soap opera, situation comedy and heritage costume dramas. However comparison of the popularity of the theatre with annual events such as the Notting Hill Carnival, Gay Pride and a range of music festivals suggests that theatre has yet to forge a significant critical or popular role within British culture. British television drama, by contrast, has become an accepted part of everyday social idioms, though individual plays or series of any critical sophistication are rare. Symptomatically a reconstruction of Shakespeare's Globe Theatre is one of the most important new theatres built recently in London.

While the ancient scenery of the British state continues to be patched up, British theatre struggles to free itself from the ideology of heritage and the wider culture industry. It remains to be seen whether the new Labour administration elected in 1997 will reinvigorate theatre within British culture. Early signs suggest that state support will be focused on tax breaks for the film industry and occasional hand-outs from lottery funding, a system which has disabled serious political discussion of arts funding, while leaving much of the financial power directing British theatre in the hands of unelected quangos. The long revolution of cultural democratisation is long indeed.

Bibliography

Acheson, J. (ed.) (1993) *British and Irish Drama since 1960*, Basingstoke: Macmillan.

Adorno, T. W. (1991) *The Culture Industry*, ed. J. M. Bernstein, London: Routledge.

Ansorge, P. (1975) *Disrupting the Spectacle*, London: Ditman.

Barker, H. (1989) *Arguments for a Theatre*, London: Calder.

Barnes, P. (1986) *A Companion to Post-war British Theatre*, London: Croom Helm.

Benjamin, W. (1992) 'The work of art in the age of mechanical reproduction', in *Illuminations*, trans. Harry Zohn, London: Fontana.

Bennett, S. (1996) *Performing Nostalgia: Shifting Shakespeare and the Contemporary Past*, London: Routledge.

Berney, K. A. (ed.) (1994) *Contemporary British Dramatists*, Detroit: Gale Research.

Bigsby, C. W. E. (ed.) (1981) *Contemporary English Drama*, London: E. Arnold.

Billington, M. (1990) *Alan Ayckbourn*, Basingstoke: Macmillan.

Boireau, N. (ed.) (1997) *Drama on Drama: Dimensions of Theatricality on the Contemporary British Stage*, London: Macmillan.

Brandt, G. W. (ed.) (1981) *British Television Drama*, Cambridge: Cambridge University Press.

—— (ed.) (1993) *British Television Drama in the 1980s*, Cambridge: Cambridge University Press.

Brook, P. (1972) *The Empty Space*, Harmondsworth: Penguin (first published 1968).

Brook, P. (1987) *The Shifting Point*, London: Methuen.

—— (1988) *A Theatrical Casebook*, ed. D. Williams, London: Methuen.

Brown, J. R. (ed.) (1968) *Modern British Dramatists*, Englewood Cliffs, N.J.: Prentice-Hall.

—— (ed.) (1984) *Modern British Dramatists: New Perspectives*, Englewood Cliffs, N.J.: Prentice-Hall.

Bull, J. (1994) *Stage Right: Crisis and Recovery in British Contemporary Mainstream Theatre*, London: Macmillan.

Chambers, C. (1989) *The Story of Unity Theatre*, London: Lawrence and Wishart.

Chothia, J. (1996) *English Drama of the Early Modern Period, 1890–1940*, London: Longman.

Cohn, R. (1991) *Retreats from Realism in Recent English Drama*, Cambridge: Cambridge University Press.

de Jongh, N. (1992) *Not in Front of the Audience: Homosexuality on Stage*, London: Routledge.

Drakakis, J. (ed.) (1981) *British Radio Drama*, Cambridge: Cambridge University Press.

Edgar, D. (1988) *The Second Time as Farce*, London: Lawrence and Wishart.

Elsom, J. (1979) *Post-War British Theatre*, London: Routledge.

—— (ed.) (1981) *Post-War British Theatre Criticism*, London: Routledge.

Esslin, M. (1980) *Theatre of the Absurd* (rev. edn), Harmondsworth: Penguin.

Freeman, S. (1997) *Putting Your Daughters on the Stage: Lesbian Theatre from the 1970s to the 1990s*, London: Cassell.

Goodman, L. (1993) *Contemporary Feminist Theatres*, London: Routledge.

Goorney, H. (1981) *The Theatre Workshop Story*, London: Methuen.

Hanna, G. (ed.) (1991) *Monstrous Regiment*, London: Nick Hern.

Hill, J. (1986) *Sex, Class and Realism: British Cinema 1956–1963*, London: British Film Institute.

Holland, P. (1997) *English Shakespeares: Shakespeare on the English Stage in the 1990s*, Cambridge: Cambridge University Press.

Hughes, D. (1996) in T. Shank (ed.), *Contemporary British Theatre*, London: Macmillan.

Innes, C. D. (1992) *Modern British Drama*, Cambridge: Cambridge University Press.

—— (1993) *Avant-Garde Theatre, 1892–1992*, London: Routledge.

Itzin, C. (1980) *Stages in the Revolution*, London: Methuen.

Jellicoe, A. (1987) *Community Plays: How to Put them On*, London: Methuen.

Kerensky, O. (1977) *The New British Drama*, London: Hamish Hamilton.

Kershaw, B. (1992) *The Politics of Performance*, London: Routledge.

Lacey, S. (1995) *British Realist Theatre: The New Wave in its Context 1956–1965*, London: Routledge.

Lambert, J. W. (1974) *Drama in Britain, 1964–1973*, London: Longman.

Levy, D. (ed.) (1992) *Walks on Water*, London: Methuen.

McGrath, J. (1981) *A Good Night Out*, London: Methuen

—— (1990) *The Bone Won't Break*, London: Methuen.

—— (1996) *Six-Pack: Plays for Scotland*, Edinburgh: Polygon.

Marowitz, C and Trussler, S. (eds) (1967) *Theatre at Work*, London: Methuen.

Marowitz, C., Milne, T. and Hale, O. (eds) (1965) *The Encore Reader*, London: Methuen.

Maxwell, D. E. S. (1984) *A Critical History of Modern Irish Drama, 1891–1980*, Cambridge: Cambridge University press.

Nairn, T. (1981) *The Break-Up of Britain*, 2nd edn, London: Verso.

Nelson, R. (1997) *TV Drama in Transition*, London: Macmillan.

Oliver, L. (1982) *Confessions Of An Actor*, London: Weidenfeld and Nicolson.

Pine, R. (1990) *Brian Friel and Ireland's Drama*, London: Routledge.

Segal, L. (1988) 'Look Back in Anger: Men in the 50s', in R. Chapman and J. Rutherford (eds), *Male Order: Unwrapping Masculinity*, London: Lawrence and Wishart.

Shank, T. (ed.) (1996) *Contemporary British Theatre*, London: Macmillan.

Shepherd, S. and Womack, P. (1996) *English Drama: A Cultural History*, Oxford: Blackwell.

Sinfield, A. (1983) 'The theatre and its audiences', in A. Sinfield (ed.), *Society and Literature: 1945–1970*, London: Methuen.

Stevenson, R. and Wallace, G. (eds) (1996) *Scottish Theatre since the Seventies*, Edinburgh: Polygon.

Taylor, R. J. (1969) *Anger and After* (rev. edn), London: Methuen.

—— (1971) *The Second Wave*, London: Methuen.

Trussler, S. (ed.) (1981) *New Theatre Voices of the Seventies*, London: Methuen.

Wandor, M. (1986) *Carry on, Understudies*, London: Routledge.

—— (ed.) (1982–5) *Plays by Women*, vols 1–4, London: Metheun.

Weintraub, S. (ed.) (1982) *British Dramatists since World War II*, 2 vols, Detroit: Gale Research.

Williams, R. (1973) *Drama from Ibsen to Brecht*, Harmondsworth: Penguin.

—— (1983) 'Drama in a dramatised society', in *Writing in Society*, London: Verso.

Zeifman, H. and Zimmerman, C. (eds) (1993) *Contemporary British Drama, 1970–90*, Basingstoke: Macmillan.

The following journals are also useful: *Encore, New Theatre Quarterly, Modern Drama, Theatre Record, Theatre Research International*, and *Plays & Players*.

Chapter 9

Resting on laurels

Andrew Crozier

Is there any reason to expect that an up-to-date account of British poetry since the war will differ in important ways, except perhaps in details of personnel, from an account of the poetry of the first twenty-five postwar years written twenty years ago? If not, then our poetic culture – represented by the poetry on view in the chain bookstores, or that taught in schools (little poetry is taught, or read, in universities nowadays) – has remained largely unchanged in half a century. This essay seeks to substantiate this proposition, bringing the perspective of 1980, as it were, to bear on the last twenty years. More controversially, perhaps, it will suggest how the canon has developed, and adapted, sustained by the discursive habits that encoded it as poetic language at the moment of its inception in the 1950s, in a period in which poetry has moved yet farther away from the cultural centre. The reason for this is obvious: as an economic activity poetry is marginal, just as is, for example, hill farming. No one wishes to admit this, least of all publicists of the contemporary canon, but the behaviour of publishers demonstrates it as matter of fact. On the one hand, less and less cultural capital accrues from sub-sidising poetry: the place of poetry in the culture industry is increasingly specialised; on the other hand, and this is the more telling point, even a modestly profitable poetry list is likely to be axed because of its insignificant position in company balance sheets. Taking poetry as an economic activity, I would hazard the guess that – the occasional bestseller notwithstanding – its most lucrative sector is the secondary market, operative in the rights departments of publishers, and the 'modern firsts' trade. (It is commonly thought that royalties from Lord Lloyd-Webber's *Cats* are what have kept Faber and Faber a going concern.)

'Thrills and frills'

In a glibly titled essay (to which this section title refers), published in Alan Sinfield's *Society and Literature 1945–1970* (Crozier 1983), I suggested that a canon of contemporary poetry had developed in the 1950s and 1960s, and cited Philip Larkin, Ted Hughes and Seamus Heaney as its foremost representatives, establishing each in turn a poetic succession from decade to decade. This was hardly contentious then, nor is it now. I proposed that despite polemic disagreements on the score of gentility, in which a poem by Hughes might be held up as significantly of the postwar world and serious, in a way that one by Larkin, by virtue of its nostalgia, was not, the canon thus constituted was homogeneous.[1] I further argued that this homogeneity consisted in those common features of canonical work – its discursive habits – that constituted it as poetry: the enunciation (as we have learned to say) of an empirical subject, and a textual insistence on figures of rhetoric as the discernible sign of the poetic. That is to say that these two features, which are related, were (and, I shall maintain, still are) generally understood to be the necessary conditions of a poem; that is to put it at its best. At the worst they were (and are) its sufficient conditions.

The relation between empirical subject and rhetorical figuration is the canon's defining nexus, in which what is figured is given as deriving from the posited experience of a self which, in turn, appears as the author of the poem's figurative scheme, in a discursively foreclosed writing. Imagery does all the hard work of the poem, subject to ratification and guarantee (as fit for consumption) by an originating self. This is true equally of Larkin, Hughes and Heaney, so that whatever their genuine differences – which are, as much as anything, a matter of temperament, inflections of an individual poetic 'voice' – they represent and define a canon of contemporary poetry with determinate horizons of social and cultural engagement and, I might add (for I think these the more important), no horizon at all for engagement with either the history of poetry as an art, or the questions of metaphysics and ontology that concern us as human beings which great poetry has addressed. This is increasingly inevitable while poetry is represented as belonging to or, indeed, bearing responsibility for a national culture. This is not strictly an issue of specific national identity, and Heaney's objections to being enrolled in an anthology of 'British' poetry were personal to him. To the extent that poetry belongs to culture (as of course it does) and culture is not exclusively national (as it never has been, despite the pretensions of the nation state) a canonical poetry identified by reference to national identity (however problematic that may prove) will be a poetry that has reduced its scope of human concern. The canon itself, being a critical and cultural construct, cannot be held responsible for this, needless to say, but the purpose of such constructs is to command assent, and the consequence of uncritical and unreflecting assent regarding the properties that constitute a written item as a poem is an instrumental logic of cultural production to standardised specification. A poem is recognisably *thus*. So our poetic culture is more than ever a matter of figuratively embellished anecdote. But whereas, in the immediate postwar world, there may have been reason for poets to wish to be seen as meaning to stand by their words, to assume responsibility for their role in an aesthetic discourse towards which they felt distrustful, we cannot suppose that reason still to apply with any urgency. Indeed, whatever reason applied, it was in the aftermath of the illusion that poetry might exert direct social agency. Auden, of course, had dealt with that issue succinctly and with equanimity when he said that poetry made nothing happen.[2]

In its account of the canon that began to be established in the 1950s my essay paid particular attention, of course, to the 'Movement' poets and the canonical anthology *New Lines* (1956), in the Introduction to which the editor, Robert Conquest, had explicitly argued for the rediscovery of a native tradition of poetry, in repudiation of a modernism that was essentially foreign, as well as various subsequent aberrations of the 1930s and 1940s. Conquest's irritable polemic misled, by its demand for a return to basics, and failed to disclose the motives (typical of the Movement poets) towards a disparagement of affect, low-key irony, and themes of thwarted expectation. That there was an ethic in all this, attuned to the postwar moment, no one can doubt, and what it conveys to us in the best of them, Larkin himself, and Donald Davie, is a subjectivity formed around not so much self-denial as dismay.[3] To articulate an ethic as poetry requires that writing a poem be itself considered an ethical activity, undertaken with a display of self-conscious control if that ethic is a predicate of the private person, and poems as I have described them to be constituted in the canon are apt for the purpose, but composition in such a mode, once the purpose of which it is formally significant has ceased to obtain, leads to disequilibrium: without the pressure of the ethical subject the tropism of figurative rhetoric becomes its own end. I thought this was to be seen already under way in Larkin's successors, first Hughes, then Heaney (and down, I suggested, to Craig Raine): their poems were different from those of their predecessors only in the sense that their motivations were no longer the same, but were nevertheless poems of the same kind, and were treated accordingly in a somewhat cursory fashion. In an equally cursory manner, but by way of contrast, I drew attention to poetry of other kinds, giving as examples specimens of writing by Charles Tomlinson and W. S. Graham: poets of quite different types, chosen because, although scarcely of the canon, both had received a modest amount of public attention. In both, I argued, the place of the subject was vacated in favour of, so to speak, an objectively grounded and embodied experience.

My assessment of Larkin and Davie, in particular, would probably now be more generous than it was, perhaps because I am better able to recognise in their reluctance, hesitation, and dismay the signs of their ethical dilemma as poets, and what they took to be the ethical dilemma of poetry in the postwar world, despite the suspicion that this was rather conveniently assumed on the basis of a tendentious construal (caricatured by Conquest) of the high art tradition in the twentieth century. (To do proper justice to Davie, he also went on to write with impressive eloquence in non-canonical modes: the verse epistle, for example, and what can best be described as the disrupted symbolist lyric.)[4] This sense of dilemma was not shared by all British poets, least of all perhaps by those who felt an affinity with other poetic traditions, and it was helpful (and still is) to recall Tomlinson's phrase of sharp reproof, in a review of *New Lines*, since it applies with equal force both to what Tomlinson thought to be its poets' 'suburban mental ratio' and what I have discerned as their posture of ethical responsibility (Tomlinson 1957: 215). Tomlinson also spoke, with more acuity than we should expect given his sneering reference to the suburbs, of the Movement poet's 'mental conceit of himself', and this is telling because reflexive self-conceit can take more than one form. What Tomlinson identifies as a 'suburban mental ratio' may well correspond to what I have inferred to be an assumed ethical dilemma, but that is not the issue, for his acuity lay in discerning the character of a poetics in which the mind of the poet is manifested as a mode of self-reflexivity. Given the ethical bearing of Tomlinson's own poems (that of the serious artist, mindful both of knowledge and its objects and their energies) we should not be misled by his recourse to an ethical terminology of personal qualities. At issue is not that poets are conceited (they mostly are, anyway), but the direct representation in the poem of the poet's controlling intelligence – or personality, idiosyncrasy, obsession, whatever it may be. To be blunt, Tomlinson's objection to the Movement poets was that they expected readers to be interested in reading about *them*, an objection that applies by extension to the entire contemporary canon. Moreover, Tomlinson's phrase might be turned around to apply equally to the reader's own 'mental conceit of himself', to make the point that our canonical poetry is designed to establish the reader's empathetic identification with the figure the poem gives of the poet.

The argument being repeated here, by which it is maintained that there exists a canon of poetry defined not so much by the excellence of the poems as by the fact that they are inclusively of the same sort, may appear, because of its persistent totalising of postwar poetry, vulnerable to fundamental objection on matters of detail: either that the poems of the canonical poets are not of this sort, or that poets whose poems are not of this sort belong in the canon. Of these the former is the weightier objection, and I shall go on to discuss an instance of it provided by David Trotter. The latter type of objection will most frequently be encountered as a quibble, indignation that a favourite poet has been somehow slighted. Objections of this sort are an attempt to have one's cake and eat it. For the truth is that a canon exists in a nebulous hinterland, as the cultural property of a host of minds and institutions, comprising both poets and poems, and will manifest itself thus as virtually *given*. The canon that I identified twenty years ago was, in effect, either given to me, or adopted by me from the ambient culture, and I recall no dissent from the flat assertion that Larkin, Hughes and Heaney exemplified it. Just because of its nebulous existence a canon must also be able to be represented as a strongly outlined construct. Is Davie canonical? Probably not, though some of his poems probably are, and the question is not one we ask when thinking about Davie's work, or any other poet's, on it own terms.

In a review of *Society and Literature 1945–1970*, Trotter suggested that the period under review did not allow my case to be fully made since my canonical poets 'were beginning, around 1970, to write in ways that challenged the projection of a mental conceit on to the world' (Trotter 1984a: 707). The allusion was to my use of Tomlinson's phrase, of course, minus the crucial element of reflexivity. My *riposte* might be that Trotter had not fully ascertained the nature of my case, which concerns poems rather more than it does 'the world'. But this would just be a point scored against a critic who had interesting things on his mind that bear on what I have say. In *The Making of the Reader*, published in the same year as his review (Trotter 1984), Trotter devoted a chapter to what he discerned as beginning around 1970, using the terms 'pathos' and 'anti-pathos' to frame what was now different, but offering it as no more than a 'significant, although perhaps temporary, change of emphasis' (Trotter 1984b: 196). (That qualification, I infer, was due to hindsight.) The opposition of pathos and anti-pathos placed Larkin and Heaney under the first category in a separate chapter, and I merely note that there the 'pathos of subjectivity' is glossed as the 'responsibility to say what one feels about things' (Trotter 1984b: 177) – and that is close to the imperative to be seen as standing by one's words. Anti-pathos, on the other hand, represented 'an opportunity for English poetry which is now in some danger of fading' – obviously, since two of the three books that stood for it, Hughes's *Crow* (1970), and Geoffrey Hill's *Mercian Hymns* (1971), had proved to be blips in their authors' careers. Trotter at least had the consolation of being able to say, in the case of his third exemplary book, that the author of *Brass* (1971), J. H. Prynne, 'has not followed the later Hughes and the later Hill back to the pathos of origins' (Trotter 1984b: 230).

Trotter's categories may strike athwart my notion of the canon, but they do not marshall the evidence to controvert my case. Quite the reverse, in fact. On his own evidence, there was no significant reorientation of the canon after the 1960s: indeed, the canon was strongly reinscribed in the 1970s, as Heaney came to the fore. *Crow* and *Mercian Hymns* were, in their way, exceptional, but as slapstick fictions, light relief for otherwise dour temperaments. Nevertheless, *Crow* strikes me as a prime example of the canonical sort of poem in a particularly etiolated manner, for surely Hughes's fictive persona is principally characterised, down to his acts of self-erasure, by his mental conceit of himself. Hill, on the other hand, I would not claim for the canon: he has his admirers, but they are too strong-minded to bother with that kind of thing, while his poetry is too recusant to be co-opted. Furthermore, Trotter's concluding chapter, taking its evidence from, on the one hand, handbooks for teaching poetry in schools and, on the other, from the poems of the 'Metaphor Men' (Craig Raine and the poets associated with him as 'Martians') found him drawn to the baleful conclusion: 'Comparison, one of the many different ways in which poems signify, has become a sign for poetry itself: for the entire scope and value of the art' (Trotter 1994b: 247–8). While I agree with this as a statement about the canon, I obviously don't accept his suggestion that this may be a consequence of the way poetry is taught in schools; there may be an element of feedback, but the phenomenon is immanent to the canon itself. The figures of rhetoric (to which comparison is fundamental), in the argument I have advanced, conferred poetic authenticity on

Movement poems, under the vigilant superintendence of the ethical qualms of the Movement poet, but their role in this transaction did not confer on them any prestige, since poetry itself was (given its recent history) an object of suspicion. In other words comparison was *already* the sign for poetry itself. Take away those qualms and the canon lets rip, for a time at least, in the way Trotter described. But we should not lose sight of its capacity to turn in a different direction, towards a poetry of mental self-conceit.

The canon rests on its laurels

I proposed at the outset that our postwar poetic culture has remained largely unchanged, and in the course of reviewing a former argument about the canon of poetry to 1970 I suggested, in passing, that the canon was geared to assumptions about its status as representative of a national poetic culture. I maintained that the canon to 1970 comprised poems of a particular sort, a poetic discourse which had once answered to specific cultural and social imperatives but which, with their passing, persisted as the exclusive sign of the poetic. My proposition now requires, therefore, arguments to show that the canon to 1970 has extended down to the present. It will not be enough to challenge anyone to deny that Larkin, Hughes, and Heaney retain exemplary canonical status, or that they are still read in terms of the poems that established them thus, even if the longevity of their esteem tells in favour of my case.

But in reviewing my diagnosis of the canon to 1970 I also antici-pated, of course, the case that now requires to be made. Although Heaney began to publish, to acclaim, in the 1960s, his exemplary prominence belongs to the 1970s. The same is to be said, moving on a decade, of Craig Raine, who began to publish in the 1970s, but whose general *réclame* was a thing of the 1980s. This is going over ground already covered, but it throws light on how the canon obtains as a cultural construct. For a start, while it persists as such, the canon will remain posited over against the poetries that antedate its 1950s incep-tion. It will not invite us to reconsider modernism, or the poetry of the 1930s, let alone that of the 1940s. Indeed, the excesses of the 1940s come to be re-duplicated in recent canonical polemic as the excesses of the 1960s. On the other hand, what the canon excludes of the recent past is less than ever represented (as it was by Conquest, for instance) as that which might constitute its other. Thus the occluded past can become a site of *ad hoc* and whimsical recuperations and fetishisings: of

Auden for example, or that perennial adolescent standby, Weldon Kees. These are signs of the canon's diminished poetic vitality, as were its raids farther afield on poetry behind the Iron Curtain, or the texts of ethnopoetics. This lack of vitality is offset, to an extent, by the spectacle of the entropic energy of the canon itself: younger poets are now less interested in the question how to write than in the question how to publish. The former question has, for practical purposes, been settled since we have had a canon in which poetry is a fully socialised cultural product. But because poetry's position in relation to cultural production and consumption is eccentric, at the very margin, it can afford no more than a handful of canonically definitive poets (more likely to be read about than read, in the culture at large, their names a litany of reproach to a reading public that thinks perhaps it ought to read some poetry). Defined thus, the canon extends over time by accretion of new names, at the rate of one per decade: from the 1950s, Larkin; the 1960s, Hughes; the 1970s, Heaney. For the 1980s, I have suggested Raine; and for the 1990s, surely, the definitive poet has been Simon Armitage.

When I suggested, twenty years ago, that the canon to 1970 'extended itself' in the work of Raine, it was merely to indicate the lie of the land: a prospect of poets being 'praised above all else as inventors of figures' (Crozier 1983: 229), and a canon falling yet more spectacularly into decline. The coincidence of my view of the poetry of the 1980s with that of Trotter, nevertheless, is merely confirmation of part of the evidence for the case that Raine's poems are of the canonical sort. In *Contemporary Poetry and Postmodernism* (1996) Ian Gregson took issue with me on this point, wishing to show 'the extent to which' poets such as Raine had 'broken with the tradition of the Movement' (Gregson 1996: 37). The metaphorised textual economy of Raine's poems was not in dispute, but he alleged (citing Bakhtin) that their 'structural principle is the interaction of points of view' rather than 'image-making' (Gregson 1996: 30). (This, I am afraid, will prove to have given the game away.) Thus while Gregson agreed with what I said about the role of the self in the Movement, he supposed that he could transfer that intact in order to refute its application to Raine by claiming that 'the Martian poetic . . . systematically undermines the authority of the self by restlessly enacting the vulnerability of its knowledge' (Gregson 1996: 37). On the one hand, Gregson did not take the force of my point that figures of rhetoric 'constitute the nature of the poem' (Crozier 1983: 229; Gregson 1986: 37), which applies equally to Larkin and to Raine; on the other hand, he failed to notice that in my argument about the continuity of the canon there was an inverse relation between the authority of the self *qua* subject and the efflorescence of figures of rhetoric. Furthermore, his assertion about Martian poetics, which connects back to his notion of interaction of points of view (how this can be a 'structural principle' in the lyric quite eludes me) was simply wrong. Metaphor can only work if the identity of its terms is recognised: Martian poetry, therefore, far from existing in a state of epistemological uncertainty can be wonderfully periphrastic because it is cognitively certain of itself. More to the point, Raine is certain of, indeed complicit with, his reader's ability to identify what is not mentioned by name – typically by transpositions of visual scale. As Trotter put it: 'In Raine's world, a packet of cigarettes looks like a miniature organ and a rose has a shark-infested stem' (Trotter 1984b: 249). Even if, as in his signature poem 'A Martian sends a postcard home' (1979), Raine represents his figures of rhetoric as originating from a cognitive set unlike ours, unfamiliar with the names of things in our everyday normality, it is far-fetched to situate such misprisions as implied dialogue, as if the poet had encountered an authentic other, whose rather precious figures of rhetoric he bore no responsibility for. To the contrary, the very attempt to project another consciousness, another point of view, by means of the figures that define the text as a poem, seems self-defeating. Raine is master in his 'Martian' house. For myself, I'd prefer my Martian more like the real thing. '*Sit ka vassisi von ka, sta'chi que v'ay qray*' (Ellingham and Killian 1998: 57).[5]

Gregson and I differ because he eschews any concept of poetry, of what constitutes something as a poem. Like most of our poetry critics, he takes whatever is handed to him on a plate and makes the best of it. No one will mistake a Martian poem for a Movement poem (not even me), their differences are clearly marked, like tabby and tortoise-shell cats, but Gregson wishes to differentiate them radically, on the basis of their different styles of subjectivity, and must indulge in fanciful hermeneutics to justify this, where I discern their radical identity in the textual role of the subject both inscribe.

If Raine does not represent a break with the canon inaugurated by the Movement, but is instead its beneficiary, what are we to make of the claims recently made on behalf of a new generation of poets of the 1980s and early 1990s, showcased in the 1993 anthology *The New Poetry*, where Armitage appears to figure as its *terminus ad quem*? This anthology was quickly followed by a complementary volume of essays by one of its editors, David Kennedy, *New Relations, The Refashioning of British Poetry 1980–1994* (1996), complete with an Appendix 'The New Poetry – A User's Guide' giving 'pointers on using *The New*

Poetry with GCSE and Advanced Level examination syllabuses for 1996 and 1997' (Kennedy 1996: 267), and was already in its fifth impression by 1996. This smacks of genuine success, and Kennedy's subtitle pinpoints the editors' claim that their anthology documents a cultural shift. That Kennedy also recuperates this new poetry for the national culture might then seem tactless, given the editors' anti-centrist claims in view of which, we might well ask, what is this poetry doing on the curriculum? Well, it 'emphasises accessibility, democracy and responsiveness, humour and seriousness, and reaffirms the art's significance as public utterance' (Hulse, Kennedy and Morley 1993: 16). That is to say (the editors are somewhat impressed by the novelty of this) it is self-consciously politically *concerned*: 'poetry and political concerns . . . are inseparable' (ibid.: 17). It is post-imperial, post-colonial, multicultural, pluralist, devolutionist, provincial, anti-authoritarian, and generally *bien pensant*. What we can all feel comfortable with, each in our own social exclusion zone. In effect we are invited to read this new poetry as a return of the repressed (culturally speaking); an outburst from the hitherto silent majority oppressed by the cultural and political system. In this populist arena for confused-identity politics we are, it becomes apparent, solicited to read their poems for the poets' mental conceit of themselves.

This however is largely window dressing, including a lot of excess baggage that Kennedy smartly drops from his exposition of an inclu-sively *British* poetry in *New Relations*. Out (but for impeccable reasons) go the Irish and Afro-Caribbean poets, and women poets are denied a separate look-in – a surprising ecumenical gesture, since while the Afro-Caribbeans were excluded because they are 'still being theorised', the same can hardly be said of writing by women. This clears the ground for a traditional configuration of British poetry, but with a grudge against the English class system, particularly as manifested in the 1982 *Penguin Book of Contemporary British Poetry*, explicitly the *terminus a quo* for *The New Poetry*.[6] Whatever its overt politics *The New Poetry*, seen in its true colours, is a foray into the village politics of British poetry, based on a shrewd appraisal of both the canon and its history and, as such, a bid for centrality and cultural legitimacy. This is implied by its editors' choice of title, claiming for their anthology affinity with A. Alvarez's 1962 anthology also entitled *The New Poetry*, which effectively subsumed the Movement's codes of discourse while denouncing the gentility of English cultural tradition in order to extend the hegemony of the canon. *The New Poetry* (1993) situates itself toward *The Penguin Book of Contemporary British Poetry* precisely as *The New Poetry* (1962) situated itself toward *New Lines*.

Kennedy's historical case runs something like this. Larkin by his example had sanctioned a degree of contemporary realism, which in the next or 'middle' generation became the privileged frame of reference. Kennedy presents this realism in terms of communities inhabiting a landscape that is a 'blighted urban pastoral of . . . industrial froth and dismantled cars', while its cultural bearing relates to 'issues of access, ownership, property and rights' (Kennedy 1996: 15). The poets of this generation speak back, as it were, to their sponsor Larkin, from marginal communities acknowledged in his poems but unknown to them. They also prepare the ground for poets of the next generation, represented by *The New Poetry* (1993), whose individual voices both continue the struggle with the central culture and its class position and, because that struggle has been won, represent a release of the poetic imagination into the pleasures of mass culture. This is both and at once an argument about ownership of the canon since the Movement, and a claim for historical and political significance. Thus it can be suggested that we are to see in this history some reflection of the break-up of a postwar consensus, and that the new generation's consciousness was forged politically within Thatcher's Britain.

What seems to me more striking is that these arguments based on exclusion are belated, for they belong to the 1950s, when they were urged – very convincingly, since they then could cite a widespread turn to realism – with reference to the theatre, cinema, and the novel. It might be countered that it is poetry that is belated (though these same arguments were once held to relate to Larkin), but that would be to miss the point, which is that these arguments ascribe to the institution of poetry a cultural authority and oppressive agency inconceivable in late twentieth-century culture. But the fiction that this is so lends legitimacy to the struggle for centrality, for possession of poetic culture, which turns on the correct representation of the 'middle' generation. For while the 'middle generation' poets who speak back to Larkin from the social margins his poems glance at, Douglas Dunn, Tony Harrison, and Heaney himself (who can seem like the joker in every anthologist's pack), are indeed represented in the *Penguin Book of Contemporary British Poetry*, their place in the true succession was there usurped, and instead Raine's Martianism and the 'secret narratives' of Andrew Motion and James Fenton were enthroned. Thus the anthology is seen by Kennedy as an attempt to draw a veil over the radical credentials of the 'middle generation' by claiming its continuity with the poetic mainstream, invoking post-modernism in order to separate it 'from a wider cultural, political and social context' (Kennedy 1996: 16). Dunn and Harrison, and Peter Reading (whose exclusion from the *Penguin Book of Contemporary British Poetry* so scandalises Kennedy), may well be forebears of the next generation's mental conceit of itself, but it is easier to detect in them a staged immiseration and the self-pathos of the elective outsider than a convincing politics. Nor is it credible to suppose that metrical verse represents, in their hands, a political gesture of cultural expropriation; rather, it serves to foreground an aestheticised disgust.

These arguments do not have to persuade in order to be successful as a tactic for establishing the poetic centrality of the next genera-tion's *new poetry* drawn from the socially excluded margins, and both Armitage and Glyn Maxwell are now safely with Faber and Faber, pub-lishers to the canon. Of the two, Armitage is by far the more frequently spoken of, and he is by virtue of that representative of his generation, and also representative of the canon by virtue of the sort of poem he writes. He serves therefore to close my case. Whereas in Raine the discursive subject is axiomatically the poet, there as the originator of a steady drip of metaphoric events, the Armitage *persona* is somewhat various, but invariably demotic, an average citizen or common man. This is the poet who is like his readers to the extent that they don't normally read poetry, and are pleasantly surprised that it deals with the routine stuff of everyday life: probation officers, football, drugs. Discursively, that is to say, Armitage's poems are directed by an intransigent fiction of the ordinary person. So far so good. But these ordinary people, it turns out, possess a transformative imagination attuned to remote comparisons, and can speak like Raine's Martians. In 'You may turn over and begin', for example, the straddled legs of a female pillion rider, suddenly *sans* motorbike, resemble a wishbone; in 'B & B' a dead mole is both like a pocket and like a purse; in 'Parable of the dead donkey' an empty grave fills with rain water like a bath. Such poetry was new only in the sense that it was waiting to be recuperated by the canon, prime cuts resting on Movement laurels.

Notes

1   The comparison was made by A. Alvarez, see A. Alvarez (ed.), *The New Poetry*, Harmondsworth: Penguin, 1962.

2 'In memory of W. B. Yeats'.
3 See, for example, Philip Larkin, 'I remember, I remember', and Donald Davie, 'Rejoinder to a Critic', both in R. Conquest (ed.), *New Lines*, London: Macmillan, 1956.
4 See, for example, *Six Epistles to Eva Hesse* (1970), and *The Shires* (1974).
5 Purportedly a specimen of Southern Martian, but the authors' informant was recalling an occurrence some forty years in the past. The speaker, who had been drinking Red Cap Ale, was a passenger on a train to Los Angeles, and was taken for an Australian by other passengers (who, like the inform- ant, had also been drinking).
6 This was the anthology at which Seamus Heaney balked, its editors having nevertheless identified 'the new spirit of British poetry' as having begun 'to make itself felt in Northern Ireland during the late 1960s and early 70s' (B. Morrison and A. Motion (eds), *The Penguin Book of Contemporary British Poetry*, Harmondsworth: Penguin, 1982: 12). Fractious disputes on the score of national difference, however, can have no bearing on an argument (such as mine) concerning the canonical identity of poems.

Bibliography

Alvarez, A. (ed.) (1962) *The New Poetry*, Harmondsworth: Penguin.

Conquest, R. (ed.) (1956) *New Lines*, London: Macmillan.

Crozier, A. (1983) 'Thrills and frills: poetry as fibures of empirical lyricism', in A. Sinfield (ed.), *Society and Literature 1945–1970*, London: Methuen.

Ellingham, L. and Killian, K. (1998) *Poet, Be Like God*, Hanover, N.H.: Wesleyan University Press.

Gregson, I. (1996) *Contemporary Poetry and Postmodernism*, Basingstoke: Macmillan.

Hulse, M., Kennedy, D. and Morley, D. (1993) *The New Poetry*, Newcastle upon Tyne: Bloodaxe.

Kennedy, D. (1996) *New Relations: The Refashioning of British Poetry 1980–1994*, Bridgend: Seren.

Morrison, B. and Motion, A. (eds) (1982) *The Penguin Book of Contemporary Poetry*, Harmondsworth: Penguin (12).

Tomlinson, C. (1975) 'The middlebrow muse', *Essays in Criticism* 7, 2: 208–17.

Trotter, D. (1984a) 'Cut-off Points', *TLS* no. 4, 238 (22 June): 707.

—— (1984b) *The Making of the Reader*, Basingstoke: Macmillan.

Index